The Third Reich

The Third Reich

K. HILDEBRAND

Translated from the German by P. S. Falla

London and New York

Die Originalausgabe erschien unter dem Titel Klaus Hildebrand,
Das Dritte Reich im R. Oldenbourg Verlag München Wien, © 1979
by R. Oldenbourg Verlag GmbH München

This translation first published in 1984
by George Allen & Unwin (Publishers) Ltd
Third impression 1990

Reprinted 1991, 1994, 1999 by Routledge
11 New Fetter Lane, London EC4P 4EE
29 West 35th Street, New York, NY 10001

Transferred to Digital Printing 2004

British Library Cataloguing in Publication Data

Hildebrand, K.
    The Third Reich.
    1. Germany – History – 1933–1945
    I. Title   II. Das Dritte Reich, *English*
    932.086   DD256.5
    ISBN 0 415 07861 X Pbk

Library of Congress Cataloging in Publication Data

Hildebrand, Klaus.
    The Third Reich.
    Translation of: Das Dritte Reich.
    Bibliography: p.
    Includes index.
    1. Germany – History – 1933–1945.   I. Title.
    DD256.5.H47713   1984   943.087   84–6229
    ISBN 0 415 07861 X (pbk.)

Set in 10 on 12 point Plantin by Fotographics (Bedford) Ltd

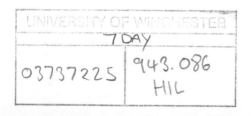

Contents

Preface

It is undoubtedly a bold enterprise to seek to present the history of the Third Reich in such a short compass as the present volume. The difficulty of the subject and the complexity of its problems, which have been the subject of voluminous research, make it hard to keep within the prescribed limits of space. Some selection must be made; the choice is to some extent a personal one, but is defined in principle by the area of debate covered by international historiography. Thus primary attention will be devoted to those elements and problems of the history of the Third Reich which have been identified as important by a research tradition of over thirty years' standing.

While problems of the political history of the Nazi period will thus occupy the centre of the stage, account will naturally be taken of economic and social questions in so far as they are necessary for an understanding of politics. According to the course of events, internal developments will come to the forefront at one time and external ones at another. However, the two constantly react upon each other and are to be regarded as complementary aspects of the history of the Third Reich; and it is our object in this way to give as full and balanced an account as possible of the origin, development and collapse of Hitler's totalitarian dictatorship.

Apart from the problem of selecting the right material, a still greater difficulty should be mentioned at least briefly. This lies in the fact that a historian accustomed to intellectual categories, when confronted with the monstrous phenomena of the Third Reich, finds his sense of method strained to the utmost. It is a painful task for such an historian to treat National Socialism with objectivity based on sympathy, as the classic rules of German historiography would require. Consequently scholars have for the most part chosen one of two ways of approaching or avoiding what Golo Mann has called 'the repellent subject'. The first of these – the condemnatory point of view, an essentially negative process of 'demonising' the Nazi period – reflected a postwar need which was often only too understandable on the part of individuals and was no doubt also necessary for the community; but, while it certainly answered to political needs, it can no longer satisfy the claims of scholarship. Secondly, many contemporaries and historians adopted the attitude of Benedetto Croce, who in 1950 declared in effect that he would never write the history of Italian fascism because he hated it too much to treat it with the necessary objectivity. The tendency, which deserves every respect, to flee from the horrors of Nazism to more tranquil realms of study has for some time been less prominent, if only since a new generation of historians has come on the scene. From the political and the academic point of view there is no longer any need to de￼ ate the morality or amorality of the Third Reich – that issue is settled once and ￼or all. Our task is rather to present the history of Nazi Germany as broadly as possible, using the methods of contemporary historiography – not in order to moralise, but in order to judge the Third Reich, like any other regime, with understanding of its historical roots and relation to the era as a whole. In this way alone will it be possible to assess Hitler's dictatorship 'in the light of its own nature and conception of itself', and thus 'to compare this alien spirit with that of its own context' (E. Troeltsch). For, as Cesare Pavese once said, the only way to escape from falling into the abyss is to survey and measure it, to descend into and plumb its depths.

In writing this history of the Third Reich I have received valuable advice and criticism from Professor Andreas Hillgruber of Cologne, to whom I owe special thanks. I am grateful to Dr Jost Dülffer (Cologne), Stefan Martens (Münster, Westphalia), Dr Wolfgang Michalka (Frankfurt am Main) and Dr Gregor Schöllgen (Münster, Westphalia), who took the trouble to read my manuscript and furnish expert comments. I also owe thanks to Professor Lothar Gall of Frankfurt am Main, co-editor of the series in which this book appears, for suggesting the subject and for careful scrutiny of the first draft.

Finally I must not omit to extend my warm thanks to Frau M. Hopmann for the promptitude and accuracy with which she turned the manuscript into legible form.

K.H.

Münster, June 1978

The Expansion of the German Reich, 1935-43

- Allied and incorporated territories
- Occupied areas
- Neutral states

List of Abbreviations

Arch. f. SozG	*Archiv für Sozialgeschichte*, Bonn.
GiWuU	*Geschichte in Wissenschaft und Unterricht*, Stuttgart.
HZ	*Historische Zeitschrift*, Munich.
JCH	*Journal of Contemporary History*, London.
MGM	*Militärgeschichtliche Mitteilungen*, Freiburg im Breisgau.
NPL	*Neue Politische Literatur*, Frankfurt am Main.
Saec.	*Saeculum*, Freiburg im Breisgau.
VfZg	*Vierteljahreshefte für Zeitgeschichte*, Munich.

PART ONE

Historical Survey

(A) SEIZURE OF POWER AND *GLEICHSCHALTUNG*, 1933–5

1

The Creation of Totalitarian Dictatorship

When Hitler was appointed Chancellor on 30 January 1933 by President von Hindenburg, he became head of a coalition government of 'national concentration', in which conservatives seemed clearly to predominate. Apart from Hitler there were at the outset only two Nazis in the Cabinet. Wilhelm Frick became Minister of the Interior; Hermann Göring was at first Minister without Portfolio and on 28 April became Minister of Aviation. Göring also took over the Prussian Ministry of the Interior on an acting basis, and on 10 April became Prime Minister of Prussia, the largest state in the Reich. Nazi membership of the Cabinet was increased by one when Joseph Goebbels, on 13 March, became head of the newly created Ministry of Popular Enlightenment and Propaganda, but to the outward eye this scarcely affected the balance of power. For, in addition to what appeared to be the strong men of the government – Hugenberg, Minister for the Economy and Agriculture, and von Papen, Vice-Chancellor and Reich Commissar for Prussia – the government contained four more members of Papen's 'Cabinet of barons': von Neurath, the Foreign Minister, Count Schwerin von Krosigk, Minister of Finance, Gürtner, Minister of Justice, and Freiherr von Eltz-Rübenach, Minister of Posts and Communications. Together with von Blomberg, the Army Minister, and Seldte, the Stahlhelm leader who became Minister for Labour, these members of the 'old guard' were expected to keep the Nazis under control and ensure conservative policies. Papen's idea of taming Hitler seemed to have succeeded. 'We have roped him in' (*wir haben ihn uns engagiert*). In these terms von Papen dismissed conservative misgivings on the subject of Hitler and Nazism, and his self-confident assessment was accepted by most observers at home and abroad. 'In two months we'll have pushed Hitler into a corner, and he can squeal to his heart's content.'

Despite Papen's self-congratulation the Nazi leader, on the very day of the take-over and immediately before the new government was sworn in by Hindenburg, had won a decisive victory over his conservative ministers and especially Hugenberg, the leader of the German National People's Party

(DNVP). Hitler thus showed from the outset that he was by no means a puppet of powerful army and landowning circles, the bureaucracy and big business. Contrary to an agreement reached between the Nazis and the Nationalists during the negotiations which led to the coalition, after the new government was formed Hitler demanded the right to dissolve the Reichstag elected in the previous November and to hold fresh elections. These, as Hugenberg rightly feared, were unlikely to improve the position of the DNVP; in any case Hugenberg was opposed on principle to further elections and wished to see an extension of presidential power. Since the last election the Nazis and the Nationalists together controlled over 42 per cent of Reichstag votes, while the Centre (Catholic) Party held out hope that they would tolerate the new government if not actively support it. There was thus no compelling reason for new elections, but Hitler demanded them in the hope of using government power to gain a clear majority. He finally gained his point with Hugenberg, as otherwise the coalition seemed in danger, and the aged von Hindenburg, who stood ready to effect the ceremonial transfer of power, could not, it was felt, be kept waiting any longer.

The Reichstag was dissolved on 1 February 1933, two days after Hitler's appointment as Chancellor. During the election campaign which lasted till the country went to the polls on 5 March, Nazi terrorist tactics, endorsed by the power of the state, were openly exercised against all political opponents, especially communists and social democrats. There now set in a progressive seizure of absolute power, in which it was often difficult to distinguish terroristic from legal measures. A decisive factor was that, in accordance with the modern recipe for a totalitarian *coup d'état*, the Nazis controlled the Ministry of the Interior, and hence the police power, in the Reich as a whole and also in Prussia. Göring, as head of the Prussian police apparatus, even created an auxiliary police force numbering 50,000, of whom 40,000 belonged to the SA or the SS. In this way police powers were conferred on strong-arm Nazi gangs. Then, in a notorious order of 17 February 1933, Göring instructed the Prussian police to 'make free (*fleissig*) use of firearms' (Hofer and Michaelis, 1965).

From the beginning of February onwards the new rulers used emergency decrees based on Article 48 of the Weimar constitution to restrict the activity of other parties, to limit press freedom and to ensure the docility of the civil service by means of purges. The process of reducing the bureaucracy to subservience was accomplished by party interference and by prudent self-adaptation on the part of civil servants. The law of 7 April 1933 'for the restoration of the professional civil service' gave the party and state full powers over officials who were in any way objectionable: it provided for the more or less arbitrary dismissal of any whose professional competence was in doubt, who were of 'non-Aryan' descent, or whose record suggested that they might not be prepared to act 'single-mindedly and at all times' in the interests of the national state.

However, it was after the Reichstag fire of 27 February 1933 that Hitler took his most decisive step towards practically unlimited power. The disputed question of who caused the fire (cf. Part Two, Section 4, p. 137 below, and works in the bibliography by W. Hofer and others, 1972 and 1976. H. Mommsen, 1972a, and Tobias, 1964) is not of prime importance in this connection: the main point is the use made of it by the Nazis to seize and consolidate their power. On the day after the fire, which profoundly shocked the general public, von Hindenburg on the advice of the Cabinet issued a 'decree for the protection of the people and state' which in effect abolished the basic political rights conferred by the Weimar constitution, although this remained theoretically in force throughout the twelve years of Nazi rule. The decree created a permanent state of emergency and thus gave a cloak of legality to the persecution and terrorisation of the regime's political opponents.

The last 'semi-free' election in Germany took place in this climate of legalised insecurity and open terrorism, exercised in the first instance primarily against the Communist Party (KPD). The two parties of the left, the communists and the social democrats (SPD), were already prevented from taking part on a regular footing. Yet even in these elections, which were illegal by the standards of European parliamentary democracy, the Nazis gained only 43.9 per cent of votes. Thus the party was never returned to power by a majority of the German people. As for the plebiscites held during the Third Reich, which regularly acclaimed the Führer with over 90 per cent of 'Yeses', these took place under the political and psychological conditions of a well-advanced or firmly established totalitarian dictatorship, in which such percentages are all in the day's work.

The coalition of the Nazis and nationalists obtained 51.9 per cent of votes in the election of 5 March 1933, and in accordance with the constitution it could thus have governed with the approval of the Reichstag. However, on 21 March Hindenburg issued a decree supplementing that of 28 February and entitled 'law for the repelling of treacherous attacks against the government of national recovery'; and on 23 March Hitler proposed an 'Enabling Law' designed to terminate once and for all the effective authority of parliament and the constitutional organs of control. The new measure, which required a two-thirds majority of the Reichstag, was to confer on the government for four years the right to enact laws without requiring the consent of the Reichstag or the Reichsrat (Senate). The parties ranging from the Nationalists to the Catholic Centre and the other bourgeois groups were thus confronted with the decision whether to abdicate their own powers. With much hesitation they finally acquiesced in what they regarded as inevitable, believing that their only hope of influencing the government and avoiding worse evils lay in a policy of consent and co-operation, not of resistance. They hoped by their conduct to keep the government within the bounds of legality and thus influence the application of the Enabling Law; by adapting themselves they expected to save their own party apparatus and avoid personal damage to their leaders, officials and members. These hopes sprang from ways of thinking based on the concept of the *Rechtsstaat* (rule of law), which in principle had not been violated even by the authoritarian Cabinets of Brüning, von Papen and von Schleicher, but which was sharply at variance with the practice of the Nazi dictatorship. The non-Nazi parties lacked the experience to realise that with a totalitarian regime there could be no question of helping to frame events, but only of resistance or subjection. Only the SPD under its chairman Otto Wels courageously voted against the Enabling Law, which was finally passed by the requisite two-thirds majority.

The social democrats' 'No' was seen by conservatives and the bourgeoisie as confirmation that under Nazi leadership they themselves were on the right side of the front uniting all non-Marxist forces. The adversary was clearly on the political left; and on 21 March, two days before the vote on the Enabling Law, this seemed to be confirmed by a major demonstration of unity between Hitler's new Germany and time-honoured Prussian traditions. At a solemn ceremony in the Garrison Church at Potsdam, Chancellor Adolf Hitler paid homage to the aged President, Field Marshal von Hindenburg, who was revered as a symbolic figure by the majority of Germans. The reconciliation of old Prussia with the new movement seemed complete; conservative and bourgeois Germany identified with the Chancellor's party, not suspecting that the scene had been planned and stage-managed by Goebbels as a 'sentimental comedy' with the object of emphasising Hitler's seriousness and lulling the apprehensions of his right-wing associates.

Hitler had long ceased to be what the conservative 'gentlemen riders' had intended, namely, a faithful steed that would carry them swiftly to their objective. By now the position was reversed, though the fact was not yet obvious in the 'dual state' (Fraenkel, 1941) that was coming into being. For the majority of citizens life continued in a normal fashion, often with less disturbance than in the stormy last days of the Republic. The price paid for peace and quiet was unduly high, however, since it meant law giving place to terror in the political sphere. The Nazis began to honeycomb society with party associations and institutions: at the outset these competed with existing bodies, but by degrees they got the upper hand and either absorbed or displaced them. Such bodies as the SA and SS, the Hitler Youth and women's organisation, the Nazi associations of students, teachers and professors, doctors, civil servants, technicians, and so on, all served the purpose of totalitarian organisation and party control of the German people. All this regimentation gave an impression of order which had long been lacking. The nation marched steadily and in unison towards dictatorship; the new system did away with the inconveniences and incalculability of parliamentary procedure, and for this reason alone many Germans found in it something familiar and not unwelcome.

In the same way the boycott of Jews on 1 April 1933, directed *inter alia* against Jewish shops, appealed to feelings of antipathy that had long existed in Germany as elsewhere in Europe and which might be classed as 'normal anti-Semitism'; it was not hard to fan such feelings into something stronger. In the last years of the Weimar Republic Nazi propaganda had been fairly restrained in its anti-

Semitism and had preferred to stress the battle against communism as more likely to win conservative votes; but now the anti-Semitic component of Hitler's philosophy and of the Nazi state came to the fore. The 'scapegoat' aspect of racial agitation was calculated to have a rallying effect on the SA, whose restless and discontented members were seeking to discover their proper role in Hitler's state, and in addition it reflected the essence of Nazi thinking and the Führer's radical objectives. The regime began to introduce 'eugenic' measures immediately after the seizure of power, and the 'Nuremberg Laws' of 15 September 1935, together with the Law on German Citizenship and Law for the Protection of German Blood and German Honour, degraded the Jewish population to the rank of second-class citizens and subjected them to discrimination and deprivation of rights. In these ways Hitler's racial policy became manifest at a fairly early stage. This policy, with the demand for the destruction of 'useless lives' and for the breeding of a biologically superior race, defined the historic task and ideological purpose, in short the motive force of Nazism in its negative aspect. The anti-Jewish measures aroused some uneasiness, but anti-Semitism also commanded a degree of popular support.

Political emigration from Germany began at this time, as did the witch-hunt against disaffected intellectuals, writers and academics: this reached a first peak in the public 'burning of un-German literature' organised by Goebbels and carried out by Nazi student leaders in the Berlin Opernplatz on 10 May 1933. This too was accepted by the general public, and the loss it represented to the nation's intellectual life was hardly appreciated at the time. Cultural life was largely steered into Nazi channels by the Reich Chamber of Culture, set up by Goebbels for the purpose on 22 September 1933.

Alarm at the new rulers' increasingly evident claim to a monopoly position was felt in conservative circles when the *Gleichschaltung* ('co-ordination') of the German component states (*Länder*) was carried out shortly after the take-over, between 31 March and 7 April 1933. The Nazis played on anti-particularist feelings and represented their action as a step towards unifying the Reich. No notice was taken of the fact that the independence of the *Länder* was destroyed in favour of a brand of particularism run mad, namely, the duality of state and party in Germany as a whole. This was a distinguishing feature of Hitler's dictatorship, as was 'what appears a curious lack of structure in the Nazi system of command' (Hofer and Michaelis, 1965). The confusion of functions among a multitude of mutually hostile authorities made it necessary and possible for the Führer to take decisions in every case of dispute, and can be regarded as a foundation of his power. The *Länder*, and not least Prime Minister Held of Bavaria, offered resistance to the law of 31 March 1933 'for the co-ordination of the *Länder* with the Reich'; but in the last resort this resistance was in vain, because their police powers had been invaded by the Nazis during the election campaign and they had thus already lost much of their independence. *Gleichschaltung* was soon to be extended to the local level in the Municipal

Ordinance of 30 January 1935. For the present it took the form of appointing Reich Governors for each *Land* under the law of 7 April 1933. This was followed on 30 January 1934 by the Law for the Reorganisation of the Reich, and on 14 February 1934 by the abolition of the Reichsrat.

While the *Gleichschaltung* of the *Länder* may have had a sobering effect on many of Hitler's conservative allies, the traditional ruling class and the bourgeoisie applauded the measures of 2 May against trade unions, which marked a further decisive step towards totalitarian dictatorship. The Nazi Party evidently feared the power of the unions, which they had not been able to overcome in the works council elections held in March 1933. Accordingly they avoided open confrontation with the ADGB (the German TUC) and organised labour, and resorted to a double strategy alternating friendly gestures with persecution and violence. May Day was proclaimed a holiday in honour of national labour, with huge mass demonstrations organised in co-operation with the unions. Like the non-Nazi parties, the ADGB under its chairman Leipart, notwithstanding encroachments by the SA against his members, chose to conform in order to survive and above all to save the organisational structure of the unions. Accordingly the executive of the free unions declared that it would keep entirely out of politics and confine itself to the social sphere, 'whatever the nature of the state regime'. Its leaders hoped that in return for this the Nazis would permit the existence of a unified trade union system. On 1 May this expectation seemed justified, but it proved to be an illusion on the following day, when, in accordance with a prearranged plan, union premises were occupied by force and leading officials were arrested. The unions were then incorporated, not into the appropriate party organisation – the *Betriebszellenorganisation* – which already existed, but into the German Labour Front (DAF), founded on 10 May and headed by Robert Ley, chief of staff of the political organisation of the Nazi Party. After its reorganisation in November 1933 the DAF became in practice, though not in law, a compulsory association of employers, clerical and manual workers, in short 'all persons involved in working life irrespective of their economic and social status' (proclamation of 27 November 1933). With the destruction of the unions, the power of employers and employees to negotiate salary and wage rates also came to an end. This function henceforth belonged to a new institution, the Public Trustees of Labour (*Treuhänder der Arbeit*), set up under a law of 19 May 1933.

This development is clear evidence of the fact that, although the Third Reich was friendly to employers, it is not to be regarded simply or mainly as an instrument of counter-revolution. In the first place, it is impossible to overlook certain features of Nazi policy tending towards social equality and the elimination of class differences: these gave the regime a political complexion of its own, indicating that it was not primarily pro-employer or anti-worker. Secondly, from 1933 onwards the state and party began to display their power on the shop-floor *vis-à-vis* employers as well as workers. For, despite the regime's bias towards employers in wage disputes, it could not be overlooked that the boss's traditional position of 'master in his own house' was in some ways more restricted by the party's new measures than it had been by the unions in Republican days. These measures included the appointment of 'labour trustees', protection against dismissal, paid holidays and the obligation to provide increased welfare benefits. In addition the leisure organisation *Kraft durch Freude* (KdF: Strength through Joy), set up under the DAF on 27 November 1933, brought innovations particularly in respect of holidays and the use of leisure-time by the masses, including the system of saving to buy a 'people's car' (*Volkswagen*). These measures were felt to be progressive and were calculated to excite popular gratitude. They also had to some extent an egalitarian effect, being designed to eliminate class differences in the 'national community' (*Volksgemeinschaft*) of the Third Reich; a similar purpose was served by the State Labour Service introduced on 26 June 1935, which was compulsory for all young people. Such measures went beyond politics in the direction of economic and social reform, the modernising effect of which was not fully visible until later, but which meanwhile helped the regime to dominate all sections of the population and to further its aims in regard to war, expansion and racial policy.

At the same time it could not be overlooked that employers were considerably favoured by Hitler's economic policy, which was largely the work of Hjalmar Schacht, president of the Reichsbank from 17 March 1933, and from 30 July 1934 also Reich Economic Minister and Minister for the Prussian Economy. Wages, for instance, were frozen at the level which prevailed during the world-wide slump of 1932. This was not much altered in the second half of the decade, when skilled workers became scarce and a 'grey market' came into existence, with employers evading the ban on wage increases so as to attract and keep employees by means of covert rewards and indirect grants.

After the Nazi take-over the German economic situation on the whole improved, and unemployment fell. As the world economy gradually recovered, the new regime vigorously pursued work-providing schemes that had been begun under previous governments. The policy of creating employment was accompanied by a call to combat the 'folly of rationalisation' and to dispense with 'mechanical aids'. Laws of 1 June and 21 September 1933 for the reduction of unemployment, loans to young couples, a 'repair and maintenance programme' with tax advantages for private and commercial building, and the building of the first Reich autobahn under a law of 27 June 1933 – all these paved the way for the reduction of unemployment, as did 'voluntary' labour service, the employment of those out of work as rural labourers for a low wage, or their engagement in 'badly paid relief works' (Hofer and Michaelis, 1965). Other factors were compulsory military service, introduced on 16 March 1935, Reich labour service (also compulsory) from 26 June 1935, and the economic effects of rearmament after the turn of the year 1933/4. As a result of all this, between January and July 1933 the total of those out of work fell by over a million to less than 5 million, after which it sank steadily and rapidly to 1 million in the autumn of 1936. At all times it was a combination of favours and terrorism, the stick and the carrot, that won the regime popular support and accounted for its dynamic progress.

While the trade unions had been forcibly incorporated in the DAF, associations representing farmers' interests were absorbed into the Reich Food Corporation (*Reichsnährstand*) set up by a law of 13 September 1933. This was operated at the consumer's expense, in the interest of achieving autarky in foodstuffs and because imports were hampered by lack of foreign exchange. In order to increase agricultural production as fast as possible, the regime abandoned its plan to carve up the large estates. Richard Walter Darré, the Reich Minister for Food and Agriculture and Prussian Minister of Agriculture, preached the Nazi agrarian philosophy of 'blood and soil' and protection of the peasantry as the 'life-source of the Nordic race'. Under the Hereditary Farms Act of 29 September 1933 farms of more than 7·5 hectares (18·5 acres) and, as a rule, less than 125 hectares (308·5 acres) were declared 'hereditary' provided the owner could furnish evidence of 'racial purity' as far back as 1 January 1800. They were thus 'in principle inalienable and exempt from encumbrance' and could not be partitioned on the owner's death; at the same time they were sheltered from the effects of commercialisation. But the law 'was often applied less rigorously than it might have been' (Farquharson, 1976).

Unlike the workers and rural labourers, heavy industry was at first exempt from party interference. Although the party's ideology was a middle-class one, it refrained for the time being from tampering with the big concerns, chain-stores and banks which threatened the existence of an independent middle class. On the contrary, such enterprises continued to develop and concentrate under the Third Reich, and for the present escaped the *Gleichschaltung* applied in other fields. The Reich Association of German Industry changed its name on 19 June 1933 to Reich Corporation (*Reichsstand*) of German Industry in deference to the 'corporative' ideology of the Third Reich, which in fact was largely confined to propaganda, but it remained relatively independent under the leadership of Krupp von Bohlen and Halbach. This situation was unaffected by the law of 27 February 1934 'on preparing the organic structure of the German economy' – with the basic object of making the economy substantially more dependent on the state – or the reorganisation of industrial associations in the Reich Chamber of Industry (*Reichsgruppe Industrie*) which also took place in 1934. The Third Reich needed the co-operation of big business, which was still a major factor in the land, and allowed it a certain autonomy even after 1936, which year marked a turning-point in the relationship between the economy and politics. After that time the primacy of politics over economic interests was made clear, and both employers and employees were impartially deprived of their rights in the spirit of 'full Fascism' (Schweitzer, 1965).

At the outset Hitler was acutely dependent on the voluntary co-operation of both industry and the army in order to start effecting his ambitious and utopian aims in the sphere of racial and foreign policy. In the first years after the take-over the 'economic dictator' Schacht made rearmament possible by risky methods of procuring credit, the so-called *Mefo-Wechsel*. These were bills which could be drawn by armament manufacturers on a Metal Research Company (*Metall-Forschungs-GmbH*), founded for the purpose with a modest capital, in return for supplies to the state; the latter guaranteed the bills *vis-à-vis* the Reichsbank, which was obliged to discount them. Schacht mistakenly believed that he could discontinue the process at a stroke when the economy had recovered sufficiently and it was necessary to effect a consolidation of social policy. He realised too late that Hitler's ideas on rearmament, economics and politics were basically different from his own, and that the Führer had no notion of stopping rearmament once the economy had revived and society was once more on an even keel. On the contrary he wanted to go on arming in order to make war, wiping out debts by old-fashioned methods of plunder, and finally to destroy the existing social order both nationally and internationally. Schacht did not yet realise that he was playing Hitler's game. His 'new plan', based on the 'decree on commercial exchanges' dated 4 September 1934 and in force from 24 September, provided essentially for the bilateralisation of foreign trade; it involved quotas and the planning of imports according to a 'scale of national urgency' (H. Flaig) and promoted exports on a barter and compensation basis. The plan introduced an export offensive which served the purpose of promoting social consolidation at home; its author accepted the risk of conflict, for example, with the USA in areas such as South-East Europe and Latin America, where economic ambitions overlapped. In general it represented a more realistic political alternative to Hitler's bellicose and ideological aims. The Third Reich, as far as its relations with big business were concerned, was still in a state of 'partial fascism' (Schweitzer, 1965). Hitler had no interest in embarking on a collision course with the powerful industrialists: his interests in part coincided with theirs, and by co-operating in their sphere the conservatives helped the regime to increase its power and thus worked for their own overthrow. Although the state regulated the competence of the various 'Reich industrial groups' – for example, by the system of supervision and auditing in respect of allocations of foreign currency and raw materials, developed from summer 1934 onwards, and also by price control – and although it could always use as a threat the charge of industrial sabotage, none the less it seemed that politics and industry, the party and big business, which had only come together during the last weeks of the moribund Weimar Republic, were in general on pretty good terms. It was by no means the case, however, that 'capital' and big business played a decisive part in bringing Hitler to power. They did not support him with funds to any great extent until after the take-over, when the March elections had to be financed. At that time the big industrialists contributed 3 million Reichsmark to Hitler's movement and the other pro-government parties. This was when the Nazi Party had already become the decisive political factor; moreover, after the Führer had addressed a select circle of business representatives in the palace of the Reichstag president, Göring had assured a meeting of industrialists and financiers on 20 February that the coming election would be the last for ten or even a hundred years. By contrast, at the end of the Weimar Republic the industrialists, while certainly not friendly to the dying regime, gave their support not to the Nazis but to von Papen's model of a 'new state', and in general were ready to come to terms with any political force that was not committed to the abolition of private property.

Against the background of a totalitarian dictatorship that already existed in essential respects, there followed in June and July 1933 the 'self-*Gleichschaltung*' of the political parties, which lost heart and capitulated to Nazi power and Nazi terror. After the SPD was banned on 22 June 1933 the Catholic Centre, the last of the democratic parties, on 5 July yielded to the monopolistic claim of what the new rulers had already, on 14 April, declared to be a 'one-party state'. According to a view which some dispute (Scholder, 1977), an important reason for the surrender was the prospect of the Concordat of 20 July 1933, which seemed to offer the Catholic church in Germany favourable terms and a legal basis for resistance to the Third Reich.

While the Catholic church could present a united front to the Nazi state, among the Protestants there was open conflict between those who represented older and newer attitudes: liberal theology and religion-based socialism on the one hand, and on the other the 'Evangelical National Socialists' who styled themselves 'German Christians'. The conflict was in full swing when, on 25 April 1933, Hitler publicly endorsed the latter movement and appointed Ludwig Müller, an army chaplain for the Königsberg area, as his 'plenipotentiary for the affairs of the Evangelical churches'. A conflict then arose over the post of bishop for the proposed new 'Reich church': the German Christians supported Müller and announced his appointment in opposition to Pastor Fritz von Bodelschwingh. Among other acts of interference in church matters by the state and party, the Nazi Party gave massive support to the German Christians in the campaign preceding the church elections on 23 July 1933. The national synod which was elected as a result duly appointed Müller Reich bishop on 27 September. This inaugurated a contest which was to last as long as the Third Reich. Resistance to the new authorities and the German Christians was organised by the Pastors' Emergency League founded at Berlin/Dahlem in September 1933 by Martin Niemöller, and by the Confessing church which developed from it and which first met as a body at Ulm on 22 April 1934. A protest by the Synod of Barmen (29–31 May 1934) was also of importance in the development of the dispute. This was the first occasion on which voices of opposition were raised by conservative and bourgeois Germany, which – on a basis of injured interests and disregarded knowledge – complemented and varied the resistance of the communists, which was essentially ideological. But it must be recognised that these protests were not on the whole very successful: cf., for example, Papen's Marburg speech of 17 June 1934.

After Hitler and Frick had, on several occasions from July 1933 onwards, declared the revolution to be at an end, the Führer still had to cope with a challenge from within his own movement. It was becoming more and more urgent to decide what was to be done with the SA (*Sturmabteilung*: Storm Detachment), the strong-arm force which, in its devotion to the Führer, had played an important part in destroying the Weimar Republic, fighting political opponents in the streets and enabling Hitler to seize power. It now claimed its reward, and from its ranks was heard a half-articulate cry for a second, social revolution, reflecting the tradition of the 'left-wing' National Socialists who had left the party or been expelled from it in 1930. The SA leaders, especially the chief of staff Ernst Röhm, wanted to command a people's militia to be created by merging the conservative army with the revolutionary SA, in such a way that the 'grey rock' of the *Reichswehr* would be submerged by the 'brown flood' of Nazi troops. The corps of officers, headed by von Blomberg, naturally viewed this demand with suspicion and hostility. Hitler, who wanted Germany to be ready for war as soon as possible, preferred to ally himself with the conservative officers against the social romanticism of the SA. Röhm's alleged intention to carry out a putsch was used as a pretext to remove the SA leaders with the army's help, to reward the latter and consolidate Hitler's power. The conservatives who desired to see an end to the revolution had their wish; the military were relieved of a troublesome rival institution, whose place in the Nazi scheme of things was henceforth taken by the SS (*Schutzstaffel*: Defence Echelon). This body was not only Hitler's praetorian guard but increasingly became the ideological spearhead and prime defender of Nazi racial policy. Within a year of Hitler's accession to power the SS under Himmler had already wrested control of the political police from the SA in all the constituent German states. In Prussia, where Göring created the Secret State Police (*Geheime Staatspolizei*, Gestapo) on 24 April 1933 as an instrument of state terrorism, one of its duties being to establish concentration camps, the SS also succeeded in gaining decisive control over this body. Göring, who was appointed head of the Gestapo by a law of 30 November 1933, was obliged in April 1934 to accept Himmler as deputy to himself, and the latter appointed Heydrich, his subordinate in the SS, to head the Gestapo.

The army's role as sole defender of the nation was safeguarded by the elimination of Röhm. In return, the officer corps raised no objection to the arbitrary murders of opponents of the regime which were perpetrated at the same time as the 'Röhm putsch', though the henchmen of Göring and Himmler included among their victims two generals, von Schleicher and von Bredow. Altogether the effect of the putsch was to strengthen the Reichswehr outwardly but to leave it in a highly demoralised state.

Among those murdered in addition to the SA leaders were conservative opponents and critics of the regime such as Edgar Jung and von Bose – two of von Papen's closest collaborators; also Gustav von Kahr, the former state commissioner in Bavaria, and Erich Klausener, head of Catholic Action in Berlin. Hitler's claim that he had the SA leaders shot because homosexuality had been rife among them was a threadbare excuse to cover a political showdown. However, few members of the public realised this, and political leaders including von Papen commended Hitler's action. Carl Schmitt, then the leading German expert on public law, justified it in an article entitled 'The Führer defends the right': this maintained that judicial power belonged to the 'true leader' of the nation and that in emergency he was entitled and bound to enforce the law in his capacity as supreme judge. In this way the dictator's will was given force of law, and Hitler's power was henceforth accepted as being essentially unrestricted.

Shortly afterwards, on 2 August 1934, Hindenburg died and Hitler assumed in his own person the offices of both President and Chancellor. The take-over of power was thus complete: no institution or personality any longer offered any competition to him in practical or prestige terms. On the same day the Reichswehr was made to take an oath of loyalty to Hitler personally: this was arranged by the zealous War Minister von Blomberg, to ensure Hitler's favour towards the army and himself. It was the oath of loyalty to the Führer and Chancellor, instead of to the country or the constitution, which was to cause such heavy conflicts of conscience to the officers who later took part in the resistance to Hitler. In summer 1934, however, his regime seemed to be consolidated, his dictatorship over Germany was established and the 'brown revolution' of the Nazis followed its course within what were still largely traditional forms. In this way the profile of the Third Reich was equally made up of tradition and revolution, and the same may be said of the beginnings of Hitler's foreign policy.

2

The First Phase of Nazi Foreign Policy

In foreign affairs the new government held to the demand of its predecessors for the revision of the peace treaty, but its methods and objectives were unmistakably different. Stresemann's nationalist policy of treaty revision and great power status for Germany had remained within the framework of European policy and international law. In this respect the later authoritarian Cabinets already differed perceptibly from Stresemann, and Hitler's Nazi policy was to go further still. In the atmosphere of the world economic crisis the governments of Brüning, von Papen and von Schleicher took a tougher line than their predecessors and aimed to secure a revision of Versailles by 'going it alone' on a national basis. This marked a completely fresh stage in the history of Prussian and German foreign policy; it contrasts with Stresemann's nationalist but peaceable line with its emphasis on economic ties with foreign countries, and also with Hitler's expansionist, warlike and racialist strategy. The conservative von Neurath continued to be Foreign Minister after the take-over on 30 January 1933, and largely for this reason foreign statesmen and diplomats gained the impression of continuity in Germany's foreign policy. Thus German diplomacy to a large extent obscured, without intending to do so, the sharp difference between the revisionist great power policy of the past and the Nazi policy of aggression and racism. To some extent, indeed, Foreign Office officials also tried to pursue a course of their own. But their revisionist views were so similar to parts of Hitler's policy that they could not at the outset take a substantially different line, while the dictator himself took firm control at a comparatively early stage in such important matters as the reorientation of policy towards Russia and Poland.

The new emphasis in foreign policy was already seen on 3 February 1933, when Hitler declared in a speech to senior army officers that it must be the aim of German foreign policy to conquer 'fresh *Lebensraum* (living space) in the East', and that this area must be 'ruthlessly Germanised'. Alongside this objective Hitler seemed to put forward as equally valid the idea that Germany's space problem 'might be solved by seizing fresh opportunities in the export field': this was in harmony with Schacht's efforts to solve Germany's internal and external, social and national problems by means of a foreign trade offensive (see above, pp. 9–10). Hitler supported these efforts and let Schacht have his way provided the latter aided Hitler in his political plans, especially as regards rearmament and the resulting need for foreign currency. Moreover, the ostensible alternative based on economic expansion enabled Hitler, while proclaiming his warlike aims, at the same time to reassure his audience by professing a love for peace. This theme was repeatedly stressed at the outset of his chancellorship, for example, in his speech to the Reichstag on 23 March 1933 apropos of Mussolini's proposal of 17 March for a four-power pact, and especially in his major 'peace speech' of 17 May 1933.

At the same time Hitler, who treated foreign affairs almost entirely as his private preserve, immediately took up the theme of his objectives as set out in *Mein Kampf* and his second work, known in postwar translation as *Hitler's Secret Book*. In accordance with these, the ultimate purpose was to establish a global Pax Germanica 'by the conquering sword of a master race' which would 'bring the whole world into the service of a higher civilisation'. Given the premises of anti-Semitism, anti-Bolshevism and the fight for *Lebensraum*, the Soviet Union was presented as Germany's arch-enemy in the sphere of power politics and ideology. A war was envisaged which would destroy Bolshevism, solve the Jewish question and provide the German people with the space it needed. Unlike his conservative associates in the government of 'national concentration', Hitler was not content with the objective of recovering the 1914 frontiers and restoring Germany's position as a European great power. He intended, step by step, to advance beyond treaty revision, to establish German predominance in Central and Eastern Europe and, after conquering the Soviet Union, to set up a continental empire in which France, hitherto the strongest power in Europe, would either be subjugated or reduced to the role of a junior partner. As early as the 1920s Hitler made clear his long-term political dream: future generations of Germans, leaders of a racially purified Europe, would in the end be capable of challenging even the USA – which Hitler at that time still viewed with great respect – and exerting influence overseas as a world power with a strong navy. At that time, which still seemed far away, it might be desirable to reassess the plan for an alliance with Britain, which Hitler regarded as essential to his objective of conquering the Soviet Union, and which he bent all his efforts to obtain. From the point of view of ideology and power politics, Britain seemed to him the right partner for his foreign policy and warlike enterprises. The two peripheral powers of the international system, the USA and the Soviet Union, were an economic, military and ideological threat to Britain's imperial interests; in view of this threat, Hitler was convinced that Britain would abandon her traditional policy of holding the balance in Europe and would consent to an alliance with Nazi Germany on the basis of spheres of interest. Under this plan Germany would have a free hand in Eastern Europe while Britain would concern herself with her empire, undisturbed by naval and colonial demands such as the Kaiser's Germany had made upon her. The idea of co-operation with Britain always loomed larger in Hitler's mind than that of alliance with Mussolini's Italy, which he also entertained from an early stage. Even before his accession to power he repeatedly put the idea of an alliance before British visitors, and after January 1933 he endeavoured to achieve it by diplomatic means and, still more, by initiatives of a highly unorthodox kind on the part of some of his closest followers. Although visits to England by Ribbentrop and Rosenberg as unofficial envoys were unsuccessful, British policy showed much sympathy for German revisionist demands, and there seemed to be grounds for hope that his basic plan would find acceptance. In actual fact the motives and objectives of the British 'appeasement' policy were quite different from Hitler's ideas of an alliance, but he refused to believe this even after Sir John Simon, the Foreign Secretary, visited Berlin on 25–26 March 1935. Whereas Hitler hoped to conclude a bilateral agreement with Britain so that he could attack the Soviet Union, the British aim was, by showing sympathy for revisionist demands, to induce Germany to conclude multilateral agreements that would be binding in international law and thus ensure peace in Europe.

Still hoping that Britain would see the light, Hitler pressed on with the rearmament which was so important for his plans. On 14 October 1933, not without pressure from the conservatives in his government, he terminated Germany's participation in the disarmament conference and announced her withdrawal from the League of Nations, thus freeing the Reich from the restrictions imposed on rearmament. Then, on 16 March 1935, he took the final step by denouncing the military clauses of the treaty of Versailles and reintroducing conscription in Germany.

In the first phase of Nazi foreign policy Hitler endeavoured, with the initial support of conservative members of his government, to pursue two major aims. On the one hand he wished to avert the threat of German isolation and to find allies in accordance with the ideas he had formed in the 1920s; on the other he sought to accelerate and turn to his own ends the disruption of the international system which had begun with Japan's attack on the Chinese mainland in 1931. As foreshadowed in *Mein Kampf* he tried to achieve a *rapprochement* with Italy, which however did not yet succeed: Mussolini was more inclined to go along with the Western powers and act as a 'trimmer' in the European balance between the Reich and the powers defending the status quo. Whereas in *Mein Kampf* Hitler had regarded the defeat of France as a precondition of the conquest of *Lebensraum* in the East, he now began not only to woo Britain but also to seek an understanding with France. The idea of limited co-operation with that country never had the same importance to him as an alliance with Britain, which played a central part in his plans, but none the less it was attractive for various reasons. In the first place it lessened the danger for Germany of the 'period of risk' of which Hitler spoke on 3 February 1933, when he pointed out that rearmament would be dangerous as long as France was in a position to attack Germany in concert with her East European satellites. Secondly, his appeals for peaceful co-operation served to weaken France's military resolve and opposition to his plans. Finally, in the early 1930s he probably no longer rated France's power as highly as he had done in the previous decade, when he had thought it essential to defeat France and thus safeguard his rear before turning on the Soviet Union. In view of the internal crises by which France was shaken, he seems to have thought in the later period that, provided Britain acquiesced in his attacking the Soviet Union, he need not make war on France before doing so but could secure France's consent to his plans by means of an agreement. Having conquered Russia he would be so powerful as master of Eastern Europe that the rest of the continent would have to acknowledge German hegemony.

While Hitler's long-term plans were firmly based on a war for *Lebensraum* in the East, as well as on racial dogma, the idea of a continental empire and eventually world supremacy for Germany, he showed much flexibility in his choice of methods. Thus on 5 May 1933 he ratified the German-Soviet treaty, signed in Berlin on 24 April 1926 and prolonged by the Brüning government on 24 June 1931; and on 20 July 1933 he concluded a Concordat with the Vatican. In this way the Third Reich acknowledged in the political sphere two powers whose ideology was diametrically opposed to each other's and to Nazism.

Hitler's objectives in foreign policy became clear, however, at the beginning of 1934, when he accomplished a diplomatic coup which averted the threat of isolation by the European powers, lessened the risk of the 'danger zone' in foreign affairs and pointed the way to his new Eastern policy. On 26 January 1934 he concluded a non-aggression pact with the Polish dictator, Marshal Pilsudski. This was a sensational reversal of German policy towards Eastern Europe, since, broadly speaking, it had till then been the objective of the Weimar Cabinets and the German foreign office to pursue an anti-Polish policy in league with the Soviet Union. Hitler's new move effected a 'change of partners' and radically altered the thrust of German policy in the East. The pact with Pilsudski helped him to break the ring of French encirclement and prevent France from co-ordinating an attack on Germany with her Polish ally. Hitler's decision caused misgivings on the part of his conservative associates, who still saw Poland as a barrier to German ambitions in the East. However, the move was a fairly obvious signal that Hitler had embarked on his ideologically motivated campaign of expansion at Russia's expense.

On 13 January 1935 a plebiscite was held in the Saarland in which 91 per cent of the population voted in favour of the province returning to Germany. This was a great success for Hitler in the foreign policy field, and had a valuable effect in consolidating the regime's position at home. At the same time, Hitler endeavoured, despite his previous failures, to reach an understanding with Britain. In November 1934 he indicated to Sir Eric Phipps, the ambassador in Berlin, that Germany was prepared to reach agreement on the basis of a voluntary restriction of her naval forces. Britain accepted the offer, welcoming it as an opportunity to avoid the naval armaments race that had been so pernicious a factor in the international situation before 1914. On this occasion Hitler managed to prise Britain away from the principle of multilateral agreements and conclude a bilateral pact with her. Its main features were that Germany agreed to limit her naval programme to 35 per cent of British forces and, as regards submarines, to accept for the time being a ratio of 45 : 100. This was clearly advantageous to Britain in view of her overextended worldwide commitments. From 1934 onwards the British endeavoured to conclude a similar agreement with Germany as regards rearmament in the air, but Hitler, significantly, never made any earnest effort in this direction. While the naval treaty of 18 June 1935 did not in itself commit the British to anything further, Hitler and his plenipotentiary von Ribbentrop believed, despite setbacks on particular issues, that they could also reach a general accommodation on wider matters, which it was always Hitler's object to achieve.

It seemed at times as if Hitler's aims in foreign policy might be realised, since their far-reaching character was not understood either by the German conservatives or by foreign statesmen. The excesses of the Third Reich in internal affairs caused revulsion in the West, however, and when Germany reintroduced conscription on 16 March 1935 the Western powers reacted by forming the 'Stresa front', following a conference at that resort on 11–14 April between the heads of government of Britain, France and Italy. The powers condemned the German procedure and the unilateral abrogation of treaties, but their protest remained ineffectual. Again and again they were reassured, however, as each new move by the German dictator was accompanied by protestations of peace, by Hitler himself and his diplomatic agents. The conservatives in the Foreign Ministry unwittingly helped Hitler to succeed in his 'grand strategy of self-deprecation' (Jacobsen, 1968). The racialist excesses at home were an indication of the ideological aspect of Nazi foreign policy and a dramatic revelation of the essence of Hitler's dictatorship, but this was still not clear to observers of the confusing pattern of German behaviour in foreign affairs. For, alongside Hitler and the Foreign Ministry, the 'Ribbentrop bureau' and the 'Rosenberg office' pursued what were virtually policies of their own, and so before long did agencies of the SS and the Propaganda Ministry. These activities often thwarted one another, producing events such as the Nazi putsch in Vienna on 25 July 1934, which Hitler at that time probably did not desire. The dynamic forces let loose in foreign affairs by the chaos of conflicting authorities may on occasion have forced the dictator's hand, but in principle they were always in conformity with the lines of 'high policy' laid down by him.

Summary

The following conclusions emerge from this account of the Third Reich from 1933 to 1935.

Hitler's appointment as Chancellor on 30 January 1933 marked the end of the Weimar Republic and introduced a new era of German history. Few contemporaries realised what can be seen in retrospect, that it was a first step towards the destruction of the Prussian-German national state founded in 1871. The Nazi leaders of the new government of 'national concentration' put their revolution into effect gradually and by seemingly legal means, using the slogan of 'national recovery' which was understood primarily as an anti-Marxist rallying-cry, and proceeding to the *Gleichschaltung* (regimentation) of political, social and public life in Germany. On the whole they showed extraordinary speed in achieving the total 'seizure of power' which profoundly transformed the Reich. Scarcely anyone at the time, no doubt, foresaw the catastrophic end to which all this would lead.

The ideas of *Gleichschaltung* and the seizure of monopolistic power by Hitler and the Nazis are repellent to us today, but many contemporaries found them attractive. The party set about achieving its ends immediately after the change of government in January 1933, and in a relatively short time the Reich was subjected to the will of its new masters. During that time recalcitrant members of the old political system were either brought to heel or deprived of their posts by terrorist means. The seizure of power was in principle effected by 2 August 1934, when Hitler, on Hindenburg's death, took over the office of President as well as Chancellor.

However, two major political and social forces, namely, big business and the army, managed to resist the party's totalitarian demands until 1936 and 1938 respectively, when they were brought under closer control. There was clearly a partial identity between Hitler's aims and the interests of these two groups, and it was only later that differences began to appear, so that for a time the economic and the military élite preserved a relatively high degree of autonomy. The regime continued to recognise them as factors of power and to some extent still respected them in the interests of co-operation.

The process of *Gleichschaltung* and the seizure of power which was essentially completed in August 1934 continued logically thereafter in two ways. In the first place the regime endeavoured to bring under its control such political and social institutions and associations as had till then been left relatively undisturbed. On the other hand it continued the process, begun in 1933, of honeycombing the country with Nazi organisations which competed notably with existing state institutions. Despite propaganda boasting of the unity of the Third Reich, these organisations reflected the dualism between party and state which was characteristic of Nazi rule, and were designed to support the party's claim to ideological leadership in the new state.

In this way existing bureaucracies were penetrated, exploited and turned to new purposes; at the same time they did for a considerable period provide 'safe areas' within which, to a limited extent, it was possible to pursue independent activities unknown to the regime and contrary to its policies. This, however, was not the only specific feature of Hitler's 'legal revolution'. The typical feature of the 'one-party state' proclaimed on 14 July 1933, in which the chaos of different authorities provided a basis and an instrument whereby the Führer's wishes were dominant in all important matters, was rather the fact that the revolutionary seizure of power took place under a cloak of tradition. The 'national revival' under the Nazis was characterised by the juxtaposition of old and new elements: tradition and revolution, legality and terror. In this sense the seizure of power and *Gleichschaltung* were conceived as a long-term objective and realised by a series of improvisations: (1) by the use of legal means, (2) by steadily widening the legal possibilities, (3) by creating new authorities, and (4) by means of organised or spontaneous campaigns from below, from street fighting upwards, under Nazi ringleaders (Schulz, 1976). In this fashion Hitler's seizure of power was a far-reaching process of transformation in home and foreign policy whereby a constitutional state based on the rule of law became a totalitarian 'dual state', though in some cases it took years before the political, social and economic implications of this became apparent. Hitler preserved the mechanism of the state based on traditional standards in so far as he needed it as a convenient cloak for the attainment of his largely ideological aims. But behind this cloak the terroristic, arbitrary rule characteristic of the Third Reich was sufficiently discernible to be an ever-present threat.

Altogether the Nazi seizure of power was 'one of the new style of twentieth-century revolutions operating, consciously and ostentatiously, with novel means of terror, mass suggestion and communication, compulsion and control' (Bracher, 1976a). The watchword of 'national revival' offered leading sections of the population the hope of liberation from the Versailles peace settlement, which was generally felt as an insult and a humiliation. Given the attachment of the German people to law and order, the fact that the revolution was apparently conducted legally was important in overcoming their scruples. Justice was violated in the name of law: the seeming legality of the take-over confused objectors and created sufficient confidence for Hitler to set up his totalitarian dictatorship. The secret of the Nazis' success was to use the threat of terror and to make it a reality whenever they could not attain their ends by stretching law to the uttermost and by taking advantage of the German people's readiness to acquiesce in a basic transformation of the constitutional and parliamentary state.

From this point of view the take-over was assisted by the marked distaste of

German élite groups for the parliamentary system. Nazi policy was also aided at the outset by an upswing in the national economy, due in part to improved conditions worldwide. In the second half of the decade those who had promoted Germany's economic revival after the seizure of power, and believed they were fully in charge of it, were for a long time unable to see that it depended heavily on rearmament, which was difficult to put into reverse and which had fatal consequences as an adjunct to Hitler's war policy. Many of Hitler's conservative patrons and associates who helped him to power and worked with him thereafter were eventually to pay with their lives for the deceptive state of public order achieved by substituting terrorism and emergency decrees for the bourgeois system based on the rule of law.

The conservative bastions were still plainly in evidence at the time of the boycott of Jews on 1 April 1933 and the Nuremberg Laws of 15 September 1935 – measures which extended far beyond immediate circumstances and revealed Hitler's racist aims as a prime motive of the Third Reich. While members of the old ruling classes still expected to use Hitler and his movement to preserve social conservatism and the traditional order of things, he and his party had already turned the tables on them: he used the knowledge and influence of the traditional élite as long as he had to and as long as they served his purpose. Thus a characteristic feature of the initial phase of the Third Reich was the co-operation, based on a clear community of interests, between the Nazis and conservatives, who were both hostile to Weimar democracy and between them sealed its fate.

In addition to general features of German political culture (cf. Concluding Remarks to Part One, pp. 93–8 below) and Hitler's political planning, the Nazis were certainly helped in the months of the seizure of power and *Gleichschaltung* by unforeseen situations and historical accidents. The party used these to assist its conquest of power, in an improvised manner but with conscious purpose. There was a firm determination to transform Germany completely, even if they scarcely had a clear picture of their aims in detail. The party and Führer were to be assured of an undisputed monopoly of power in home affairs, and the international status quo was to be revolutionised far beyond the aims of Weimar and conservative Germany. Finally, in some distant future, came the utopian aim of a racial dictatorship over the whole world. To achieve this programme the party made use of every opportunity that presented itself, combining accident and design with diabolical skill.

(B) PREPARATIONS FOR WAR, 1936–9

1

German Foreign Policy: from Revisionism to Expansionism

Four major international factors in the 1930s largely accounted for the fact that Hitler was for so long able to conduct a policy of expansion under the guise of revisionism, with undoubted success and with relatively little interference from foreign powers.

(1)   The attention of the powers, especially Britain and the USA, was constantly diverted to the continuing crisis in the Far East. This began in September 1931 with Japan's military action in Manchuria, and developed into an armed conflict between Japan and China following the Japanese attack at Lukouchiao on 7 July 1937.

(2)   The Mediterranean area became a world crisis centre owing to Italy's war against Abyssinia (October 1935–July 1936) and the Spanish Civil War (July 1936–March 1939); the latter involved all the European powers, the USSR and the USA, or at least claimed their attention more or less intensively. Together with the problems of East Asia and continental Europe, Spain became a key area for British world interests and required the constant attention of the British government.

(3)   Events in the 1930s increasingly showed up the problems and 'artificiality' (R. Aron) of the Paris treaty system of 1919–20, which had left unsolved, or created, too many conflicts between 'established victors, those deprived of the fruits of victory, and the defeated' (Hillgruber, 1973b).

(4)   The worldwide antagonism between Britain and the Soviet Union, which extended to the Far East, the Mediterranean and continental Europe, favoured the revisionist and expansionist policy of the German dictator for a considerable time. Only in 1941 was this antagonism patched up and Anglo-Soviet differences shelved for the time being in the face of Hitler's military challenge, which forced into partnership the powers whose ideological and political rivalry had dominated the international system.

By exploiting these crises, tensions and wars, and taking advantage of the diversion they offered, the Third Reich from 1936 to 1939 consistently yet flexibly pursued the dictator's systematic policy. Hitler's first endeavour was to win British support for his anti-Soviet strategy, but as Britain hesitated he turned more and more towards Italy and Japan as well.

After a period of vainly wooing the British from 1933 to 1935, in the next two years Hitler sought to make Britain amenable by threats: thus on 7 March 1936 he made his first official demand for the return of colonies. This was intended to intimidate the British into complying with Hitler's plan for an alliance; as far as Germany was concerned, the colonies themselves were a long-term objective which would only be of interest after the programme of continental conquest was carried out. From the end of 1937 onwards Hitler steered an ambivalent course towards Britain, and in a sense he did so even after 3 September 1939. On the one hand he continued to work for a British alliance as the ideal solution, while on the other, not least under the influence of his foreign affairs adviser von Ribbentrop, he became increasingly used to the idea that he might have to achieve his political ends without Britain or even against her. In accordance with his plan for separate spheres of influence for Britain as a maritime and colonial power and Germany as a land power with continental hegemony, Hitler thought it self-evident that Britain would not oppose his demand for revision of the treaty of Versailles and his plans for hegemony and expansion. While friendship with Britain was the main objective of his alliance policy, he had no intention of purchasing it at the cost of abandoning his designs in Central and Eastern Europe. In this sense he evaluated each step in the active execution of his foreign policy as a test of Britain's attitude towards his plans, the ultimate nature of which was for a long time obscure to British observers.

When the Foreign Secretary Sir John Simon visited Berlin on 25–26 March 1935 he already let it be understood that Britain was prepared to accept German designs in Central and East Central Europe. On 6 January 1936 Mussolini informed von Hassell, the German ambassador in Rome, that Italy had no objection to Austria becoming a 'satellite' of the Reich. These events charted the course which international politics were to follow. For the time being, it is true, normal diplomatic relations between Berlin and Vienna were preserved by the agreement of 11 July 1936, which re-established friendly relations. But in the published part of the agreement, the Austrian government undertook to take account in its policy of the fact that 'Austria regards herself as a German state', and in the secret clauses they promised to conduct their foreign policy 'with due regard to the peaceful aims of the foreign policy of the government of the German Reich' – a policy which culminated in the enforced union of Austria with Germany in March 1938.

Mussolini's accommodating attitude was due in large part to Hitler's skilful double-dealing over the Abyssinian war. On the one hand he supported the Duce's military measures, while on the other he secretly delivered arms to the Ethiopians. In this way he prolonged the conflict as long as possible, diverted the attention of the two world powers to the Mediterranean and Africa, increased Mussolini's dependence on Germany, not least in the economic sphere, and thus promoted Italy's *rapprochement* with Germany.

The British offered no resistance worth the name on 7 March 1936 when, taking advantage of the Abyssinian War, Hitler in a surprise move reoccupied the demilitarised zone of the Rhineland – a step which was seen in London as of little consequence to British worldwide interests. Hitler received firm support from the conservatives in his government when he used the signature of the Franco-Soviet pact of mutual assistance as a pretext for thus securing his rear as a prelude to his designs in the East. France's power to react was paralysed for reasons of military strength and internal politics, while Britain, as we have seen, indicated its indifference to what Germany was doing: it condemned methods of violence, but basically approved of German aims. The reoccupation of the Rhineland did not prevent Britain from trying once again to reach a peaceful settlement with Hitler. Meanwhile the dictator had scored a decisive success in the field of treaty revision, which increased his popularity with the German people.

While the army leaders and the Foreign Ministry had also played an important part in the Rhineland episode, it was clear that Hitler was more and more in sovereign control of Reich foreign policy, the anti-Soviet trend of which became increasingly evident in 1936. On 22 July of that year, five days after the outbreak of civil war in Spain, Hitler saw the Japanese military attaché General Oshima at Bayreuth and described to him his determination to 'once more split up the gigantic block of Russia into its original historical components'. In the same connection the Nazi regime in August–September 1936 unleashed an intensified campaign against world communism and the Soviet Union. On the one hand this was an expression of Hitler's ideological aims, and on the other it served the purpose of representing Germany as the guarantor of a broadly based anti-Bolshevik policy, and hence as the obvious ally for the Western powers, especially Britain, or, failing them, for Italy and Japan.

As the hoped-for agreement with Britain still did not materialise, Hitler proclaimed the Berlin–Rome Axis in his speech at Milan on 1 November 1936, and on 25 November concluded the Anti-Comintern Pact with Japan. These were provisional solutions, intended to serve the following purposes. In the first place the secret clauses of the treaty with Japan provided for benevolent neutrality if either partner should find itself at war with the Soviet Union. Secondly, the *rapprochement* with Japan and Italy had a substitute value in Hitler's mind in the event of Britain finally refusing to join the alliance. Japan, in particular, was already seen by von Ribbentrop as the basis of an alternative to Hitler's programme, namely, a definitely anti-British concept which envisaged a continental concentration of power, all the way from Japan to Spain, in opposition to Great Britain and the USA. Whereas Hitler's policy was anti-Soviet and pro-British, von Ribbentrop's long-term ideas, which became increasingly clear from 1938–9 onwards, were based rather on securing Soviet neutrality for an anti-British policy. However, for the time being this did not prevent Ribbentrop, as ambassador in London from 1936 to 1938, from doing his best to obtain support for German expansion eastward in accordance with Hitler's plans.

Hitler had enjoined von Ribbentrop to secure the British alliance when he sent him to London in August 1936 to succeed Leopold von Hoesch as ambassador. Hitler also confirmed his desire for a free hand in Eastern Europe in conversation with Count Ciano, the newly appointed Italian Foreign Minister, who visited him at the Berghof on 24 October 1936: at the same time the Mediterranean, the Balkans and the Near East were assigned to Italy as her sphere of influence.

Hitler's anti-communist and anti-Soviet orientation was made clear once more when, on 25 July 1936, he acceded to General Franco's request and decided to intervene on the side of the insurgents in the Spanish Civil War – an important factor in Franco's victory. After Hitler had taken this decision for political reasons Spain became the scene of much German economic activity, mainly directed by Göring, but this was a secondary element in the dictator's plans. What weighed with him most was the fear that, since the Popular Front government had come to power in France in June 1936, Spain too might adopt a course of internal policy that would incline it towards Russia rather than Germany, and might deprive Germany of the safeguard in the rear which was necessary before she could attack the Soviet Union. Thus from the ideological and strategic point of view the intervention of the Third Reich in Spain is to be regarded as part of Hitler's systematic anti-Soviet policy. Another factor was that Mussolini had overstrained his military and economic resources by intervening in Spain, and the more Italy depended on German support in this area the more closely she would be bound to the Reich. In addition Berlin closely observed Britain's attitude to the Spanish War, and noted that in this case too Britain's chief concern was to avoid a major European war: she was content to let Hitler and Mussolini do as they liked in Spain, and Stalin also. As the Spanish conflict dragged on it served the purpose of distracting the European great powers and might even involve them militarily. Thus German aid to Franco was a function of Hitler's anti-Soviet policy and of his plans for a series of lightning campaigns on the continent.

His aims were also made plain at the end of August 1936 in the directive for the Four-Year Plan. 'In four years the German army must be operational and the German economy fit for war.' Hitler still believed he could secure an alliance with Britain, and was confirmed in this belief by a visit from Lloyd George, the former premier, at the Obersalzberg on 4 September 1936. He never grasped the fact that the Conservative government under Neville Chamberlain hoped by means of 'appeasement' to achieve peacefully a European settlement that differed radically from Hitler's warlike methods and expansionist plans. However, in the course of 1937 he saw more clearly that Britain was making difficulties for him and that France was becoming more and more dependent on British policy. Hence from the end of 1937 onwards Hitler no longer excluded the possibility that in the last resort he might have to act without Britain or against her, and perhaps even, as a *pis aller* (Hillgruber, 1973b), adopt an anti-British policy based on Ribbentrop's 'world political triangle' of Berlin, Rome and Tokyo. None the less, he continued his efforts to secure the British alliance by means of interviews, conversations and contacts of all kinds.

The year 1937 lies between the period of Hitler's 'surprises' in the field of foreign policy and the crises that led directly up to the war. It marked to some extent a turning-point in Hitler's thinking. He held fast to the basic plan of a war for *Lebensraum*, but, given the shortness of time, he had to weigh the possibilities open to him in the way of alliances and was finally obliged to alter his plans in this respect.

The period was one of accelerated international developments which were advantageous to Hitler's revisionist and expansionist policy and, as we have seen, were not confined to Europe. It was not only Italy's war in Abyssinia and the Spanish Civil War that had severely shaken the international order. France's weakness as the chief power in Europe and guarantor of the Versailles settlement had been dramatically revealed. The *cordon sanitaire* erected by France against Germany in Eastern Europe had shown itself to be of a highly doubtful value, not least because of the all-overshadowing opposition between Britain and the Soviet Union; and Britain, it was plain, was playing a wait-and-see game in all matters of international policy. The global status quo was also threatened in the Far East, where Japan had invaded Manchuria on 18 September 1931; and Japanese-Chinese hostilities once more came to the forefront with the incident of 7 July 1937 at the Marco Polo Bridge in Peking, which was of the greatest concern to Britain and the USA.

As the East Asian conflict continued, Hitler decided on 18 October 1937 to abandon the Foreign Ministry's line of supporting China and attempting to mediate between the combatants, and instead to support Japan unequivocally. As in the case of Italy's accession to the Anti-Comintern Pact on 6 November 1937, apart from the propaganda emphasising the possibilities of anti-Soviet action it was clear that German policy was swinging away from Britain as a result of the latter's reluctance to conclude an alliance with Germany. However, in Hitler's mind – as opposed to Ribbentrop's plans at this time – the anti-British mood never predominated over the true ideological and strategic objective of the Third Reich, that of conquering *Lebensraum* in Eastern Europe and destroying the Soviet Union.

In accordance with this policy the fight against communism continued in the political field and with noisy propaganda. In a speech at the Reich Party Day of Labour on 7 September 1937 Hitler spoke of the 'Germanic Reich' formed by the German nation in defiance of Bolshevism and Jewry. In the last resort the foreign policy of the Third Reich was determined by the ideological motifs of anti-Bolshevism, the conquest of *Lebensraum*, and racism. These prompted Hitler to create a 'state in arms' in order to solve Germany's space problem – an intention he announced on 23 November 1937 in a secret speech at the inauguration of the *Ordensburg* (youth training centre) at Sonthofen.

The question of *Lebensraum* also figured prominently in Hitler's secret speech on 5 November 1937 to von Neurath, the Foreign Minister, and the heads of the armed services. The record of this speech by Hitler's military adjutant, Col Hossbach, is not free from doubt as to its authenticity, but agrees in substance with numerous other key documents on Nazi foreign policy. In his speech Hitler specified the objectives he hoped to attain if possible by the end of summer 1938, especially *vis-à-vis* Austria and Czechoslovakia. He also declared in general terms that the space problem must be solved by 1943–5, as Germany would then be at the height of her military strength. Hitler felt himself pressed for time, partly because of his own age (he was now 48) but also because it seemed likely that the international situation would alter to Germany's disadvantage.

For, on 5 October 1937 – exactly a month before Hitler had spelt out his views as to the need for the Reich to accelerate its programme of expansion – President Roosevelt in his 'quarantine speech' at Chicago had issued a warning to the revisionist states, calling on all peace-loving nations to unite and threatening that lawbreakers would be expelled from the family of nations; he also indicated, at least by way of a *ballon d'essai*, his determination to lead the Americans away from their policy of ignoring global conflicts and to activate the role of the USA as a world power. The British factor was of greater importance to Hitler than the still distant American threat or the USSR, which was held to be of little account since Stalin's bloody purges of the Red Army; but for the present he had to reckon Britain among the possible adversaries of the Reich. Britain, as before, was the key to Hitler's foreign policy; but as the British were not prepared for a *rapprochement*, he decided to put pressure on them in the context of international politics, so as to make them amenable to his plans.

On 19 November 1937 Lord Halifax came to the Berghof on behalf of the Chamberlain government (appointed in May of that year) and outlined to the Führer the appeasement policy envisaged by the British Cabinet. This implied territorial concessions (the questions of Austria, Czechoslovakia and Danzig to be settled according to German wishes), in return for which Germany was to be committed to a permanent European peace settlement. However, these proposals were by now of little interest to the dictator, as he already regarded East Central Europe as an area subject to German influence and hegemony. Hitler demanded all or nothing. He wanted an alliance with Britain and a free hand in the East, but British hostility would not deter him from pursuing his aims. As Chamberlain's government would neither conclude an alliance nor quietly tolerate his planned policy in the East, Hitler's attitude towards it became more and more sceptical. He was confirmed in this view by a long report on the international situation and German-British relations, drawn up by Ribbentrop at the conclusion of his embassy to Britain. Ribbentrop declared that it was impossible to reach an agreement with Britain on the lines Germany wanted, and he advised

Hitler to consider the idea of forming an anti-British front. Hitler's policy of alliances was in a precarious state: Italy and Japan were inadequate substitutes for Britain, and from time to time he still tried to reach an understanding with the latter.

The transformation of the German economy, army and Foreign Office were completed at the end of 1937 or beginning of 1938. Schacht was dismissed from his post as Reich Economic Minister on 26 November 1937. The Blomberg-Fritsch crisis of January–February 1938 brought about changes in the army high command, and at the same time Ribbentrop replaced Neurath as Foreign Minister. All these spectacular events created the necessary internal conditions for a forcible policy of territorial gains in Eastern Europe. They also had the effect of strengthening the Führer's authority and covering over the recurrent tensions and disagreements within the German leadership over the internal, foreign and economic policy of the Reich.

The first decisive action took place in regard to Austria, relations with which were governed by the bilateral agreement of 11 July 1936. As late as December 1937 Hitler declared that he did not want a 'strong-arm' solution. He no doubt hoped to assist the Austrian Nazis to seize power in the same manner as he himself had done in Germany. In order to defuse the relationship between the two countries von Papen, then German ambassador in Vienna, arranged a meeting between Hitler and the Austrian Chancellor von Schuschnigg, which took place at the Obersalzberg near Berchtesgaden on 12 February 1938. Here the German dictator bullied Schuschnigg into accepting an extremely one-sided agreement whereby the Austrian Nazis were to take part in the government, control the Ministry of the Interior and therefore the police, and be free to carry on party activities. To avert a complete Nazi take-over Schuschnigg on 9 March took the bold step of announcing a plebiscite to be held three days later, 'for a free, German, independent, social, Christian and united Austria'. The voting age was raised to 24 so as to exclude young people, who were mostly Nazis and in favour of the *Anschluss* (union with Germany). The arrangements for the plebiscite were clearly faulty and improvised, and this gave Hitler a pretext to force Schuschnigg to desist from the idea.

Meanwhile Göring and von Ribbentrop were pressing for a military invasion of Austria. Mussolini assured Hitler that this time, unlike 1934, he would not interfere in Austria's affairs. On 11 March Schuschnigg succumbed to a German ultimatum threatening that the troops would go in unless he surrendered his office to the Nazi leader Seyss-Inquart. His desperate appeal to the Western powers met with no response; he resigned, but when the Austrian President Miklas refused to appoint Seyss-Inquart Chancellor, Hitler on 11 March ordered his troops to invade. On the night of the 11th/12th Miklas at last gave in, but it was too late to avert the military solution. The pretext was furnished by a telegram dictated by Göring, in which General Keppler of the SS, Hitler's agent in Vienna, transmitted to Berlin a fictitious appeal from the new Austrian government to the Reich.

On 12 March the German units moved into Austria, after Ribbentrop had assured Göring by telephone from London that the British would not intervene. When the invasion began it was still Hitler's intention to proclaim merely a union between the two countries, but the enthusiasm with which he and the German troops were greeted persuaded him to effect the complete absorption of Austria into Germany. The precise form of union was not a major issue with him, provided Germany could use Austria to encircle the Czechs and act as a satellite in the conflicts to come. Germany was now incontestably the dominant continental power and seemed likely, together with Italy and Japan, to determine the fate of the world. Britain condemned the manner in which the *Anschluss* had been achieved, but recognised the *fait accompli* within a fortnight. Hitler had realised that he could count on Mussolini and that the British would not fight. He could be confident that Japan, whose puppet government in Manchukuo he was to recognise on 17 February 1938, would stand by him, while the attention of the USA was diverted by Japan from Europe to the Far East.

Against this background Hitler decided on 28 March 1938 to solve the Czechoslovak problem 'before too long'. Europe's next crisis loomed, and Hitler's next objective in the East became visible. In Germany rearmament proceeded by leaps and bounds; naval preparations went forward and the demand for colonies was activated, pointing to the overseas phase of German global policy, while the regime's utopian racial policy was put into effect by a fresh series of measures.

On 28 March 1938 Hitler received Konrad Henlein, the leader of the Sudeten German Party in Czechoslovakia, and instructed him to keep putting forward more demands than the Czechoslovak government could meet. The Sudeten Germans, who had been discriminated against in Czechoslovakia, were to be a springboard for Hitler's next expansionist move. The 'Sudeten crisis' duly took the course prescribed for it in Germany. On 20 May the Czechs mobilised in the mistaken belief that a German attack was imminent. Britain, in the belief that France would support the Czechs, took up a firm attitude in Berlin, although in other respects it did all it could to keep the already reluctant French from taking action. The total effect was to give the European public the impression that Hitler had knuckled under to the Czechs and British; this infuriated Hitler and made him force the pace. On 30 May he notified the army of his 'unalterable decision' to 'crush Czechoslovakia by military action in the foreseeable future'. The army was to be in a state of readiness by 1 October 1938. The accompanying propaganda campaign insisted that the cession of the Sudeten territory was the Reich's last territorial demand.

As the crisis became acute the whole world looked to Britain. At this time the budding conservative resistance movement in Germany approached the British government with plans to oppose Hitler more firmly, to bring about a setback to his foreign policy and thus create conditions for the overthrow of the Nazi regime. The government received these overtures coolly. For external and internal reasons Chamberlain preferred to achieve a European peace settlement officially with the German government and not in a conspiratorial manner with the opposition, whose emissaries he compared to 'Jacobins at the French court'. He was prepared to go a long way to meet German demands for a change in Central and Eastern Europe, and to negotiate with the Reich over economic favours and compensation in colonial matters, in order broadly to safeguard the European and worldwide status quo and above all to avert the danger of war, which he thought would be disastrous for Britain and the Empire.

At the height of the crisis, after Hitler at the Nuremberg party congress had threatened to invade Czechoslovakia, the British premier on 15 September flew to the Obersalzberg to discuss personally the surrender of the Sudeten territory, so as to keep Hitler from warlike measures and prevent Germany from swallowing up the Czechoslovak state. After consulting the Cabinet on 22 September he again flew to meet Hitler, this time at Bad Godesberg, and informed him that the British government approved the agreement reached a week previously for the self-determination of the Sudeten Germans and the cession of the area to Germany. Thereupon Hitler demanded that the Western powers should consent to an immediate occupation of the territory by the German army, together with a plebiscite in an area that was not exactly defined; he also encouraged Poland and Hungary to make territorial demands of their own on Czechoslovakia. The Godesberg conference ended in deadlock on 24 September. A European war seemed inevitable; but there was no change in the situation for Britain, in as much as British interests had been damaged to an extent that would have obliged her to go to war with Germany. Hitler had set an ultimatum for 28 September; as the Western powers prepared for war, the British government asked Mussolini to use his good offices in Berlin, as a result of which the Munich conference took place on 29 September 1938.

There the Duce proposed to Britain, France and Germany a solution which had been prepared by the Germans. It emanated from State Secretary von Weizsäcker and his associates in the Foreign Ministry, and members of the staff of the Four-Year Plan under Göring, who were interested in averting war. These circles represented a traditional 'great power' policy in contrast to Hitler, who now wanted to go ahead by military means and create conditions in Central Europe for his aggressive and racialist war against the Soviet Union. They certainly wanted Germany to predominate in Europe and to secure colonial territories, but they expected Britain to help them in this without the need of going to war; in fact she might well do so, they thought, in return for a less bellicose attitude on Germany's part. In evident contrast to Hitler's warlike designs these circles imparted their alternative plans to Mussolini, who was also anxious to keep the peace and who presented them in his capacity as go-between.

The Czechs were called upon to surrender the Sudeten territory to Germany and to cede further areas to Poland and Hungary. In return the great powers were to guarantee what remained of Czechoslovakia. The peace of Europe and the world had been saved again, and on 30 September Chamberlain and Hitler signed an Anglo-German agreement for non-aggression and consultation. This confirmed the Prime Minister in his firm belief that Hitler would after all consent to a general European settlement and be conciliated by offers of economic and colonial appeasement.

Hitler, however, had no intention of abandoning his anti-Soviet policy of eastward expansion by force of arms. This soon became clear in the negotiations between Ribbentrop and Bonnet, the French Foreign Minister, which led to a declaration of non-aggression on 6 December 1938, a kind of parallel to the Chamberlain–Hitler declaration of 30 September. In those discussions the German Foreign Minister insisted firmly and, as he believed, successfully on France showing understanding for a German policy of a 'free hand' in Eastern Europe.

The complex effects of Munich on German and European policy in the remaining months before the Second World War may be summed up as follows.

(1)   The course of the Czechoslovak crisis clearly showed up Hitler's bellicose intentions. Trusting to British neutrality, the dictator was bent on using military means to achieve the preliminary stages of his anti-Soviet policy. Britain was to be relegated to a maritime and overseas role. While seeking agreement with France he believed it was possible simply to ignore that country; he also considered the option of attacking it before turning eastward. In matters concerning colonies, naval and racial policy he ordered preparations to be made and solutions discussed so as to be ready to carry out his programme: for it was increasingly clear that time was getting short for the execution of his plans in racial and foreign affairs. Plans for becoming a global world power had till then been relegated to the indefinite future, but the Nazi leaders now began to contemplate their execution in the later 1940s, after the expected conquest of a continental empire in Eastern Europe.

The events of autumn 1938 had also shown that there were different trends of opinion in Germany as regards foreign policy. In some cases it was hard to judge at the time whether they served Hitler's plans and contributed to the dynamism of his actions, or were to be regarded as more peaceful alternatives from which the radical, utopian features of Hitler's thinking, his racial policy and worldwide ambitions, were missing. This of course would have been more acceptable to the other powers; but we know today that in the last resort the exponents of such ideas were in fact serving Hitler's designs, though not always wittingly or intentionally.

(2)   A decisive factor in relations between the European great powers was that the Soviet Union did not participate in the Munich conference. Chamberlain still regarded Europe as the centre of international affairs, and he tried to keep the two peripheral powers, the USA and the Soviet Union, from interfering in its affairs. He did not want to be directly exposed to economic competition from the USA, which appeared ready to displace Britain as a world power. Towards the

Soviet Union he was highly suspicious and hostile, and he wished to prevent the extension of its political and ideological power into Central Europe. Stalin regarded the exclusion of his country from the European concert as a sign that the Soviet policy of collective security, pursued since 1934–5, was a failure. He feared that the capitalist powers, both revisionist and anti-revisionist, would gang up against the Soviet Union, so that it was necessary to reorient Soviet foreign policy. In a natural quest for security, Stalin chose the path of *rapprochement* with Nazi Germany to prevent the formation of a united capitalist front against the Soviet Union, and if possible to involve the capitalist states in war with one another. Thus the foundation for the Nazi-Soviet non-aggression pact of 23 August 1939 was firmly laid at Munich.

(3)   The result of the Munich conference made it clear that Chamberlain and his 'inner cabinet' were wedded to appeasement as a systematic strategy dictated by the basic requirements of British home and foreign policy. Certainly they were not deterred from it by the need to make territorial concessions to the Reich in Central and East Central Europe, and to accept Germany's more or less open hegemony in that region. Chamberlain had managed to avert the threat of war in September 1938, and he now thought the time had come to achieve a reasonable and peaceful solution of outstanding problems between Germany and Britain in the economic field and in respect of colonies and armaments.

Hitler, however, stood in September 1938 at the height of his power and popularity. As regards treaty revision he had achieved what the majority of German statesmen and of the German people had longed for since 1919, and he had done so without going to war. Only a few close confidants in Berlin knew that he had not wanted a peaceful solution of the Sudeten dispute. But the motive forces of Nazi foreign policy transcended mere revisionist aims and looked towards the realisation of Hitler's more ambitious purposes.

In 1938 the German navy began to consider the problems of fighting Britain at sea, and also turned its eyes to the question of extending Germany's power overseas, which as yet took second place to continental conquests in Hitler's mind. Commenting on a 'Discussion paper concerning naval warfare against Britain' in September 1938, Admiral Carls remarked that 'If the Führer wishes Germany to achieve a secure status as a world power, we must have sufficient colonial possessions, safeguarded sea communications and free access to the open sea'. We do not know whether Carls knew in detail of Hitler's ideas of making Germany a world power by conquering Europe, including the Soviet Union, and then at once striking out overseas. Probably he did not; but the thoughts which he sought to embody in German naval planning were entirely in accord with the worldwide scope of Hitler's ultimate intentions.

Shortly after Munich, at the end of January 1939, Hitler gave orders for the construction of a large surface fleet, the navy's so-called 'Z Plan'. Thus, contrary to his plan in the 1920s, while still preparing the continental stage of his programme he also had an eye to the future overseas phase. Defensive and offensive motives were intermingled in his decision to bring the navy up to strength by the mid-1940s. It would certainly be needed if, contrary to his wishes, he had to fight Britain in the event of her opposing his continental plans, and the existence of a strong navy would, he hoped, deter Britain from anti-German moves. But apart from this rather traditional function of the German navy it was clear in the context of other, simultaneous plans that Germany expected a future showdown with the USA once she had placed herself at the head of a European empire.

To the same setting belong the intensified activities of the Office of Colonial Policy, which was to be the nucleus of a future Colonial Ministry. The overseas plans of the Third Reich were discernible in the form of colonial propaganda and demands, which on the one hand were used as a lever to induce Britain to agree to Hitler's continental ambitions, and on the other foreshadowed the direction of German foreign policy following a successful attack on the Soviet Union. On 9 March 1939 Ritter von Epp, the Minister-designate for the Colonies, received orders from Hitler through Lammers, the head of the Reich Chancellery, to push on with plans for the 'occupation of colonial territory' in Africa. The outline of the 'greater German world empire' was drawn more firmly after the seizure of Prague on 15 March 1939, when Goebbels admonished the press to reserve the use of this phrase till future occasions.

Ideas of world power were also voiced by Himmler, Reich leader of the SS, in a speech to his 'comrades' on 8 November 1938, at the time when Hitler, in his customary address in the Bürgerbräukeller in Munich, extolled the German armed forces as the instrument of his great power policy. Himmler told the SS leaders that Germany would in future be either a great German empire or nothing – a remarkable parallel to Hitler's statement in *Mein Kampf* that Germany would be a world power or nothing at all. Himmler promised that Hitler would create 'the greatest empire erected by mankind, the greatest ever seen on earth'. The *Reichsführer SS* was a prime exponent of the ideology of the new, racially superior man, which in the last resort was an obstacle to a rational calculation of power politics in the Nazi state; and in the above-quoted words he no doubt had in mind ideas of world domination by a future, racially pure Germanic empire. It is not certain whether he then knew of Hitler's 'gradual plan' (Hillgruber, 1965), which in practice hardly presented the features of a revolutionary biological policy. But, alongside the planning activities of the rather conservative navy leaders and the Foreign Ministry, the ideas of Himmler and the SS displayed a combination of revolutionary and traditional elements that was typical of the Third Reich: they increased its dynamism, complemented one another for the time being and provided the basis of Hitler's policy in peace and war.

On the day after the 'Night of Broken Glass' (9 November 1938: the destruction of Jewish shops and synagogues) Hitler made a secret speech to representatives of the German press instructing them to lay off peace propaganda and switch to psychological preparation for war. The anti-Jewish excesses in revenge for the murder of the German diplomat Ernst vom Rath in Paris by the Jew Herschel Grynszpan amounted to a country-wide pogrom and reflected the importance of the racialist strain in Nazi policy.

Anti-Semitism in Nazi Germany was not, as in the rest of Europe, a mere instrument of social and political integration: rather was it the dominant motif and purpose of Hitler's foreign policy and that of the regime. At the same time different attitudes and plans were canvassed within the conservative and the Nazi élite of Hitler's 'dual state'. Various rival solutions of the 'Jewish question' ranged from plans for emigration and deportation, handled by Göring from the point of view of the foreign exchange situation which was so vital for Germany, to the policy of Heydrich, chief of the Security Service and the Gestapo, that Jews should be expelled from the Reich and steered towards Palestine with the help of Zionist organisations. Seen in retrospect, these were intermediate stages towards the 'final solution' which was, in principle, always present in Hitler's mind and which he openly described to the Reichstag on 30 January 1939 as 'the radical, racial-ideological objective of the coming war' (Hillgruber, 1972/77) (see also Section C2, pp. 69–73 below). At that time Hitler darkly threatened that the next war would mean 'the destruction of the Jewish race in Europe'. Hitler openly proclaimed and steadfastly worked towards the objective of solving the 'Jewish question' as completely as possible. Consequently during the Second World War advantage was taken of the most varied circumstances and occasions to 'solve' the problem with increasingly drastic measures of extermination.

Meanwhile Hitler still had to achieve his power objectives, beginning in the East, which continued to involve the problem of British reactions. Hitler's further territorial aims were more and more difficult to reconcile even with Chamberlain's appeasement policy. The British looked with suspicion on Germany's naval rearmament and preparations in the field of colonial policy, while Hitler set about planning the destruction of rump Czechoslovakia and a 'solution' of the Polish question.

From 24 October 1938 onwards Germany resumed with greater intensity its efforts to induce Poland to join in an anti-Soviet alliance in return for territorial rewards in the Ukraine. This went on until 26 March 1939, when Poland refused a German offer of 21 March. From the beginning of the year, however, it became increasingly clear in Berlin that Germany must either get Poland to join her against the USSR or else first conduct a localised war against Poland herself and attack the Soviet Union thereafter. While the Polish leaders went on trying to steer an independent course between their two powerful neighbours, Hitler embarked on the next stage of his programme by absorbing what was left of Czechoslovakia. In so doing, for the first time he carried his ambitions clearly beyond what was justified by revisionist or ethnic claims.

On 15 March the German troops marched into Prague, the Protectorate of

Bohemia and Moravia was set up, and Slovakia became Germany's vassal by the 'Treaty of 18/23 March 1939 establishing a protective relationship between the German Reich and the Slovak state'. Czechoslovakia, which Nazi propaganda had constantly attacked as an 'aircraft carrier for the Soviet Union', was dismembered and destroyed. Hitler's action was a clear breach of treaty engagements and was condemned by world opinion, especially in the Western democracies. But despite the tough impromptu passages which Chamberlain included in his speech at Birmingham on 17 March, he held in principle to his endeavour to reach an all-round understanding with Germany. The Foreign Office had been vindicated in its more sceptical attitude towards Hitler's Germany and was strengthened in its opposition to appeasement. Public opinion in Britain began to swing against Chamberlain's policy, and as the year advanced the circle of his supporters in the Cabinet and Parliament became steadily smaller. In principle, however, the British government had no alternative but to pursue the policy of appeasement to the best of its ability at least until the outbreak of war in September 1939. But Britain was determined not to allow further concessions which it regarded as inadmissible to be extorted from it by force.

In accordance with this new attitude, on 31 March 1939 Britain announced a guarantee of Polish independence. This is not to be read as a sign that Britain was determined to make war on Germany; it was intended as a final warning, to deter Hitler from further warlike action, to induce him to negotiate and bring the Reich into a general peace settlement. In this way the two flanking powers of the European system – Britain and the Soviet Union – endeavoured, each in its own way, to reach an advantageous understanding with Nazi Germany. After efforts during the course of the summer to revive the old entente between Britain and Russia had come to nothing, Hitler was still prepared to reach a settlement with Britain in accordance with his own ideas; but in view of the immediate Polish problem he preferred an understanding with the Soviet Union. Whereas Britain had undertaken to come to Poland's aid if she felt her independence to be clearly threatened, Stalin for his part made a move towards Nazi Germany, which had till then been branded as a deadly enemy of the Soviet Union.

Stalin put out a first feeler at the 18th Party Congress on 10 March 1939, emphasising that the Ukraine in no way felt itself threatened by Germany. As soundings were taken by the Soviet side from 17 April onwards, there seemed increasing likelihood of an understanding for a limited period between Hitler and Stalin. At the same time attempts to reach an Anglo-German settlement went on at different levels; these emanated partly from Göring's entourage as a peaceful alternative to Hitler's policy of making war in league with Stalin, and partly from Hitler himself in the hope that Britain might after all consent to his terms. But finally the option of an agreement with Stalin tempted Hitler ever more strongly. Hence Ribbentrop's grand design for an alliance between Germany, Italy and Japan, which had been the subject of negotiations since the summer of 1938, was shelved in favour of a pact with the Soviet Union, which was then in a state of war with Japan in the Far East. Hitler confined himself to signing, on 22 May, the 'Pact of Steel' with Italy; it was not of the first importance to his military plans, and Mussolini warned him on this occasion that Italy would not be ready for war till 1942. Meanwhile the arrangement with the Soviet Union enabled Hitler to attack Poland without any fear of being caught in a vice between Russia and the Western powers. Hitler also hoped that the Nazi-Soviet pact would deter Britain and France from going to war, and it enabled him to obtain from the Soviet Union the raw materials he needed for the armaments industry and for war purposes in general.

The German *Blitzkrieg* against Poland was to bring about the fourth partition of that country and divide East Central Europe into a German and a Soviet sphere. Meanwhile, on 23 March 1939 German troops occupied the Memel zone of Lithuania. On the same day Germany concluded an economic treaty with Romania. Whatever Göring and his entourage may have intended, Hitler saw this not as an alternative to war but as a help to Germany's military economy in the Blitz campaigns that were to come. On 27 March Spain acceded to the Anti-Comintern Pact. Germany was giving a formidable demonstration to the world that it was the Axis powers that dictated the course of events in Europe.

On 23 May Hitler informed the defence chiefs of his intention to destroy Poland by force of arms. The necessary precondition was finally created when the negotiations with the Soviet Union led to the signature of a non-aggression pact on 23 August. In a secret protocol Germany declared that Finland, Estonia, Latvia, Bessarabia, and Poland east of the rivers Narew, Vistula and San lay outside her sphere of influence, while the Soviet Union declared its own disinterest in Lithuania and the rest of Poland. The pact did not, of course, mean that Hitler's anti-Soviet intentions had changed in any way; he made this clear twelve days earlier, on 11 August, in a conversation with Carl Jacob Burckhardt, the League of Nations high commissioner in Danzig. Perhaps as a last hint to the Western powers that they might after all think better of their refusal to conclude an alliance with Hitler, he declared: 'Everything I do is directed against Russia. If the West is too blind and stupid to understand that, I shall have to come to terms with the Russians, defeat the West and then turn with all my forces against the Soviet Union. I need the Ukraine so that we can never again be starved out as we were in the last war.'

That Hitler still held to his favourite idea of an understanding with Britain was shown by his 'generous' offer of 25 August 1939: this suggested that after Poland was subjected the European continent and the world overseas could respectively become the spheres of Germany and Britain, which would co-operate mutually. After concluding his pact with Stalin, Hitler seems to have had some hope that Britain would after all put up with his anti-Polish policy and war. This vague hope proved illusory, as did the peace initiatives undertaken with Göring's support by the Swedish industrialist Birger Dahlerus, which continued even after the outbreak of war.

Hitler attacked Poland on 1 September; on the 3rd Britain, and France a few hours afterwards, declared war on Germany. Hitler's situation from the point of view of alliances was now the reverse of his original plan. The effect was to confer on Stalin a key position in Europe such as he had striven for since the 1920s. The 'imperialist' powers were at war with one another, and Stalin could await developments as a *tertius gaudens*.

The campaign against Poland which began the Second World War was made immediately possible by Stalin's pact with Hitler, but it was a deliberate result of Hitler's warlike intentions. The essential causes of the war lay in his foreign and racial policy. As for the problems of economic strategy which Hitler, in his speech to the *Wehrmacht* commanders on 23 August, described as 'rational' grounds for war, they were mere consequences of the more and more forced and precarious boom caused by rearmament and, being thus secondary, can hardly be regarded as basic reasons for the campaign. Hitler's warlike policy and the rearmament programme instituted by him led to the economic and social consequences we shall examine: these gave additional momentum to the dictator's course, but they were not the cause of it and could not alter it in any essential respect.

The Consolidation of Nazi Rule
and the Arms Industry

During the phase of preparation for war between 1936 and 1939 the development of internal policy in Germany was subservient to Nazi aims in the foreign sphere and in racial matters. Although home and foreign policy affected each other, the determining factor at all times was Hitler's war policy.

Events connected with the extension of Nazi influence to industry, the armed forces and the Foreign Ministry between the summer of 1936 and the winter of 1937/8 are to be seen in this light. The establishment of Nazi dictatorship over these three institutions went hand in hand with parallel encroachments on the Catholic and Protestant churches and with intensified attacks on German Jewry.

In its conflict with the Catholic church the Nazi state violated the concordat of 20 July 1933, for example, in its proceedings against Catholic schools from 1935 onwards. From as early as September 1933 the Vatican had constantly to complain of breaches of the concordat. Open conflict between Catholicism and Nazism was expressed in the encyclical *Mit brennender Sorge* of 14 March 1937, in which the Pope voiced his 'increasing dismay' at the situation of the Catholic church in Germany, deplored the church's Calvary and attacked the anti-Christian regime.

Evangelical resistance groups, assembled at the second Dahlem Synod on 19–20 October 1934, claimed a 'right of the church to take extraordinary measures' in its conflict with the totalitarian state. There was thus an unbridgeable gulf between the Nazi dictatorship and the Protestants who gradually united to form the 'Confessing church', and between the 'Reich church' and the 'Evangelical church council' which set itself up as the 'provisional administration of the church'. The Nazi philosophy was castigated as false and anti-Christian in a message of 4–5 March 1935 from the Confessional Synod of the Evangelical Church of the Old Prussian Union to its parishes, which drew attention to the limits within which Christians were bound to obey the state. Among other things it stated that even the force of an oath is limited by the fact that God's word alone is absolutely binding. On 16 July 1935 Hanns Kerrl was appointed 'Reich Minister for Church Affairs' in order to deal with the church resistance groups on behalf of the regime and to curb them by means of 'legally binding ordinances'. In this he was not wholly successful: part of the Confessing church was prepared to co-operate to a limited extent in the numerous church committees set up by Kerrl, but others definitely refused such co-operation after February 1936. The conflict between the Protestant opposition and the Third Reich also reached its height in 1937. The autonomy of the churches was undermined by several decrees, and in that year about 800 members of the Confessing church were arrested.

After the outbreak of war the regime outwardly modified its anti-church policy so as to avoid social tension, but in reality it held to its previous line with the intention of suppressing the churches altogether once victory was achieved.

The position was reversed as regards anti-Jewish measures, which reached a peak of atrocity during the war period. Even before September 1939, however, in pursuance of the Nuremberg Laws of 15 September 1935 some 250 ordinances of various kinds excluded Jews from numerous professions and deprived them of rights. From 1938 onwards, under pressure from the radical anti-Semites in the top leadership (Goebbels, Ley), Jews were more and more excluded from economic life: particular spheres of activity were barred to them, and individuals were eased out of industrial posts, the world of commerce and the banking system.

Despite legal discrimination, racial persecution and economic disadvantages, only about 170,000 Jews, a third of the Jewish population of Germany, emigrated before the pogrom of November 1938 (the 'Night of Broken Glass'). According to a report from Heydrich to Göring on 11 November, thirty-six people were killed and another thirty-six severely injured in the outrages committed at Goebbels's instigation on the night of 9/10 November. Material damage amounted to several hundred million Reichsmark; 7,500 Jewish shops were destroyed and plundered, and about 250 synagogues set on fire or demolished.

Following the pogrom, the Nazi and government leaders discussed various ways of solving the 'Jewish problem' by emigration. But even before the outbreak of war the great majority of the 375,000 Jews in the Great German Reich lived without legal protection, unable to exercise a profession or trade and obliged to subsist by forced labour. The 'ghetto without walls' (Hofer and Michaelis, 1965) took the form of the Reich Association of Jews in Germany, set up on 4 July 1939 under the authority of the Reich Minister of the Interior or of Heydrich, head of the security service.

However, the main feature of state and party policy between 1936 and 1939 was that the regime consolidated its authority by attacking conservative bastions in industry, the army and the Foreign Ministry, so that these became at least more amenable than previously.

The differences that kept breaking out within the new Nazi élite and among political leaders as to whether policy should be more traditional or more revolutionary, and not least as regards the choice of peace or war, were in every case settled by Hitler to his own advantage. This applied especially to his decisions shortly before September 1939. Since 1936 or 1937 circles close to

Göring had leaned towards a more peaceful policy, though they never openly opposed the Führer but merely presented alternative courses in the hope of dissuading him from war; but in the last year or two of peace Hitler had reconciled these people to his own course in foreign affairs and made them serve his ends. Foreign affairs were paramount for Hitler, and in them he now exercised undisputed authority – so that the foreign policy and military strategy of the Third Reich can be judged essentially from the standpoint of Hitler's ideas and decisions.

With the inauguration of the Four-Year Plan in August 1936 the state and party began to exert a stronger influence on the economy. In order to accomplish the warlike aims of the Führer and regime the Reich was set the task of achieving economic 'autarky' to an extent that was hard to attain even in particular sectors. Stocks of certain raw materials had to be created and supplemented by the production of synthetic fuels, and so on. To obtain foreign exchange for rearmament purposes the export offensive towards South America and South-Eastern Europe, initiated by Hjalmar Schacht in 1934, was vigorously pursued. Economic leaders no doubt regarded this offensive in part as an alternative to the regime's policy of autarky and war, but meanwhile it led to conflicts not only with the USA and Britain but also with Germany's Italian partner.

In the relations between the state or party and industry, 1936 marked the transition from 'partial Fascism' to 'full Fascism'. The relative independence of the economy was limited by political interference and demands, although one cannot speak of an economy planned by the state in Germany at that time. Industry was subjected to the dictator's will, but it remained on a capitalist basis. 'In the particular way in which it was intertwined with state interests, industry took on a form quite different from the economic order vaguely foreshadowed in the corporative ideology of the Nazis' (Erdmann, 1976a). But the relationship cannot be properly described as state capitalism either: for often it was hard to tell 'where the autonomy of private interests ended and the system of state orders began' (Broszat, 1981). In Hitler's armament programme there was no hard and fast division between state control and private initiative, between the regime and the economy. At the same time, industry and politics were no longer on an equal footing. In 1936 the state and party gained firm control of the economy and in 1938 of the army, reducing their previous partners to a secondary role (Schweitzer, 1965). The latter now lived constantly under the threat expressed unmistakably by Hitler in his memorandum of August 1936 on the Four-Year Plan: 'It is for the Economic Ministry to state the requirements of the national economy, and for private enterprise to meet them. If private enterprise finds itself unable to do so, the National Socialist state will be able to accomplish the task by its own efforts.' Henceforth the political *Gleichschaltung* of the big industrialists was complete, though their economic privileges for the time being remained intact.

Industry was geared more and more to war preparations. The capitalist principle of obtaining maximum profit with minimum resources took second place to the Reich's political and military aims, as it was expected that the debts and waste would be made good from war booty in a few years' time. This policy was highly repugnant to the 'economic dictator' Hjalmar Schacht, who had been regarded as a worker of miracles in the first years of the Third Reich, and on 26 November 1937 he resigned his post as Economic Minister. He remained president of the Reichsbank till 20 January 1939, but was unable to influence events in accordance with his own ideas, which differed more and more from those of the Nazis. Walter Funk succeeded Schacht as Reich Economic Minister and Reichsbank president, but it was Göring who became the decisive force in economic affairs. On the one hand Göring whole-heartedly supported Hitler's policy of rearmament and war, which flew in the face of all economic considerations. But on the other hand, probably under the influence of Helmuth Wohlthat and other experts on the staff of the Four-Year Plan, he advocated alternative economic and foreign policies which were more or less consciously similar to those of Schacht. Not least on this account, in 1938–9 many contemporaries at home and abroad thought of him as representing a traditional form of great power policy with a strong economic tinge, in favour of peace and far removed from Hitler's warlike plans rooted in ideological fanaticism.

While Schacht had always respected the economic possibilities and limitations of German industry, it was now directed towards arms production at all costs. Although Hitler emphasised that the needs of civilian consumption, which were important for the maintenance of his internal prestige, should not be unduly neglected, expenditure on arms grew steadily at the expense, for example, of private building, and soon accounted for a percentage of the budget far higher than in the Western democracies. In the context of the Four-Year Plan the population was appealed to, insistently and not without effect, to put up with food restrictions for the sake of armaments, with the prospect that hardships would be made up for by war booty and *Lebensraum* in the future. Compared to the arms industry, the consumer goods industry shrank considerably in the course of the decade. In 1928–9 it accounted for 31 per cent of total industrial investment; in 1934–5 it fell to 25 per cent, and in 1937–8 to only 17 per cent. The laws of economic profitability were consciously set aside for the sake of rearmament; costly processes were employed to develop artificial raw materials such as Buna (synthetic rubber), and additional fuel was to be obtained by the hydrogenation of coal.

Despite evident discrepancies between Nazi propaganda and the reality of the Third Reich, the aim of 'preparing for war in peacetime', proclaimed by Hitler in his directive on the Four-Year Plan, was more or less realised. Göring, the new plenipotentiary for the Plan, made clear in a speech to leaders of commerce and industry on 17 December 1936 that they must henceforth recognise without reserve the primacy of Hitler's policy. The armaments policy might lead to unusual and harmful consequences for the capitalist economy – some contemporaries already thought they would prove fatal to the system – but these must be accepted for the sake of political and military gains to come. 'The contest to which we look forward calls for enormous efficiency. No end to rearmament is in sight. All that matters is victory or defeat. If we conquer, the business world will be fully indemnified. We must not reckon profit and loss according to the book, but only according to political needs. There must be no calculations of cost. I require you to do all you can and to prove that part of the national fortune is in your hands. Whether new investment can be written off in every case is a matter of indifference. We are playing for the highest stakes. What can be more profitable than rearmament orders?'

The combination of unbridled rearmament with an economy still endeavouring, despite restrictions, to cater for consumer needs led to much tension, contradiction and moments of crisis in relations between politics and the economy, resulting not least from the growing shortage of raw materials, foreign currency and labour. The economy of the Third Reich, working as best it could for the needs of both peace and war, did not base its plans on a 'long' war of attrition which would have required a correspondingly planned programme of 'armament in depth'. Planning for the war economy was based on the assumption of short *Blitzkriege* separated in time, for which the first requisite was a broadly based armament system. Hitler's idea of the *Blitzkrieg* was partly derived from his political technique of first isolating an adversary diplomatically and then destroying him with a decisive blow, the action being limited in both space and time. Apart from this, the limited economic potential of the Third Reich made this form of warfare the most obviously suitable, unless private consumption was to be throttled back to a degree which Hitler never contemplated and which might have shaken the dictatorship to its foundations.

As it was, the headlong course of rearmament caused economic difficulties which posed a fairly serious challenge to the regime. These were ultimately to be resolved by using the new armaments in battle and compensating industry with the spoils of war. Hitler was well aware that his political decisions for rearmament and war had set the country on an accelerated economic and social course which in turn virtually compelled the Third Reich to embark on war as the *ultima ratio* of its policy. He spoke of this state of affairs in an address to the defence chiefs on 22 August 1939, a few days before the outbreak of war. His policy was one of permanent economic crisis, initiated by himself in full awareness of the consequences; he intended it to lead to war and to ensure that opposition groups and others had no alternative but to accept the risk of warlike adventure. According to the Hossbach memorandum, he clearly saw the future of his regime on these lines as far back as November 1937. 'On the one hand there was the great *Wehrmacht* and the necessity of maintaining it at its present level . . . and, on the other, the prospect of a lowering of the standard of living and a limitation of the birthrate, which left no choice but to act . . . It was his unalterable resolve to solve Germany's problem of space at the latest by 1943–5.' For despite certain successes in the field of commercial policy, and efforts at agrarian protectionism looking towards wartime autarky and the preservation of the peasantry as the core of the German race, it could not be overlooked that armament in defiance of economic laws faced the nation with a more and more desperate choice between war and bankruptcy. From 1936 to 1939 the problems this created were felt in practically all sectors of the economy. For instance, instead of the unemployment which had prevailed at the beginning of the Third Reich there was soon an acute labour shortage due chiefly to the needs of the armament industry. With the extension of the period of compulsory military service to two years on 24 August 1936, the construction of military works on the Western frontier (the *Westwall* or 'Siegfried Line'), and, beginning in 1938–9, the addition of naval rearmament to the army and air force programmes, the situation became so acute as to necessitate the direction of labour.

Although the mass of the working class were better off than in the period of distress and unemployment between 1929 and 1933, during the years of intensified preparation for war there was discontent and unrest especially among overworked labourers in the armament industry. This pointed to a basic contradiction between propaganda and reality in the Nazi regime. Although the population of the Reich was supposed to be too large for its territory, it was not large enough to support the regime's ambitious plans for rearmament and war. In subsequent years of territorial conquest the gap was partly filled by foreign forced labour, but it was increasingly clear that Hitler was not in charge of a 'people without space' but rather of an enormous 'space without people'.

Among the many economic difficulties was rivalry between different interests, particularly heavy industry on the one hand (which had dominated the scene in 1933) and industrial chemistry, which came increasingly to the fore from 1936 onwards; there were also conflicts from time to time between the regime and factory workers, those in shipyards and in the building industry. But all these difficulties were ultimately overcome by Hitler's personality and powers of integration. In the end they always yielded to Hitler's political will and were channelled into the regime's political and social impetus towards war, which Hitler had consciously inspired and which now increasingly drove him forward. As for the German workers, it has been justly remarked that they were made almost completely unable to resist being 'harnessed to a production process geared to a war of conquest which the majority of them did not want' (Erdmann, 1976a).

Meanwhile the youth of the nation were being increasingly organised for labour and indoctrinated with Nazi principles. An ideological slant was given to the curriculum of traditional schools, and to them were added the 'Adolf Hitler Schools' and *Ordensburgen* (training centres), both with a somewhat anti-intellectual bias, and also the Hitler Youth, set up in 1933 and converted into a state agency on 1 December 1936. Membership of this body was compulsory for all young people between the ages of 10 and 18; by 1939 it had about 8 million members and was regarded as a breeding-ground for future leaders of the Third Reich and their trusty followers. (The female section was the BdM: *Bund Deutscher Mädchen.*) These educational and training organisations for the mass of young people served an important purpose in undermining the values and privileges of the traditional élite and obliterating social and intellectual distinctions among classes which were alike dominated by the political claims of the dictatorship. On 26 June 1935 a compulsory period of six months' manual labour was introduced for youths (it was afterwards extended to girls); between 1936 and 1939, as the labour shortage made itself felt, the purpose was no longer to cure unemployment but to inculcate the Nazi doctrine that manual and intellectual labour were equally honourable: an egalitarian process designed to further Hitler's 'social revolution' (Schoenbaum, 1966). All traditional class differences were to be sacrificed to the all-powerful dictatorship, until eventually the racially pure élite of the new order should come into being. As we shall see in due course, this grandiose process of levelling served another purpose that was not in the regime's plans, namely, the modernisation of German society.

Partly as a reaction to the regime's more and more stifling claim to a monopoly of ideological training, resistance began to spring up within what had traditionally been the ruling circles of the Reich. This movement, which generally began with opposition on practical points of detail, gradually spread to those who had been Hitler's allies in the conservative camp. After the influence of state and party over industry had been enhanced in the summer of 1936, at the turn of the year 1937/8 the conservatives began to feel Nazi encroachment in the sphere of defence, which had till then been largely immune, and in the Foreign Ministry, which had also remained to some extent free from Nazification.

Field Marshal von Blomberg, the Reich War Minister and commander-in-chief of the armed forces, had zealously promoted the adaptation of the army to the new regime at the beginning of the Nazi period. At the end of 1937 he contracted what was regarded as an indecorous marriage, and Göring, who wanted his job, intrigued with Himmler to bring about his resignation on 27 January 1938. For similar reasons Göring brought to Hitler's notice charges of homosexuality (which were in fact false) against Colonel-General von Fritsch, commander-in-chief of the army. During the crisis Hitler decided to assume personal command over the armed forces: he now took the opportunity to get rid of Fritsch, who was in any case an obstacle to his war plans. Fritsch was forced to resign ignominiously on 4 February 1938, and was later rehabilitated by Hitler in an equally dishonest and inadequate fashion. His successor in the army command was the more pliable Colonel-General von Brauchitsch.

Meanwhile Hitler as commander-in-chief assumed direct control of the armed forces. General Keitel, who was wholly subservient to the dictator, became head of a new command organisation, the *Oberkommando der Wehrmacht* (OKW).

The head of its planning staff from August 1939 was Major-General Jodl, who became Hitler's chief operational adviser during the war. Hitler subjected the reorganised command to his own will, and thus contributed to a confusion of authority between the insufficiently co-ordinated instruments of command: the OKW (defence), the OKH (army) and its general staff, the navy, the air force and subsequently the SS also. This had an adverse effect on the conduct of the war, but Hitler's personal power was increased by the administrative chaos which called for frequent decisions by the Führer.

The corps of officers had meekly accepted the murder of their comrades von Schleicher and von Bredow in the 'night of the long knives' in 1934, and by maintaining an equally passive attitude in the Blomberg-Fritsch crisis they largely abdicated to Hitler the remnant of political and social power that they still enjoyed. Their surrender was no doubt due to the unquestionably high popularity of the Führer, who had scored one success after another in home and foreign affairs and had moreover exacted a personal oath of loyalty from the *Wehrmacht*. In addition, younger officers increasingly tended to identify with the Nazi regime. The main reasons for the generals' surrender lay, however, in their ignorance of the details of the smear campaign which led to the downfall of Blomberg and Fritsch, which was simply beyond the imagination of many Prussian officers. Careerism also played a part, as did the Prussian tradition of obedience and discipline, long since divorced from the system of moral values which had once inspired it. From this time on, only a handful of officers in the more and more subservient *Wehrmacht* harboured any notion of resistance to the regime, and those that did were to have little success. However, on 18 August 1938 Ludwig Beck, head of the army general staff, resigned his office primarily as a protest against Hitler's war policy.

At the same time as the reorganisation and changes of personnel in the high command of the defence forces, the Foreign Ministry underwent similar changes which subjected it to Nazi domination still more completely than before. On 4 February 1938 Ribbentrop, who had been ambassador in London, took the place of the conservative Foreign Minister von Neurath. While the main lines of foreign policy had long been determined by Hitler's sovereign will, the ministry itself, which had till then been regarded as an outpost of conservatism, was henceforth increasingly penetrated by Nazi influence.

Thus, after the seizure of power in 1933 and the elimination of rival groups within the party in the summer of 1934, the *Gleichschaltung* of traditional social groups and political institutions took place in two further stages between 1936 and 1938, clearing the ground for Hitler's policy of warlike expansion. From the point of view of the general public, not the least noticeable indication of an impending military conflict was the rationing of consumer goods, introduced on 27 August 1939.

Summary

Developments in home and foreign affairs from 1936 to 1939 may be summed up as follows.

While the first years of the regime were dominated by far-reaching internal changes, in 1936–9 the emphasis was on foreign affairs. Hitler's Germany had become a force in European politics, to a large extent determining and forcing the development of international events. Certainly the internal aspects of the dictatorship were not to be overlooked: the process of *Gleichschaltung* and the consolidation of Nazi rule continued. The regime's ideological and political aims were not least apparent in its conflicts with the Catholic and Protestant churches and its measures concerning the 'Jewish problem'.

With the inauguration of the Four-Year Plan in August 1936 industry was subjected to a tighter control by state and party. The military high command was reorganised at the beginning of 1938, thus weakening another bastion of conservatism, and Nazi influence in the Foreign Ministry increased with the appointment of Ribbentrop in February of that year.

All these developments, as well as the intensified arms drive which Hitler himself set in motion and which increasingly became an uncontrollable force in its own right, were intended to serve the dictator's ambitious and utopian schemes in the field of foreign policy, war and racialism. For some time these aims were not clearly distinguishable from traditional revisionist demands; only within a short period of the outbreak of war did their true expansionist character come to light, based directly on Hitler's systematic policy in the international field and in the matter of racism. Today we can see that the revisionism of the Third Reich was a foil for the racist 'utopia' of Hitler's *Lebensraum* policy. As we study the political crises and diplomatic conferences of those years we cannot fail to recognise that – in conformity with ideas, statements and actions during the first years after the seizure of power – plans were being made and measures taken towards fulfilling the racial policy of the regime and achieving its global aims. Plans, albeit conflicting ones, were worked out for the solution of the 'Jewish problem', the destruction of 'racially inferior' forms of life, and the creation of a Nazi élite which should embody and realise the ultimate claim of the Third Reich to universal and absolute world domination. The urgency with which international events were pushed forward, but also the normality of the immediate issues, often concealed the true motives of Hitler's systematic policy. The regime's plans for world domination related essentially to a later stage, but in the sphere of naval and colonial policy, for instance, individual agencies of the state and party were already beginning to devise and follow up plans on their own initiative and without instructions from above; such plans were nevertheless in harmony with the final aims of the Nazi dictatorship.

As a symptom of ambivalence in the Third Reich, it is notable in retrospect that Hitler made use of all the instruments of technology with the intention of one day doing without them in an agrarian utopia, and, in general, that he used the experience of history in order finally, as he hoped, to escape from it. This paradoxical policy in the economic and technical sphere developed a momentum which tended to contradict Hitler's own philosophy and the themes of Nazi propaganda: however, in the last resort these contradictions were reconciled with the dictator's aims and made little difference to his policies. They thus served only to emphasise the fact that Hitler's ideas at all times dominated the course of events in the Third Reich, despite all its complexities and frequent contradictions. Many developments in the social practice of the regime seemed for a time inconsistent with its ideology, and it sometimes appeared as though the technical apparatus of the modern world might come to prevail over Hitler's doctrine. But in the last resort everything in the Third Reich was dominated by Nazi philosophy and Hitler's policies at home and abroad, in the economic and the social sphere.

In this sense it was characteristic of the Nazi dictatorship that consumer interests were sacrificed to rearmament in a high degree as compared with the Western democracies, but far less than in the Soviet Union, which was rapidly pushing on with industrialisation under Stalin. Hitler had no intention of jeopardising his great popularity among the German people and the working class in particular; and in any case he did not reckon on a major conflict on the lines of 1914–18, which would have required an armaments industry and a war economy capable of standing the strain for years on end. His object was rather to maintain an economy capable of both preparing for war and also meeting consumer needs, and to achieve domination of the continent by means of short *Blitzkriege* conducted at intervals. He also originally hoped that his attack on the Soviet Union would be supported or at least tolerated by the Western powers – a hope which proved illusory. Thanks to his non-aggression pact with Stalin on 23 August 1939 he was able to go to war against Poland, but this brought in the Western powers and involved a conflict on the wrong front from his point of view. Then, as the European war turned into a world war at the end of 1941, the contrast between the Third Reich's ideological and racial dogma and its politico-strategic calculations came to dominate Hitler's foreign policy and conduct of the war, as well as the internal development of Nazi Germany, its racial policy and that of its occupying forces in Europe.

(C) GERMANY IN THE SECOND WORLD WAR, 1939–42

1

Hitler's Foreign Policy and Conduct of the War

When Hitler unleashed his war against Poland on 1 September 1939 the objective, according to Nazi propaganda, was the recovery of Danzig and the Corridor. However, Hitler had made it clear to his military commanders on 23 May 1939 that 'Danzig is not the subject of the dispute at all. It is a question of expanding our living space in the East, of securing our food supplies and also of solving the problem of the Baltic States. Food can only be got from sparsely populated areas.' However, the decision to invade Poland, which provoked the British and French to declare war on 3 September, worsened Germany's situation in international terms, in sharp contrast to Hitler's foreign policy triumphs of 1938–9. This fact could not be obscured even by the annihilation of Poland in a four weeks' campaign. Instead of being allied with the British Empire as he had intended, Hitler found himself at war with it.

The conclusion on 23 August of a non-aggression pact with the Soviet Union, which was still the arch-enemy of the Third Reich in terms of ideology and power politics, put Stalin in an extremely favourable position as the *tertius gaudens* profiting by the conflict between the 'imperialist' states. Soviet deliveries of raw materials were necessary to Hitler's war machine, and thus placed him in a state of considerable dependence on the USSR. Stalin sent the Red Army into Poland on 17 September and thus accomplished the 'fourth partition' of that country which was envisaged in the secret protocol to the treaty of 23 August, but he did not join Hitler in fighting the Western allies. If he had done so it would have crowned with success Hitler's tactics embodied in the Nazi-Soviet pact, enabling him to put pressure on Britain throughout the world to make her comply with German conditions. In this way the 'false' situation of an anti-British front could have been remedied, and the two powers might one day have joined forces against the Soviet Union. But in fact nothing more eventuated than a German-Soviet declaration on 28 September (the day following the surrender of Warsaw) announcing the conclusion of a pact of friendship and demarcating the frontier in occupied Poland. As in the agreement of 23 August, concessions were made by the German side which Hitler regarded as favouring the Soviet Union. The secret protocol was modified in such a way that the Bug river became the boundary between the German and Soviet spheres of interest. This meant that the Soviet Union made over to Germany the Polish provinces of Warsaw and Lublin and a triangular area at Suwalki, but in exchange Lithuania, except for its south-western tip, was assigned to the Soviet sphere. Altogether Germany gained a territory of about 45,500 square miles and the Soviet Union 77,000 square miles. Western Poland became the domain of the SS, the SD (Security Service) and the Gestapo. No decision was taken as to its ultimate political status, but on 25 September a provisional military administration was set up under Colonel-General von Rundstedt, with Hans Frank as the supreme civilian authority. On 12 October the military administration was dissolved and Frank became Governor-General of the territory conquered by Germany, except for those parts of it which were annexed to the Reich on 1 November, namely, the Free City of Danzig, the territory that had been ceded by Germany to Poland under the treaty of Versailles, the Lodz area, Upper Silesia (with an extension eastward) and the Ciechanów district.

The German-Soviet declaration laid the blame on the Western powers for continuing the war and stated that Germany and the Soviet Union would 'consult regarding necessary measures'. Britain and France could not ignore the danger that they might one day be confronted by the joint military might of the two totalitarian regimes, and in fact they continued to entertain such fears until the Nazi attack on Russia on 22 June 1941.

The Nazis' internal situation was not free from problems, as even after the victorious campaign in Poland many sections of the population were lukewarm towards the war. Externally Germany was threatened with isolation, as Italy and Japan showed no haste to assist Nazi plans. Moreover Germany was insufficiently prepared for a major war, for which it would not be properly equipped till 1942 at the earliest, and despite the efforts made under the Four-Year Plan it still depended economically on foreign supplies. For all these reasons Hitler felt compelled to undertake a 'dash for freedom' by attacking in the West. He believed that time was working for the Western powers rather than for Germany, and he thought that if France could be defeated in war by November 1939 it might be possible to eliminate British influence from the continent. Once the British had come to perceive their 'true' interests he hoped to reach an understanding with them in the sense of his basic plan of the 1920s, with Britain as the leading maritime and colonial power and Germany predominant on the continent. In this way Britain would, he thought, be relieved of a double threat: the ideological and strategic challenge from the Soviet Union, and also the risk that the USA might take over from her as a world power.

Thus Hitler in October 1939 already looked beyond the conflict with the West European powers, believing that his intention to create a German empire in continental Europe was threatened essentially by the USA and the Soviet Union, the two peripheral powers of the international system. From the point of view of geo-strategy and military economy Germany was hemmed in by these two powers, which could put a stop to her expansion at a comparatively early stage. As he put it on 9 October 1939, 'No treaty and no agreement can ensure lasting neutrality on the part of Soviet Russia ... The best security against Russian attack is to make a clear display of superior German strength and a quick demonstration of our power ... The attempt of certain US circles to lead the continent in an anti-German direction is at present unsuccessful but might not be so in future. Here too we must realise that time is working against Germany.'

Feeling obliged for these reasons to make an early move, Hitler fought down the opposition to his plan to attack France without delay and thus neutralise Britain's continental partner. As early as 27 September 1939 he characteristically stated that the object of the planned campaign in the West was 'to destroy France'; as to Britain, he only wished to 'bring her to her knees' and make her comply with his plans. In this way he returned to his ideas of the 1920s. To clear the way for German expansion eastward, France was to be eliminated and Britain thus made amenable to Hitler's designs. Thus the dictator saw the Western campaign as a way of achieving by military means the alliance which he deemed necessary for the achievement of his programme.

For various reasons the date of the attack on France was postponed several times. The Soviet invasion of Finland, which began on 30 November, was watched by Hitler with interest and suspicion. On 9 April 1940, shortly before the German attack in the West, he sent his troops into Denmark and Norway to forestall a similar move by the Western powers and prevent them cutting off the vital supply of Swedish iron ore which reached Germany via Norwegian waters. In this way Hitler enlarged the area of operations of the German naval forces, hitherto hemmed in by the Baltic, the North Sea and the Channel. Germany henceforth enjoyed a better defensive and offensive base for warfare in the Atlantic and for her future world strategy as a naval and colonial power.

The German attack on Holland, Belgium and France finally took place on 10 May 1940. Contrary to the expectation of military experts, the campaign in Western Europe was a triumph for Hitler's strategy. This placed him at the height of his popularity in Germany and enabled him to crush opposition within the officers' corps. Henceforth he enjoyed unbounded authority and prestige among many representatives of old Germany and the élite of the Nazi state, some of whom had had misgivings both before and since September 1939 as to the wisdom of Hitler's foreign and economic policy.

A crucial year for the outcome of the war elapsed between 22 June 1940, the date of the German-French armistice, and 22 June 1941, when Hitler attacked the Soviet Union. During this period 'the primacy of the political element ... was ensured to an extraordinary degree' (Hillgruber, 1973b). The internal conditions for Hitler's foreign policy decisions in the weeks and months after the fall of France have been correctly described thus: 'With the victory over France, the progressive concentration of Hitler's power in Germany and the recognition of his leadership by traditional circles in the army, diplomacy and business – two processes which had not always gone hand in hand – were now united. In the ensuing months Hitler had greater freedom than ever before or since to establish a broad framework for the plans and forecasts of economic organisation, military leadership and diplomacy. The centres of resistance which had enjoyed wide-spread sympathy among the population in the crises of 1938 and the winter of 1939/40 were now diminished and completely isolated from a nation which acclaimed the Führer with greater unanimity than ever' (Hillgruber, 1973b).

But the decisive problem in the field of strategy and foreign policy remained unsolved after the victory over France. Hitler was still tormented by the question why Britain would not agree to his proposal to 'divide up' the world, or when the British would finally see reason. Compared to this problem he took little account of any other events and developments, however favourable to the Reich. Germany now held sway from the Atlantic to the Russian border, and could dispose at will of the resources of the Central European 'greater economic area'. The various party and state offices and planning staffs already directed their attention beyond this to what were regarded as complementary colonial areas overseas, thus anticipating a later stage of Hitler's 'gradual plan' with which they were probably not familiar in detail.

Meanwhile the prestige of victory enhanced the Reich's power of attraction. On 10 June 1940 Italy abandoned the standpoint of 'non-belligerence' which it had adopted to Hitler's disappointment in 1939, and claimed its share of the spoils from defeated France, a move which was likewise unwelcome to the Führer. Even the cautious Franco came forward in June 1940 with an offer to bring Spain into the war on Germany's side; but his territorial and economic demands were so exorbitant that Hitler could not take the offer seriously. From mid-June onwards Japan also came closer towards Germany, thus reinforcing Ribbentrop's ideas of a continental bloc from Spain to the Far East, directed against Britain and the USA. But events confirmed Hitler's more conservative forecast that Japan would function primarily as a political and military instrument with the role of pinning down the Americans in the Pacific and preventing them from intervening in Europe. For, despite all the power wielded by the Reich in Europe and all the respect it now enjoyed from neutrals, it remained clear that Britain, which had been under Winston Churchill's premiership since 10 May 1940, was holding out stubbornly against Hitler's Germany.

None the less, according to Hitler's judgement Britain was faced with the basic choice of reaching an understanding either with Germany or with the USA, and so becoming the junior partner of one or other of the two world powers of the future. Whether under the *Pax Germanica* or the *Pax Americana*, Britain could only hope for a subordinate position and scarcely one of equality: such was Hitler's view even while the French campaign was still in progress, when he confidently expected that Britain would yield to German pressure. It was in this belief that he focused his attention on the Soviet Union, the true objective of his ideological and strategic policy, as early as 2 June 1940 (during the 'battle for Dunkirk', 27 May–4 June, when he was at Charleville, the GHQ of Army Group A) and again on 30 June. On these occasions – as recorded by Halder, chief of the general staff – he expressed the firm conviction that he could end the war with Britain which had been forced on him against his will, and thus at last have his rear covered for an Eastern campaign in accordance with his overall plan. The war for *Lebensraum* at Russia's expense must be begun as soon as possible, without a pause which could only be detrimental to the warlike spirit of the German people.

An important motive in Hitler's mind was to forestall any intervention in Europe by the USA, which he still feared despite the Japanese presence in the Pacific, and where the tussle between isolationists and interventionists was still in progress. But at this period he had come to reckon more and more with the possibility of a conflict with the USA during his lifetime. This was a contrast to his ideas in the 1920s, when he rather expected that some future generation would have to undertake a more or less defensive struggle for world supremacy between the USA and Germany, once the latter was racially and politically dominant in Europe. His revised views may have prompted him to approve the proposal, put before him by Admiral Raeder on 11 June 1940, for a reactivation of the plans for a large surface fleet which had been shelved at the outbreak of war. But, while at the end of June and beginning of July 1940 Hitler had more and more come round to the idea of conquering *Lebensraum* by a war against Russia, and even after Roosevelt in the second half of July had put into practice with Congress's approval his policy of 'all aid short of war' in the Atlantic, Hitler's orders to the navy were still to observe the greatest restraint in the face of multiplied US provocations. At the same time, from a mixture of defensive and offensive motives, in the light of possible war developments and his own long-term objectives, he spurred on naval preparations for a more aggressive strategy in the Atlantic, a system of overseas bases and the construction of a large-scale fleet.

This did not mean, however, that Hitler had adopted Raeder's strategic conception, which in many respects was close to that of von Ribbentrop, based on reaching an understanding with Russia against Britain and the USA. Hitler continued to regard the conquest of the Soviet Union as central to his plans. At the same time, by way of supplementing the decree of March 1939 on colonial matters he gave orders in June 1940 that plans were to be brought to a 'speedy conclusion', as 'the present situation' required Germany to be able before long to take over and administer a colonial empire in Africa. There was indeed no time in 1940 when Hitler saw overseas expansion as an 'alternative' to his programme in the East: this holds good despite the colonial ambitions expressed during the Western campaign, Hitler's ideas in August 1940 of a 'continuous colonial territory from West to East Africa', or Ribbentrop's plan for concerted 'southward expansion' by Germany, Italy, Russia and Japan. None the less, till the end of June 1940 Hitler confidently hoped for a separate peace with Britain, and he seems to have thought in this context of acquiring colonial territories for use in a later stage of his policy of world dominion. But Britain persisted in fighting on, though Hitler expected her to make peace and saw her as a junior partner rather than an equal one in future international relations. Appeals and sanctions, peace offers and peace feelers, were as ineffective in bringing Britain 'to her senses' – as Quartermaster-General Wagner once put it – as the threat of invasion, preparations for which Hitler authorised with inner reservations on 16 July 1940, or the *Luftwaffe* offensive which began on 13 August.

From the second half of July onwards Roosevelt unequivocally supported Churchill's 'tough line', so contrary to Hitler's expectations, and armed his country for what he regarded as the inevitable showdown with Germany and Japan. This meant that Germany must use the time which remained, while the USA was still not adequately armed and was to some extent hampered by Japan's presence in the Far East, to defeat the Soviet Union and make the German continental empire impregnable *vis-à-vis* the Anglo-Americans. Britain, which was challenged by the Americans in world politics, in her imperial interests and in foreign trade, and was in danger of falling into second place generally, would in this way be separated from the USA and induced to make peace. As Hitler saw things, he must now again take an offensive line as he had done after the Polish campaign – this time on a global scale, so as to destroy the last remaining continental power in Europe and make himself proof against the expected Anglo-American attack, and/or to carry out the overseas phase of his 'programme' and make Germany a world power in the fullest sense. While Hitler was considering these plans, the Soviet Union proceeded systematically to create a glacis against its German ally by occupying the Baltic States on 14–16 June 1940 and Bessarabia and the Northern Bukovina on 28 June.

On 31 July Hitler addressed the *Wehrmacht* and army chiefs on the world situation and declared that 'If Britain's hope in Russia is destroyed, her hope in America will disappear also, because the elimination of Russia will enormously increase Japan's power in the Far East'. Against this background Hitler evolved his overall plan of autumn 1940 which envisaged attacking and destroying the Soviet Union in another blitz campaign. In this way he expected to achieve the central objective of his racial and political programme and to deprive Britain of her 'sword on the continent' so that she would be ready to come to terms. Whereas formerly British neutrality or a British alliance had been the precondition of attacking Russia, the end and the means were now interchanged in a politico-military gamble: victory over Russia would help to realise his central ideological ambition and at the same time force Britain to make peace. Thereafter he would be ready for further brushes with the Americans, actual or threatened, which might directly follow the Russian campaign or occur after a longer or shorter interval.

In the conference at the Berghof on 31 July 1940, at which war with Russia was envisaged as both an end and a means, Hitler clearly referred to the threat from America, against which he could at that time only take indirect measures in the hope that Japan would ensure US neutrality. In the summer and autumn of that year Hitler thought the USA would not be ready for war till 1941 or 1942. Just as the belligerents in 1914–18 had given thought during that war to how they could best prepare for the next, so Hitler became more and more preoccupied at this time with the 'American factor', and this had a foreshortening effect on his programme as a whole. In the summer of 1940 he came more and more to envisage an 'all or nothing' strategy in which he would retain the political and strategic initiative by means of a military solution in the East. After the battle of France, Hitler and most of his officers thought a campaign against Russia would be scarcely more than a 'sand-box exercise'. Victory would be attained in a few weeks and Britain would at last make peace; Europe would be economically self-sufficient, and Hitler could then snap his fingers at America.

However, from mid-September to the end of October 1940 at latest there was a period during which Hitler reluctantly accepted Ribbentrop's idea of a 'continental bloc' as an alternative to his own design. During those weeks Hitler came to realise that Britain could not be softened by the *Luftwaffe* offensive or the threat of invasion; American support for Britain was on the increase, but it was by then too late to attack the Soviet Union in 1940. The Tripartite Pact between Germany, Italy and Japan was concluded on 27 September with extravagant propaganda, but it did not place German-Japanese relations on a truly solid basis. In any case Ribbentrop's idea of an anti-British and anti-American front based on Soviet neutrality was defeated by several factors: the resistance of the Spanish and French, who were envisaged as potential satellites, Japan's independent war plans, Stalin's territorial demands and, not least, Hitler's preference for a military solution in the East as both an end in itself and a means of winning the global war.

Hitler's conversations with Franco and Pétain at Hendaye and Montoire respectively, on 23 and 24 October 1940, were unsuccessful in bringing Spain and Vichy France into the war on Germany's side; and he took this as a confirmation of the rightness of his long-contemplated decision to attack the Soviet Union. Four days later Mussolini invaded Greece without prior warning to Hitler, which must have increased the latter's doubts of the feasibility of a chain of alliances extending from East Asia to Southern Europe. Apart from the scarcely reconcilable territorial claims of Spain, France and Italy, Mussolini's ambitious move had turned the Balkans into a zone of acute military conflict.

Accordingly, a week before Molotov's visit to Berlin on 12–13 November 1940, Hitler informed his advisers that all preparations must be set on foot for a 'major showdown' with the USSR, which still constituted the 'whole problem' of Europe. The talks with Molotov (at that time Prime Minister and Foreign Minister of the Soviet Union) were a last opportunity to find out whether the

Reich and the USSR stood 'back to back or shoulder to shoulder'. Molotov, however, showed no disposition to be tempted by Ribbentrop's plans, which were to all appearances difficult of achievement, for a concerted southward expansion of the great powers. Ribbentrop's idea was that Germany should extend her rule from East to Central Africa; Italy would take the Mediterranean area and North-East Africa; Japan, with China under her control, would have the Pacific and South-East Asia as her sphere of influence; and the Soviet Union would have India and the rest of Southern Asia. In reply to all this Molotov advanced Soviet territorial claims in East Central Europe and Finland, the Balkans and Turkey: these were a clear encroachment on Germany's sphere and were calculated seriously to impair German interests.

Thus Hitler once more felt confirmed in his long-cherished intention of attacking the Soviet Union. Not long after, on 11 March 1941, the Lend-Lease Act was passed, reaffirming America's support for Britain. Hitler regarded with suspicion Soviet and British activities in the Balkans, especially Yugoslavia. Time was working against him on all fronts, and only a victory over the Soviet Union would, he thought, give him freedom of action for the present and security in the future. As early as 18 December 1940 he had issued 'Directive No. 21' for 'Operation Barbarossa', ordering preparations for an invasion of the Soviet Union and declaring that 'The German armed forces must be prepared to crush Soviet Russia in a quick campaign even before the end of the war against England'. Practically all Hitler's military experts assured him that Russia could be overthrown in a few weeks, and this was also the view of the American and British general staffs.

While preparations for 'Barbarossa' were going on, Germany invaded and crushed Yugoslavia and Greece in the Balkan campaign of April 1941. This action was improvised in order to secure Germany's flank for the attack on Russia and to prevent the formation of an Allied front in South-East Europe. But Hitler's thoughts were already ranging far into the future, not least because of the increasing threat from America. On 17 December 1940 he had told General Jodl, chief of the Operations Staff of the armed forces, that 'we must solve all continental problems by the end of 1941, as the USA will be in a position to attack us from 1942 onwards'. Hitler was planning for the period after a successful invasion of the Soviet Union, when he would be on the defensive against the British and Americans but might also go over to the offensive and thus pursue what had originally been no more than long-term, visionary objectives.

Once he was the ruler of a continental empire bounded by the *Ostwall* (Eastern fortification) on a line from Archangel to the Caspian Sea, Hitler believed that the Tripartite Pact powers could defend the strategically important areas of the Eastern hemisphere against the Anglo-Americans, while bastions in the Near and Middle East and in North-West Africa would protect the Greater Germanic area. With this in view, the greater part of Germany's infantry, armoured and air force units were to be withdrawn from Russia by August–

September 1941, and the emphasis switched thereafter from land armaments to naval and air forces. Fifty or sixty divisions were to secure the occupied Russian territory and be prepared for a military operation beyond the Caucasus, in the direction of Iran and Iraq. An advance from Libya into Egypt and from Bulgaria and Turkey into Syria would encircle and destroy the British position in the Near East. India could be threatened from Afghanistan, where a German base of operations was to be created in accordance with Hitler's directives of 17 February 1941. Gibraltar was to be captured in the autumn of 1941 and positions occupied in North-West Africa and the Azores, thus bringing America within range of *Luftwaffe* attacks. Altogether the upshot of Hitler's calculations on the eve of the Soviet campaign, as expressed in his statements and in defence staff plans dated 9 January, 17 February and 11 June 1941, was that once the USSR had been conquered and Europe made autarkic and proof against any blockade, Germany would extend her operations on to a wider stage. In that way, by means of a 'global *Blitzkrieg*' (Hillgruber, 1965a), Germany would build up a strategic position with bases in North-West Africa and the Atlantic islands, protected by greatly enlarged naval and air forces and equipped for the expected conflict with the USA. Thus Germany's defensive position would be turned into a spring-board for either defensive or offensive operations, from which Roosevelt's America could be defied at any time.

The last attempt to induce Britain to join hands with Germany and avoid the necessity of a war on two fronts took the form of the flight of Hitler's deputy, Rudolf Hess, to Scotland on 10 May 1941: Hitler did not order this move, but may have approved or at least tolerated it. It produced no effect, and on 22 June Hitler unleashed the war against the Soviet Union. Shortly before the attack, on 11 and 21 May, he was confirmed in his resolution by intercepted telegrams between the Soviet leaders and their missions in the Far East, which spoke of delimiting new spheres of interest *vis-à-vis* Germany and also 'using' the Third Reich to combat the Anglo-Americans.

Despite the British-Soviet treaty of mutual aid concluded on 12 July 1941, the German leaders had scarcely any doubt that, as Halder put it on 3 July, 'the campaign against Russia would be won in a fortnight', after which 'the further objectives of the war against England' could 'once again come to the fore and be pursued'. Accordingly on 14 July Hitler gave orders to switch the emphasis of the armaments programme from army needs to the naval and air forces that would be decisive against Britain and America.

As the initial operations in Russia appeared so successful, Hitler began to extend his plans beyond his improvised ideas of the previous autumn. On 14 July 1941 he proposed to the Japanese ambassador, General Oshima, a general offensive alliance against the Soviet Union, which was regarded as already defeated and which was to be occupied by the two countries. According to Ribbentrop's idea, the Japanese would advance from Vladivostok to Omsk and include conquered Siberia in their sphere of influence. Then – Hitler went on, to

Oshima's surprise – Germany and Japan would together turn against the other peripheral power of the international system, the USA. 'America with its imperialist policy was a threat both to the European and to the Asian *Lebensraum*. From Germany's point of view Russia was a threat in the East and America in the West. The Führer therefore thought we must jointly destroy them. The lives of nations sometimes involved heavy tasks, but these could not be overcome by ignoring or postponing them.'

As a rule Hitler, unlike Ribbentrop, preferred the idea of relegating Japan to the Far East, so that the USA would be tied down in the Pacific and unable to turn its main forces against Europe at a time inconvenient for Germany. Hitler regarded the campaign against Russia as 'his' war and preferred to win it without the help of the 'yellow men', whom he considered untrustworthy and racially inferior. He returned to this view when the Russian campaign began to falter in August 1941, and did not depart from it again until the war situation changed radically in the winter of 1942/3. The first setbacks in Russia also postponed to a distant future the idea of an offensive against the USA. On 27 March 1941 the latter power had decided that if it was drawn into the war it would pursue a 'Germany first' strategy, and on 14 August it signed with Britain the Atlantic Charter, thus staking out its claim to a position of leadership in the postwar world. On 25 July Hitler had still envisaged 'dealing sharply with the USA' after the conclusion of the Russian campaign, but in 'table talk' at operational head-quarters on 10 September he repeated the view he had held in the 1920s that it would be for future generations to fight the decisive battle against the USA. 'I shall not live to see it, but I rejoice for the German people that one day Britain and Germany will march together against America. Germany and England will know what each expects from the other. When that happens we shall have found the right ally.' On 25 October 1941 he repeated this idea to Ciano, the Italian Foreign Minister: 'A later generation will have to deal with the problem of Europe versus America. By that time it will not be a question of Germany or England, of Fascism, National Socialism or conflicting systems, but of the common interests of Europe as a whole within the European economic sphere with its complementary areas in Africa.'

Within the next month it became clear to the dictator that the Russian war could not be won on schedule, and on 19 November he expressed for the first time his expectation 'that the two enemy groups will realise they cannot destroy each other, and will conclude a negotiated peace'. Thus he acknowledged the failure of the overall strategic plan he had improvised in the autumn of 1940; and on 27 November, consistently with the social-Darwinian logic of his 'all or nothing' policy, he declared that if the German people was not up to its task it must perish: 'If the German people is no longer strong enough and ready to make sacrifices, to shed its blood to preserve its own existence, it must be destroyed and replaced by another, stronger power. It would have shown that it no longer deserved the place it has today conquered for itself.' Such was to be the uncompromising keynote of Hitler's military and political strategy over the next few years.

From November 1941 onwards Germany's situation was characterised by resignation and by tension and crises in the military leadership. Against this background Hitler's declaration of war on the USA on 11 December 1941 appears as a forced reaction rather than a free decision in line with his overall programme. The underlying compulsion was overshadowed by the bravado of the gesture, which came three days after the US declaration of war on Japan, four days after the Japanese attack at Pearl Harbor, and ten days after the German failure to capture Moscow. On 19 December 1941, when the leadership crisis at the head of the *Wehrmacht* was at its height, Hitler took over personal command of the army. Previously, on 21 November, he had reaffirmed to the Japanese his double assurance of support against Russia and America, dating from March–April 1941. In reply to Tokyo's inquiry whether Germany would support Japan if she went to war against the USA, he instructed Ribbentrop to say that Japan could count on Germany's help 'in cases additional to those specified in the Tripartite Pact'. When Germany gave this blank cheque to the Japanese it was probably not easy to perceive the consequences with accuracy, and Berlin was unaware that the Japanese were conducting secret negotiations with the USA behind the back of their German allies. Hitler thought, however, that by giving the Japanese this guarantee he had, at least for a time, removed the danger of a Japanese-American *rapprochement*. Apart from this he intended to involve the Americans in a second front as soon as they went to war with Japan, for fear that they might defeat the Japanese quickly and then be able to turn against Germany without major hindrance. As early as 3 January 1942 Hitler expressed to Oshima his anxiety lest Japan might be defeated by the Anglo-Americans, and also his perplexity as to how to fight the USA: 'he did not yet know how the Americans were to be conquered'. What he hoped to achieve in his desperate race against time was (1) by providing military aid to Japan, to tie down America in the Far East for as long as possible; (2) with Japanese help, to safeguard the 'Eastern hemisphere' against the USA in the summer of 1942; and (3) by advancing south from the Caucasus and threatening India, to compel Britain to conclude a separate peace and thus split the 'unnatural coalition' of his enemies.

In the first half of 1942 German hopes of victory again revived. During the summer Hitler's armies swept forward almost irresistibly in Russia and in North Africa. The Japanese advance, which was not co-ordinated with the Germans, led to the spectacular fall of Singapore on 15 February 1942 and reached the peak of its success in the following month, but from the beginning of August onwards it became clear that the Japanese tide was ebbing. On 6 January 1942 Roosevelt, who had long been a deadly enemy of the aggressors, had reaffirmed his determination to resist them, and on 14 January, the last day of the 'Arcadia' conference in Washington, Churchill and Roosevelt had jointly confirmed the 'Germany first' strategy.

While Japan had reached its fullest extent and Hitler was predicting the destruction of the Red Army, in March and April 1942, not least in response to pressure from Stalin, the British and Americans began to envisage the creation of a second front in France and North-West Africa so as to attack the Axis from the rear. Time was still clearly working against Hitler's policy and strategy. None the less, he firmly repulsed Japanese attempts to mediate between Germany and the USSR, which began at the end of 1941 and continued into 1944. Hitler felt that he must attain his central objective of defeating Stalin, as the whole of his strategic and political programme stood or fell by it. Once again, in the summer of 1942, his calculations seemed justified. Although the Japanese had been driven on to the defensive by the Battle of Midway Island on 4–8 June and still more clearly by the American landing on Guadalcanal on 7–8 August, the German troops meanwhile won victory after victory, advancing to the Caucasus and towards Alexandria.

However, in the early autumn the German attack in Russia ground to a halt, while on 5 November the British victory at El Alamein forced Rommel's Africa Corps to retreat. On 19 November the Soviet counter-offensive began at Stalingrad, and the British and Americans meanwhile began to occupy bases on the fringe of Axis-controlled territory. The Americans, as already mentioned, landed at Guadalcanal, and in May–September 1942 the British occupied Madagascar. France's African colonies did not as a whole transfer their allegiance from Vichy to de Gaulle's 'Free France' until after the Allied landing in North-West Africa in November 1942. Meanwhile, in June 1942 Churchill and Roosevelt discussed the possibility of relieving the Russians by opening a second front in Europe at an early date. Hitler could only avert this threat by putting a speedy end to the war in Russia. However, when Mussolini advised the Führer on 1 December 1942 to conclude a separate peace with the Soviet Union, Hitler regarded this as unacceptable. Although in his strategic calculations he had already expressed the belief that neither group of adversaries could hope to win, throughout 1942 he tried repeatedly to achieve his programme of conquering Russia and gaining Britain as an ally.

Hitler's plans were thwarted, however, not least because of the racial dogma which inspired the policy and war methods of the Third Reich, and which had long helped to keep alive the spirit of resistance in Hitler's immensely power-ful opponents and so to undermine the bases of German strategy. The monstrous and radical character of Hitler's racial policy far exceeded the enormity even of his ambitions and plans to achieve great power status or world dominion. As the war continued, the true motives and character of the Nazi regime became visible in its racial policy and treatment of the occupied areas. This was inextricably interwoven with the power policy of the Third Reich, but as time went on it gained the upper hand and finally frustrated Germany's political ambitions. Directed towards racial supremacy on a worldwide basis, it was a prime agent of the destruction of the Third Reich.

2

Internal Developments, Racial Policy and the Treatment of Occupied Territories

The outbreak of war in 1939 affected the German people with a sense of depression very different from the enthusiasm of August 1914. Hitler's achievements in the political and economic fields, in military matters and to some extent in social policy had been widely admired; it was now suddenly clear what a price had to be paid for them, and how precarious they were. Food rationing made it possible to supply basic needs until 1944, partly at the expense of the occupied territories; but, under war conditions, the regime's claim to ideological domination and its use of terror to subdue the German population became more and more oppressive. Above all the power of the SS increased steadily. From the beginning of the war it controlled 'an institutional apparatus that overshadowed all governmental and military control' (Bracher, 1970). In September 1939 the amalgamation of the SS and the police was further completed. The two had been united at the top since 1936 in the person of Himmler, who was Reichsführer SS and Chief of the German Police; this union was now extended to middle levels of command, the senior SS officer in each military district being appointed 'Senior SS leader and chief of police'. In addition, on 27 September the Security Police (Sipo), comprising the Gestapo and the detective branch (*Kriminalpolizei*), was merged administratively with the Security Service (*Sicherheitsdienst*, SD) of the SS, a party organisation, to form the Reich Central Security Office (*Reichssicherheitshauptamt*, RSHA), which was also particularly concerned with racial matters.

Last but not least, the development of the 'SS state' was marked by the advance 'from the improvised terror of the early years to the gigantic concentration-camp system of the extermination era' (Bracher, 1970). At the beginning of the war there were six of these camps controlled by the SS in Germany; by 1942 there were fifteen, and three more were added later. At the outset, 'political and religious opponents' of Nazism were deported without trial and imprisoned 'for reasons of security, re-education, or prevention', according to the official formula. Apart from this type of 'preventive arrest' in the concentration camps there were numerous labour camps whose inmates worked as slaves for the benefit of war production and of the SS. The camps were increasingly important for the German armaments industry, especially from the spring of 1942 onwards. The number of inmates rose from about 21,000 in 1939 to nearly 800,000 at the end of the war, by which time it included criminals, prisoners of war and hostages from the occupied countries. Many were victims of Hitler's 'Night and Fog' order of 7 December 1941, whereby those suspected of belonging to resistance movements could be deported to the camps without their families knowing anything of their fate. The SS enjoyed absolute power in the extermination camps: for instance, deportees who had served their sentence or been acquitted by special courts could be turned over to the Gestapo on the basis of other ordinances and so remained in Himmler's power.

As far as the German population was concerned, a police apparatus was constantly being enlarged and perfected so as to ensure obedience to the laws, decrees and orders designed to safeguard the Nazi regime – measures of 'internal warfare', as they have been called (Hofer and Michaelis, 1965). Severe penalties, including the death sentence, were inflicted for offences against the laws on food rationing and consumption restrictions which preserved the country from the dire scarcities of the First World War. The 'mental attitude' of the population was also strictly controlled. Under Article 5 of the Wartime Emergency Penal Code (*Kriegssonderstrafrechtsverordnung*), which dealt with 'Demoralisation of the Armed Forces', the regime could treat as a capital crime any critical remark about the progress of the war. The 'Broadcasting Order' forbade citizens to listen to foreign stations and made them liable to the death penalty for spreading information obtained therefrom. Criminal offences committed under cover of the wartime blackout could be punished with death under the 'Decree concerning Enemies of the People' (*Volksschädlings-verordnung*).

Despite this concentration of power, however, the Third Reich continued after the outbreak of war to present a chaotic picture of conflicting and over-lapping authorities. This was not remedied by the establishment on 30 August 1939 of the Reich Defence Council under Göring's chairmanship, representing all political agencies of the regime except for military strategy and foreign policy, which Hitler reserved for himself. Until the last phase of the war, when military defeats came thick and fast and Hitler increasingly avoided taking decisions, the state of 'authoritarian anarchy' served as an instrument safeguarding the dictator's absolute supremacy, which was formally endorsed at the last session of the Reichstag on 26 April 1942 in the following terms: 'The Führer, without being bound by existing legal provisions, in his capacity as leader of the nation, as commander in chief of the armed forces, as head of government and the supreme source of executive power, as the highest judicial authority and as leader of the Party, must at all times be in a position in case of need to use any means that seem to him appropriate to compel any German . . . to fulfil his or her obligations.' Hitler's unlimited dictatorship was supported by a terroristic judicial system which entered its last and bloodiest phase, designed to establish the rule of 'National Socialist jurisprudence', on 24 August 1942, when the presidency of the People's Court (*Volksgerichtshof*) was assumed by Roland Freisler, whom Hitler significantly called the 'Vyshinsky' of his regime.

As already mentioned, the exploitation of conquered territories was of major importance to the German war economy. The regime's war aims for the 'Greater Germanic Reich' included the creation of an 'enlarged European economic area' (*Grosswirtschaftsraum*) extending from the Atlantic to the Pacific coast and completed by a colonial empire in Central Africa. Such plans were already put forward by the Foreign Ministry during the Battle of France, on 30 May and 1 June 1940 (cf. Section C1, pp. 53–4 above). In addition, from the outset of the war Hitler's plans assigned decisive importance to the link between military success and the exploitation of conquered territories. Contrary to the views of, for example, General Georg Thomas of the Armaments and War Production Office of the *Wehrmacht* high command, Hitler believed it was sufficient for Germany to be equipped for *Blitzkriege* but not for a long war, since each successive conquest would help provide the economic basis for the next. The 'Speer era' did not set in till 1942, when the blitz campaigns came to an end and Germany had to resign herself to a long war of attrition against an adversary far superior in manpower, equipment, raw materials and economic production. During this period the war effort was placed on a more intensive and comprehensive basis, but Germany remained hopelessly behind the Allies, not least because her preparations had till then been so inadequate.

Nevertheless, both during the blitz campaigns and the later war of attrition, thanks to the plundering of foreign territory in Western Europe and the Soviet Union the supply of food and raw materials did not collapse but functioned with considerable efficiency. Not least on account of the deportation to Germany of between 6 and 7.5 million workers from all parts of Europe, agricultural and industrial production were kept going during the war. Although a labour shortage was increasingly felt, the Nazi Party for ideological reasons was reluctant to permit women to work in the arms industry in 1939–45, as they did in Britain and as they had done to a greater extent in Germany during the First World War.

On the whole it was possible to keep the civilian population, the armed forces and the foreign workers fed adequately until 1944. As already mentioned, this was helped by the measure of 27 August 1939 which, taking account of experience in the second half of the First World War, introduced extensive control especially of consumer goods but also of other products of all kinds. Moreover farm production had been increased during the prewar years and the food supply was considerably increased by imports from occupied territory, especially the Ukraine.

The raw materials position remained difficult, but it too was aided by supplies from conquered territory as well as expensive measures under the Four-Year Plan, for example, for the production of Buna, synthetic fuel and steel from low-grade German ore. At the same time the occupied territories could not continue functioning and producing without themselves consuming raw materials on a large scale, and in some cases productivity declined considerably under occupation conditions. However, the fuel shortage, for instance, only became critical during the summer campaign of 1942, when the invading forces were unable to get at the Caucasian oil supplies, so that the increasing demand from all three services had to be met from German and Romanian production. Western bombing attacks did considerable damage in this respect, and the capture of the Ploiești refineries by Soviet forces on 30 August 1944 spelt the end of Germany's war effort from the economic point of view.

In general it is characteristic of the Nazi dictatorship that Hitler only agreed with extreme hesitation and reluctance, from 1942 onwards, to limit consumer goods production for the benefit of the arms industry. Britain had done this as soon as war broke out, and waged 'total war' in this respect much sooner and more intensively than Germany. The British democracy could demand sacrifices from its people, since all alike felt they were defending a just cause and there was virtually no challenge to Parliament's authority. Hitler, on the other hand, was constantly aware of the needs of the civilian population of Germany, which he was concerned to meet for fear of provoking an internal revolution. 'Total war' in this respect was only embarked on to a limited extent even after 18 February 1943, when Goebbels issued a proclamation which was intended psychologically to offset the shock of the Stalingrad disaster (cf. Section D2, p. 82 below). Hitler throughout took an indulgent line as regards the production of consumer goods, sensitive as he was to the reactions of the German people – whom he kept under by means of terror and concentration camps, while offering them the ultimate goal of world domination or destruction. In the same way he was averse to financing the war by increasing taxes or imposing special duties on consumer goods, preferring methods of indirect borrowing which caused inflation but did not inflict immediate hardship on the population. Meanwhile, despite the propaganda slogan of 'total war', much of the new Nazi élite lived in a style of disproportionate luxury. The administrative chaos dating from before the war, and enhanced by the decline of Göring's power, was also not calculated to promote the harmony and efficiency of the country's war economy.

Only after the great military setback of the winter of 1941/2 was Fritz Todt, the head of the Ministry of Armaments and War Production set up on 17 March 1940, instructed to place the economy of the Third Reich on an all-out war footing, a task which was taken over by Albert Speer after Todt's accidental death on 8 February 1942. Between then and the middle of 1944 Speer succeeded in improving the organisation and efficiency of German arms production, but was unable to overcome its fundamental state of chaos. General Thomas's office continued to watch jealously over its own interests, although Speer managed to integrate it into his own ministry. Formally he himself, as 'Plenipotentiary for Armament Matters under the Four-Year Plan', was subordinate to Göring, the 'economic Tsar' of the Third Reich, whose influence was on the decline but who, as commander-in-chief of the air force, again and again flouted the authority granted to Speer by Hitler. The same was true of naval armaments, at least as long as Grand Admiral Raeder was commander-in-chief (till 31 January 1943). Sauckel, the Gauleiter of Thuringia, was appointed by Hitler on 21 March 1942 special plenipotentiary for labour allocation and for recruiting foreign workers, and increasingly rivalled Speer's authority. In 1944–5 he succeeded in pushing Speer completely into the background with the help of Bormann, who became director of the party chancellery after Hess's flight to Britain on 10 May 1941 and came more and more to dominate internal policy. Thanks to a policy of allowing extensive self-administration in industry, Speer was able in 1942–4 to keep armaments production steadily rising despite Allied air raids. It was far below that of the Allies, however, and in 1942 German and Japanese arms production together was only 40 per cent as high as that of the 'unnatural alliance'. In general Speer endeavoured to absorb branches of the economy that were not useful to the war effort and to make them serve the needs of all-out warfare.

In the last months of the war, however, as Speer was gradually ousted from power, the Nazi Party recovered the control over industry that it had exerted between 1936 and 1939–41. The 'Speer era' had been more efficient and more friendly to big business; it had reintroduced a minimum of rationality and helped to meet the demands of a war of attrition. This policy was now brought to an end, and the party renewed its threats to nationalise branches of the economy. The tendency of the party and state to assume control over industry was a steady feature of the Third Reich, manifest from an early stage on the part of the 'anti-capitalist' wing of the Nazi movement, and gaining continuously in strength except for the interlude of the 'Speer era'. It cannot be ignored in retrospect, nor can the fact that the war, in contrast to Nazi ideology, tended to favour the process of industrial concentration at the expense of smaller businesses. The claims of ideology were for a time sacrificed to war production. But this should not blind us to the fact that heavy industry, despite its high profits, was no more than an instrument used to establish, by military means, a social hierarchy which would in the last resort have posed a challenge to its very existence. From this point of view we are brought back to the political aims of the Third Reich, which were expressed not least in its racial policy and treatment of the occupied countries.

Poland was the first conquered land to feel the 'heavy hand of German rule' (Hans Frank). The purpose of Nazi racial policy was first and foremost to subject the 'incorporated Eastern territories' to rigorous Germanisation. This task was entrusted by the Führer to Himmler, who on 7 October 1939 was appointed 'Reich Commissar for the Consolidation of German Nationhood' (*Volkstum*). He set about deporting, resettling, or exterminating the native Polish inhabitants and 'Germanising' the conquered territory by the assimilation of persons of mixed Polish and German stock and by introducing Germans from the Baltic States, now under Soviet occupation. Poles were almost completely deprived of civil rights and reduced to the status of 'protected persons'. In the part of Poland annexed outright to the Reich there immediately took place a campaign of annihilation against the Polish people, especially its intellectual and cultural élite, aimed at destroying the Polish character of the area, on similar lines to the policy later pursued in occupied Soviet territory. In the rump Polish territory known as the *Generalgouvernement* (see Section C1, p. 50 above), a somewhat different policy was at first pursued, the emphasis being on economic exploitation. Here too, however, Himmler's police system soon began to put the 'nationality' policy into effect by means of terror and murder, the extermination of leading Poles and the persecution of Jews, who were concentrated into large ghettos in 1939–40. The German military protested at the inhuman behaviour of Himmler's units; this opposition between the military and to some extent the civil administration on the one hand and Himmler's SS and police on the other was to be typical of German occupation policy in general, illustrating the contradiction between traditional and revolutionary elements in the politics and war methods of Nazi Germany.

Altogether, the policy of the occupation in Poland differed to a marked extent from that in Scandinavia and Western Europe. In Denmark, for instance, the government was allowed to remain in office till 28 August 1943. The German envoy, von Renthe-Fink, stayed at his post with the title of 'Reich plenipotentiary', being succeeded on 5 November 1942 by Dr Werner Best. As resistance to the occupation regime increased towards the end of the war, in August 1943 Best took over the administration of the country, with the military commander, General von Hanneken, as chief of the executive power. On 29 August 1943 a state of emergency was declared, the Danish army was disarmed and the fleet scuttled itself.

The Norwegian government and King Haakon escaped on 7 June 1940 to England, whence they organised resistance to Germany. In Norway itself only the unrepresentative 'Nasjonal Samling' (National Assembly) of the former War Minister, Vidkun Quisling, was prepared to collaborate with the invader. Despite his sympathy for Nazism Quisling was never able to obtain Hitler's consent to Norway keeping its independence in a future 'League of Germanic Peoples' under Reich leadership. On 1 February 1942 he formed a government which purported to abrogate the Norwegian constitution, but he was never more than a puppet of Josef Terboven, the former Gauleiter of Westphalia, whom Hitler appointed Reich Commissioner for occupied Norway on 24 April 1940. In his attempts to bring about a 'National Socialist revolution in Norway' (Loock, 1970) Terboven had to cope with a confusion of rival institutions and agencies, and to answer the protests against the behaviour of the civilian government and police from Colonel-General von Falkenhorst, the commander-in-chief of the German armed forces in Norway, and Admiral Boehm, the naval commander. Grand Admiral Raeder endeavoured to have Boehm promoted to Reich

Commissioner so that Norway would be primarily under naval influence, an idea not unrelated to the plans of Alfred Rosenberg and his Foreign Policy Bureau in the 1930s to incorporate the country into some kind of Nordic entity. But these efforts were unavailing, as Hitler would not take any final and unambiguous decision about Norway's future, and Terboven kept the upper hand in the battle for authority, despite increasing criticism from the Foreign Ministry and, after 1941, from the *Sicherheitsdienst* also.

Holland was likewise governed by a civilian administration after a short period of military rule. The Reich Commissioner appointed on 19 May 1940 was Seyss-Inquart, who had been Governor of the *Ostmark* (Austria) in 1938–9, and who administered the country through a body of civil servants. Belgium, on the other hand, was kept under the military administration of General von Falkenhausen, which also included the French departments of the Nord and Pas-de-Calais. On 18 July 1944 an order was issued to transform this military administration into a civilian one with Gauleiter Grohe as Reich Commissioner, but it did not take effect owing to the Allied victories in France. Luxemburg was ruled by Gauleiter Simon as head of the civil administration under Hitler's direct authority; his efforts to recover this 'ancient imperial territory' for Germany brought him into much conflict with the military. On 6 August 1940, however, Luxemburg was attached to the Gau of Koblenz-Trier, and on 30 August 1942 it was for practical purposes incorporated into the Reich.

The armistice of 22 June 1940 divided France into a zone under military occupation and one which remained unoccupied until 11 November 1942. The former comprised two-thirds of French territory, including Paris and the industrial region of the north. It extended southward to the Loire and included the Channel and Biscay coasts as far as the Spanish frontier. Occupied France was governed by the military commander in Paris, General von Stülpnagel, while the government of unoccupied France under Marshal Pétain moved to Vichy in the Auvergne. Hoping to induce Pétain's authoritarian government to throw in its lot with Germany against Britain, the Nazis treated him with some lenience and allowed him to retain sovereignty over the French colonial empire. In sharp contrast to the policy of understanding, however, were attempts to use France's economy, manpower and arms industry as far as possible in the service of the Nazi war machine. The *de facto* reannexation of Alsace-Lorraine was also not calculated to persuade Pétain to abandon his wait-and-see attitude and enter the war on Germany's side.

As regards South-Eastern Europe, the Reich allowed its Italian ally to occupy Greece subject to some reservation of authority. In Yugoslavia, which the Axis powers on 8 July 1941 declared to have ceased to exist as a state, an independent Croatia was established with Ante Pavelić as its *poglavnik* (leader): its existence had been proclaimed on 10 April by the Ustashi leader, Kvaternik. The authoritarian state under the patronage of Mussolini's Italy adopted a policy of savage nationalist and religious persecution, chiefly aimed against the Orthodox

Serbs in Croatian territory. In Serbia itself a German military administration was set up, a very restricted degree of authority being exercised under its aegis by a government established on 30 August 1941 under General Milan Nedić, formerly War Minister. Montenegro became 'independent' as an Italian protectorate, and Slovenia was partitioned between Germany and Italy, Lower Styria and parts of Carniola being annexed to the Reich.

In Scandinavia, Western Europe and South-Eastern Europe, the fact and the character of the occupation, as well as the persecution of Jews which from 1942 onwards affected the whole of Europe under German control or influence, provoked movements of national resistance which steadily increased in scope and hampered Germany's conduct of the war. While the Nazi 'battle for nationhood' continued in Poland, as far as Scandinavia and Western Europe were concerned German occupation policy until 1944 was dominated by economic exploitation rather than racial policy; but racialist ideas on the future of the 'Greater Germanic Reich' were ever present and were to some extent put into practice even there. However, with the preparation and beginning of the Russian campaign the Nazis' war and occupation policy was characterised not only by economic exploitation, as practised, for example, most intensively in the Ukraine, but also by a new quality which may be described as a 'racial war of extermination'.

In his address to over 200 senior officers on 30 March 1941 Hitler laid down as a war aim in the coming invasion of Russia the 'annihilation of Bolshevik commissars and the communist intelligentsia'. Commissars and GPU men were 'criminals' and must be treated as such. The battle 'would be different from that in the West: in the East, severity at the present time would mean mercy in the future'. Hence orders were issued regardless of the accepted laws of war and traditional morality. A notorious example was the so-called 'commissar order' of 6 June 1941, according to which political commissars of the Red Army, 'if captured in battle or offering resistance, were in principle to be put to death at once'. Such orders made clear 'that the separation between the powers of the military and the SS, which had been still maintained in the war in Poland and in the West, was now no more than a fiction, and that the effective merger of these two institutions was related to a breakthrough in the sense of achieving the regime's "ultimate objectives" ' (Hillgruber, 1973b). Nazi racial policy reached a peak of intensity during the attack on Russia, first when victory seemed to be attained between June and August–September 1941, and afterwards when 'Operation Barbarossa' was in evident danger of failure.

Hitler, at the height of his confidence in victory, had unfolded his ambitious plans to Oshima, the Japanese ambassador, on 14 July. On the following day Meyer-Hetlich, head of the central planning office in the Reich Commissariat for the Consolidation of German Nationality, submitted the 'General Plan for the East' which Himmler had called for on 24 June and which he was to approve with modifications on 12 June 1942. The intention was to settle Poland, the

Baltic States, White Russia and part of the Ukraine with Germans over a period of thirty years: 31 million of the existing population were to be deported to western Siberia, and 14 million of 'good stock' permitted to remain. On 16 July 1941 Hitler developed his plan for four 'Reich Commissariats' comprising the Ukraine, the *Ostland* (Baltic States and White Russia), 'Muscovy' and the Caucasus – only the first two were in fact created. Addressing Göring, Keitel, Rosenberg, Bormann and Lammers, that is, all the chiefs of the army, party and state apparatus except Himmler, on the future of the Soviet Union, Hitler declared that 'There must never again be any question of a military power arising west of the Urals'. On 17 July 1941 Rosenberg, Reich Minister for the Occupied Eastern Territories, issued directives for their administration. More important, however, was the fact that on the same day Himmler was made responsible for the 'political security of the newly occupied territories', so that the SS was from the outset the dominant authority in the conquered *Lebensraum* to the east.

In the next few days Hitler, still confident of victory in Russia, indicated to the Croatian Defence Minister, Kvaternik, that the Jewish population of Europe would be deported to Siberia or Madagascar. 'For, if even one state for any reason tolerates the existence of a single Jewish family, this would become the seat of infection and bring about a new decomposition. If there were no Jews left in Europe at all, the unity of the European states would be assured.' On 31 July Göring on behalf of the Führer instructed Heydrich, 'in consultation with the appropriate central authorities, to make the necessary preparations for an overall solution of the Jewish question in the German sphere of influence in Europe'. This applied to Western Europe as well as to the Soviet Union, where extermination by task forces of the SD and Sipo had already begun.

The Jewish policy of the Third Reich went through three increasingly radical phases, which began at different times but overlapped and coexisted to some extent. The first phase lasted from 1933 till the outbreak of war and in its different stages took the form of legal discrimination, deprivation of economic power and threats to the person (see Sections A1 and B2, pp. 4–25 and 71–86 above). With German victory in the West came a second phase envisaging a 'final solution' on a territorial basis: the idea originally favoured was to remove Europe's Jews to Madagascar, then a French possession.

The Madagascar plan was to some extent connected with deportation plans that had been considered in 1938–9 by the top Nazi leaders, who were by no means unanimous in their ideas of policy towards the Jews (cf. Section B1, p. 35 above). Hitler mentioned the plan to Mussolini and Raeder on 18 and 20 June 1940, and it figured among studies for a future peace settlement in a memorandum, dated 3 July 1940, by Legation Secretary Rademacher of the home affairs section of the Foreign Ministry. This included the practical argument that Jews deported to Madagascar and kept there under SS surveillance would constitute a 'pledge in Germany's hands' for use in future world power diplomacy. The defeat of France brought into the foreground the possibility of obtaining the use of Madagascar; but it lost its significance in the light of the Russian campaign, which presented Hitler with an opportunity, immediate in space and time, to realise his political calculations and ideological aims. The Madagascar plan was not formally abandoned, however, till 10 February 1942, when the Foreign Ministry was informed of Hitler's decision that 'the Jews should not be sent to Madagascar but to the East', as the war with the Soviet Union had 'now made it possible to use other territories for the final solution'. True, Hitler in his 'table talk' at headquarters on 29 May 1942 once again spoke of its being better to deport the Jews of Western Europe to an African climate intolerable for Europeans, and on a previous occasion during the 'racial war of extermination' he mentioned the Madagascar plan as a possible solution. But the plan definitely faded into the background with the outbreak of the Russian war, which was always closely connected in Hitler's mind with the destruction of Bolshevism and Jewry. In the context of a 'territorial final solution' there was now vague talk of sending European Jews to Siberia, in full awareness of the heavy physical casualties they would sustain in the inhospitable areas east of the Urals.

Alongside this plan, however, which Hitler mentioned to Kvaternik on 21 July 1941, Nazi Jewish policy entered its third phase. This went beyond the idea of deportation to Madagascar or Siberia (admittedly involving the liquidation of a large number of Jews) and envisaged a direct, systematic 'physical final solution'. Hitler's decision to this effect was part of the preparations for the Russian war and was carried out from 22 June 1941 onwards by the SD and Sipo units in conquered Russia, at the same time as plans still existed for a territorial solution (Madagascar or Siberia). From then on there was no question of, for example, persecuting only Jews of a particular origin or from certain classes of society: those systematically shot were exterminated simply because they were Jews.

Also in June 1941 Himmler, invoking Hitler's authority, ordered the commandant of the Auschwitz concentration camp to construct gas chambers of the largest possible capacity for extermination purposes. This was the ultimate expression of the 'physical final solution', the advanced technical apparatus which, from December 1941 onwards, was eventually to put to death over 4 million European Jews. In the course of preparing for the Russian war Hitler had decided on the physical liquidation of the Jews; the radicalisation of this scheme with all the resources of technology took place at a stage in that war when military defeat could already be foreseen. The gas chambers that had been tried out in the course of the euthanasia programme (cf. p. 73 below), which was suspended at the end of 1941, were now turned over, with their operators, to SS Brigade Leader Globocnik, the former Gauleiter of Vienna, and the previous practice of extermination by firing squads was extended from Russian to West European Jews. The 'physical solution' was certainly planned on Hitler's orders – though they are nowhere found in writing – not later than the summer of 1941, and from December 1941 onwards it was put into effect with the highest technical efficiency. This development was encouraged, though certainly not caused, by the setback to the German war effort in Russia in October–November 1941.

At the 'Wannsee conference' on 20 January 1942 instructions were issued to the State Secretaries of the principal German ministries by Heydrich, head of the Reich Central Security Office. These still referred to the 'evacuation' of Jews to the East as a part of the territorial solution that had by then been effectively superseded. But they left no doubt that the mention of 'other measures' and such formulations as 'natural decrease' or 'appropriate treatment' of the Jewish population were nothing but a smoke-screen for the process of physical extirpation which was now under way.

The 'final solution' of the Jewish question as it was practised until October 1944, with the methods used from the end of 1941 onwards, cannot be directly and conclusively deduced from *Mein Kampf*. But in its most radical form it can be found in embryo in Hitler's mind and philosophy and in his blueprint for future rule. The destruction of the Jews of Europe was the central aim of his policy from the outset of his career: on 16 September 1919 he spoke of his 'unshakable demand for the removal of all Jews', and in the last sentence of his will on 29 April 1945 he called on his followers to 'offer unrelenting resistance to international Jewry, the worldwide poisoner of all nations'.

During the war Hitler repeatedly and publicly proclaimed the racial aspect of his 'programme' for world domination. For instance, on 24 February 1942 he stated: 'I prophesy that this war will not lead to the destruction of Aryan humanity but to the extermination of the Jews. Whatever the fight may bring or however long it may last, that will be its final result.' A month later, on 27 March, Goebbels noted: 'The prophecy which the Führer made about them [the Jews] for having brought on a new world war is beginning to come true in a most terrible manner.'

Hitler's policy and conduct of the war were more and more influenced by his dogmatic racial ideas. Even in the summer of 1942, when German hopes of victory again revived, Hitler could not bring himself to recognise unequivocally that power politics were more important than 'racial measures'. At the height of the Russian campaign, during the advance on Stalingrad, 'when it might have been thought that every resource of labour and transport was needed for this one aim, long trainloads of West European Jews were rolling across Europe, almost with the regularity of a timetable, to extermination camps in the East, to be murdered there with their fellow-victims. This was at a time when the front urgently needed every armaments worker and every item of rolling stock. The military transport authorities and those of the Central Security Office, which was responsible for the final solution of the Jewish question, fought each other for priorities, only to be told that they were both equally necessary to the war effort' (Jäckel, 1969).

The 'final solution' was still pursued in the second half of the war, when the

German troops were being driven back on all fronts by the superior force of the enemy coalition. It was almost as if the defeats of the *Wehrmacht* were to be counterbalanced by Hitler's racial 'victories'. Until October 1944 the Führer and the SS steadily increased their efforts to exalt racial dogma above the demands of the political and military situation, in the hope of realising at least one of their overweening aims, namely, to destroy European Jewry as a prelude to the regeneration of Germany and Europe. This aim of National Socialism basically determined the course of events in the second half of the war; it constantly provoked the resistance of the conquered but undefeated peoples, and made the chances of peace more and more remote. It was expressed clearly in Himmler's notorious speech to SS Group Leaders at Poznań on 4 October 1943, in which he referred 'in all frankness . . . to a painful subject, namely, the extermination of the Jewish people'. This task, assigned to the SS and performed by it, Himmler described as 'a glorious page in your history, which never has been written and never can be'. Two days later, on 6 October 1943, Himmler gave another address to Reich leaders and Gauleiters at Poznań, which was not published until 1974 (in the edition of his speeches by Bradley F. Smith and Peterson). In that very restricted circle Himmler, as the 'true executive agent of the most intimate idea of Hitler and the Third Reich' (from the introduction by J. Fest), again addressed himself to the Jewish problem. What was said on that occasion by Himmler and within the SS 'was never anything but the direct execution of Hitler's express wishes or the consequence of his intentions' (Fest, ibid.). The SS thus embodied the regime's policy as Himmler repeated 'The Jews must be stamped out' and continued:

> I ask you only to listen to what I say to you in this group, and never to speak about it. The question will be asked: 'What about women and children?' I did not consider myself entitled to exterminate the men, to kill them or have them killed, and then allow their children to grow up to revenge themselves on our own sons and grandsons. The painful decision had to be taken, to remove this people from the face of the earth. For the organisation that had to perform it, this task was the hardest we have ever faced. It has been performed, I believe I may say, without our men and our leaders suffering any harm of mind or spirit . . . That is all I wish to say about the Jewish question. You know how things stand, and you will keep the knowledge to yourselves. Much later, perhaps, it may be considered whether to tell the German people more about it. I believe it is best that we, all of us, have borne this for our people, have taken the responsibility upon us – responsibility for a deed, not only an idea – and that we carry the secret to our graves.

With this triumph of dogma over rational policy it can truly be said that 'the reality and irreality of National Socialism were given their most terrible expression in the extermination of the Jews' (Bracher, 1970).

The murder of European Jews cannot be brought under the category of terrorism against a political opponent or compared with the war crimes committed on all sides in 1939–45: it was regarded as the extermination of 'worthless life', a dogmatic racial war with the object of creating a new, biologically superior type of 'Germanic' man. As such it ranks with other measures of Nazi racial policy. Too little research has been devoted to the regime's efforts to breed a new élite, for example, by means of the marriage regulations for SS-men or the 'consanguine fishing expeditions' and plan to re-Nordicise the Germanic population of France (Bracher, 1970).

In addition reference should be made to the 'euthanasia' programme, which would more properly be called a programme for destroying life. In a decree of October 1939, backdated to the beginning of the war, Hitler instructed Bouhler, the head of his chancellery, and Brandt, his chief medical adviser, 'to confer authority on certain named doctors to perform mercy killing on invalids who are incurable so far as human judgement goes, after a critical examination of their condition'. This was an extension of the peacetime law 'For the Protection of Hereditary Health', and among the criteria determining the fate of victims was not only their medical state but also their racial origin and capacity for work. Despite elaborate concealment the measures became known to the German population in the form of rumours and aroused firm resistance on the part of the clergy, including Count von Galen, the Catholic Bishop of Münster, and Pastor von Bodelschwingh, director of the institutions of the Evangelical Home Mission at Bethel, Westphalia. As a result the programme was to a large extent abandoned at the end of 1941.

This resistance to the euthanasia programme caused Hitler, with anger and resignation, to declare that the German people was not yet mature enough for the policy he had designed for it. Together with his reverses in the East, his vexation over this issue caused him to speak more and more frequently and angrily to the effect that if the Germans were not prepared to follow him to victory they must perish.

Summary

Our conclusions about the history of Germany in the Second World War from 1939 to 1942 may be summarised as follows.

With the military attack on Poland in September 1939 the Third Reich achieved one of the dictator's aims, even though it was contrary to his plans to be involved in a war with the Western powers, especially Britain. By military expansion he hoped to achieve European hegemony and to acquire *Lebensraum* in the East. However, with the outbreak of war the destructive elements in the Nazi philosophy and in Hitler's programme became effective in a special degree. Having long coexisted with the means and ideas of Germany's traditional great power policy and contributed to the dynamism and success of the Nazi regime, from 1939 onwards these elements became increasingly independent and in the end, by a kind of fatality, brought about the self-destruction of the Third Reich. As the ideological components of Nazism came into fuller view, the interrelation between tradition and revolution, conditioning yet opposing each other – a relationship so typical of the Third Reich – once again manifested itself in a new and accentuated form.

Under the specific circumstances in which the European war turned into a world conflict in December 1941, it seemed for a time as if politico-strategic calculations and racial and ideological dogma were compatible within Hitler's state. In fact they coexisted, but in the last resort they were mutually exclusive. As this became increasingly evident, the Reich's policy and conduct of the war were finally frustrated. The existence and development of its ideological dogma, which became a power in its own right and threatened to prevail over politico-military calculations, helped to stiffen the resistance of European nations and of the Allies far beyond Germany, and thus had a destructive effect on the Reich and its international status. While the regime was still at peace, its two pillars of politics and ideology had strengthened each other, and any conflicts between them had been absorbed in the dynamism of the Nazi state: they were smoothed over by the regime's successes in economic and domestic policy and not least in foreign affairs, and were also concealed by the dictatorship's use of terror, actual or threatened. In this way the representatives of old Germany, who willingly supported Hitler at the beginning of his rule and were thereafter gradually deprived of power by the Nazis, helped for a considerable time to make possible his successes in home and foreign affairs.

In the first war years, too, the country's traditional leading groups and the new élite of the regime – the officer corps on the one hand and the party on the other – seemed at first to work together without friction and with visible success. They continued in this way to embody the dynamic co-operation of the rational and dogmatic, the strategic and ideological aspects of the Nazi state. After the military triumph over France, which was little expected by the old élite in particular, Hitler became the acknowledged, undisputed and much admired Führer not only for the mass of the population but also for many representatives of the old Germany, who in the late 1930s had regarded him with increasing reserve and distrust and had even been prepared to go to the length of political opposition.

But the regime's politico-military needs and its racial and ideological aims parted company when Hitler embarked on his war for *Lebensraum* in Russia and at the same time began to put into practice the key feature of his ambitious racial policy. During the 'normal European war' (Nolte, 1965) in the West it was possible to reconcile the claims of the Nazi racial and occupation policy with the military and political requirements of the German war machine and foreign policy, though the two had already come into conflict in Poland. But after the beginning of the Russian campaign in June 1941 they diverged more and more widely, as the aims and assumptions of doctrinaire ideology came more and more to predominate. This dominance impelled the Reich with increasing speed along the path prescribed for it by Hitler, which was ultimately a self-destructive one both at home and abroad, and finally drove the country to ruin.

From this point of view Hitler's racial policy has a character all its own, over and above the development of the Nazi dictatorship at home and the occupation policy of the Third Reich in Europe. To an extent that was previously unknown and still has its effect today, that policy determined the course of events in Germany, in international affairs and in Europe as a whole. It would not be conceivable if it had not been willed, designed and commanded by the dictator, or at least approved and tolerated by him – the same dictator who, when military defeat was in sight, resolved to lead the German people to destruction because, according to his radical conviction, it had failed to meet the challenge of the fight for world power.

(D) 'WORLD POWER OR DESTRUCTION', 1943–5

1

Hopes of Final Victory in 'Total War'

From the turn of the year 1942/3 Germany was strategically on the defensive. Hitler, the prisoner of his own doctrine and actions, declared himself to be the defender of 'fortress Europe'. From this point on the regime gave a European slant to the struggle, claiming that the Third Reich was defending Western civilisation against the 'pluto-democracies' and above all against Soviet Bolshevism; but this was little more than a threadbare cloak for its own designs of conquest. Such propaganda met with very limited response in the occupied countries, where it had been too obvious in the preceding years that Hitler's sole object was to establish a brutal, alien and racist regime. In Russia immediately after the invasion it might have been possible, for example, to win over the Ukrainian population, which at first welcomed the German troops as liberators from the Stalinist yoke, but such opportunities were squandered by the Nazis' foolish and criminal policy. Before long it was clear to the peoples of the USSR that the new masters were at least as cruel as Stalin's henchmen, if not more so. Choosing between two evils, they rejected the aggressor who had proved not to be a liberator and fought to preserve Stalin's dictatorship in the 'great patriotic war'. While Nazi propaganda strove with little success to enlist volunteer units from all the continental countries for the war in the East, it was clear to all that Nazi doctrine was a more and more decisive factor in the policy and strategy of the Third Reich, and that there was no thought of sacrificing it to rational calculations based on European solidarity or the need to increase Germany's military striking-power. Hitler's ultimate aims were at all times so dominant in his mind and in the regime's policy that they were bound in the end to challenge the whole world and consequently to prove unworkable for that very reason.

The dogma of the superiority of the German people and the Germanic race led Hitler and the other German leaders constantly to overestimate their own strength and underrate that of other nations, with the possible exception of Britain, which they hoped to gain as an ally. Thanks to this attitude and the racial fixation of the regime, Hitler and the German army also failed to solve the problem of keeping a coalition together in war. As time went on Germany's client states fell away from her, dropped out of the war, or joined the Allies, with the result that Hitler – who from start to finish refused to entertain the idea of surrender – was obliged to extend German rule to other territories such as Italy in September 1943 or Hungary in March 1944 (see below), and thus resort to hasty improvisation to defend the periphery of 'fortress Europe' from Allied encroachment.

In 1943 the development of events compelled the German leaders to take the following basic decisions.

(1) All Hitler's ideas concerning the second, overseas and Atlantic stage of his programme were shelved after the 'crucial failure to capture Moscow' (Reinhardt, 1972) and were finally given up in 1942/3. With the Reich having to defend itself against the Soviet Union in the East and against the British and Americans in Western Europe, Africa and the Atlantic, plans for colonies and offensive-defensive bases for the attainment of global power were relegated to the distant future.

(2) After U-boat operations against North Atlantic convoys were stopped on 24 May 1943 it became evident that Hitler's strategy was confined to defending 'fortress Europe', which he was fanatically determined to hold until the 'final victory' that Nazi propaganda never ceased to promise the German people. He thus had to accept the enormous damage arising from the fact that, as Roosevelt put it, the 'fortress' had no roof and could be pounded by the vastly superior Anglo-American air force.

(3) Hitler firmly believed that the fortunes of war would be reversed by the collapse of the 'unnatural coalition' between the Western powers and the Soviet Union. This speculation was not wholly absurd in view of the ideological and power-political tensions between East and West which made themselves felt in the 'cold war' soon after the defeat of Germany and were fully manifest by 1947.

The tradition of Prussian-German history on which Hitler's expectation was based had, for instance, led the Kaiser's Germany constantly to exaggerate the rivalry between Britain and Russia and consequently the freedom of action which Germany enjoyed between them. After 1917 there were, in addition, ideological reasons for supposing that Germany's Eastern and Western neighbours would fall out to her advantage. In the Second World War there was tension between the Allies over Stalin's demand for a second front and for recognition of the Soviet territorial gains of 1939–40; this issue was not resolved at the Moscow conference of 12–15 August 1942 between Churchill, Harriman and Stalin, and became more acute after the Tehran conference of 28 November–1 December 1943. Relations between the Soviet Union, Poland and the Western Allies were strained by the discovery at Katyń on 13 April 1943 of the mass grave of over 4,100 Polish officers, who according to neutral experts must have been shot in the spring of 1940, that is, before the German invasion of the area. But even this tension did not lead to a breach between the Allies such as Hitler impatiently hoped to see and increasingly regarded as the all-sufficient answer to his problems. The world outside Germany was held together, not least by the atrocities committed by the Third Reich in the occupied countries and in pursuit of its racial and population policies. The thirst of the Nazi regime for hegemony and conquest seemed to the Western Allies at all times to present a greater threat than Stalin's territorial demands, sweeping though they were. In view of the German danger to Europe and the world it was understandable that Roosevelt and Churchill made concessions to the Soviet dictator and agreed to compromise formulae at the Yalta conference (4–11 February 1945), and that Truman and Attlee behaved similarly at Potsdam (17 July–2 August 1945).

(4)   However, while Hitler's expectation that the enemy coalition would collapse and restore Germany's freedom of manoeuvre was expressed in an increasingly monomanic fashion, it must still be considered in the light of his overall programme. During the second half of the war he repeatedly voiced the hope that one day Germany and Britain together would challenge the world. In this respect he held to his basic idea of winning Britain over and, at the last moment, joining forces with her against the Soviet Union. While this remained his favourite notion, in the desperate atmosphere of the Berlin bunker during the last weeks of March–April 1945 he also speculated on the further idea of combining with the USA against Russia. Nor were these the only permutations that came into his mind in the last days of the 'Thousand-Year Reich'. Goebbels in 1943 had floated the idea of coming to terms with the Soviet Union, and Stalin, whether for tactical reasons or in earnest, had previously put out peace feelers. In March–April 1944 Hitler for the first time half-considered the possibility – which of course had long ceased to exist – that he might, as it were, repeat the coup of 23 August 1939 and ally himself with his political and ideological arch-enemy so as to redress his position *vis-à-vis* the Western powers.

Until 1944, however, Hitler had refused to explore the possibility of peace with the Soviet Union. Nor had anything come of ideas for a separate peace in the West, such as Antonescu, the Romanian Deputy Prime Minister, had urged on Mussolini in January 1943. From that year onwards all hopes of a separate peace were illusory, as Allied superiority became more and more overwhelming, and the matter was sealed by the demand for 'unconditional surrender' put forward by Roosevelt and Churchill at the Casablanca conference (14–25 January 1943). The Americans had long shown sympathy for Stalin's territorial claims in Eastern and East Central Europe and against Germany, which the Soviet leader repeatedly put forward during and after Eden's visit to Moscow in December 1941. Western bombing raids were reducing Germany to rubble, and Nazi reprisals in occupied countries, such as those at Lidice (10 June 1942) and Oradour (10 June 1944), made it certain that the peoples concerned would not forget why they were fighting Nazism and Germany.

After the Anglo-American landing in North Africa (7–8 November 1942) and especially after the surrender of the Sixth Army at Stalingrad (31 January–2 February 1943), the German people, despite endless Nazi propaganda and their remarkable confidence in the Reich leadership, began to realise that there was little hope of winning the war. Yet despite enormous losses, especially in Russia, the *Wehrmacht* was able once more to consolidate the Eastern front to some extent in the spring of 1943. Hitler tried for the last time to recover the initiative against the Russians with 'Operation Citadel', an assault on the Kursk salient. When this came to a halt after a few days he planned to keep the existing front stable at all costs and to accept a war of attrition in Russia. While the Anglo-American invasion was to be held by the Atlantic Line in the West, he thought of building a similar line of fortifications in the East (*Ostwall*) so as to entrench himself in 'fortress Europe' with its fronts extending over hundreds of miles; thus the enemy would perceive the uselessness of his attacks and the West would eventually knuckle under.

As the Soviet armies reconquered the Ukraine between August 1943 and April 1944, Hitler decided for the time being to shift the weight of his military defence westward. On 3 November 1943 he issued Directive 51 calling for a show of German strength in the West which, he hoped, would induce the British to throw in their lot with him or would at least split them from America and the Soviet Union. The idea of a separate peace in the West was also canvassed in the army and in Himmler's SS. Goebbels for his part thought of coming to terms with Stalin's totalitarian dictatorship, so close in its nature to the Nazi system, while Ribbentrop speculated, in line with his previous plans, on the possibility of enlisting Japan's military or diplomatic help to put an end to the fighting in Russia. Hitler himself believed that his last chance lay in winning a decisive success in the West, for example, by defeating the expected Anglo-American invasion, so as to effect an arrangement with Britain after all.

From this point of view we can understand Hitler's reaction to the Allies' invasion of France on 6 June 1944, which he had long expected and which now came as a kind of relief, enabling him once again to demonstrate German strength to the British in particular. The war situation was more and more desperate: in the same month US troops had landed on Saipan in the Marianas, and in Russia on 22 June the Red Army launched a tremendous summer offensive preceded by partisan activity on an unprecedented scale. Nevertheless Hitler clung to the hope that a show of strength against the West might still turn the tables in Germany's favour. His hopes were based partly on the 'miracle weapons' – the V1 and V2 – which in fact were only partially successful, but which still kept alive the expectation of final victory that persisted among the German people.

The same purpose was to be served by the Ardennes offensive, the last major assault by Germany on the Western front. Meanwhile King Michael of Romania had given orders on 23 August 1944 to cease operations against the Red Army, and on 19 September Finland signed an armistice with the Soviet Union. In the same month Soviet troops occupied Bulgaria, and by 2 November the German forces evacuated Greece (except Rhodes, western Crete, Melos and some smaller islands). Hungary, which had been occupied by German troops on 19 March 1944, attempted to negotiate an armistice with the USSR on 15 October; this was prevented by the Germans, but by the end of the year Soviet military units reached the outskirts of Budapest.

The last German troops in North Africa had surrendered on 13 May 1943. On 10 July the Allies landed in Sicily; on the 25th Mussolini's regime collapsed, and the new premier, Marshal Badoglio, signed a separate armistice with the Allies on 3 September (for military reasons it was not announced till the 8th). The German forces in Italy thereupon disarmed the Italian troops under their control and prepared to resist the Allied advance. The Allies took Rome on 4 June 1944 and moved north as far as the German position on the Apennines, where fighting continued till 29 April 1945.

In Western Europe the Allies advanced steadily. On 25 August 1944 General de Gaulle at the head of French units entered Paris, which the Germans had evacuated, and by September the British and Americans reached the Western frontier of Germany. In October the Russians advanced into East Prussia, and Japan was decisively defeated by the USA in the battle of Leyte Gulf in the Philippines (22–25 October 1944).

While the German military leaders on the Western front wished to stand on the Meuse and await developments, Hitler's plan was to follow up the Ardennes offensive by advancing to Antwerp, so as to show that Germany's strength was still unbroken and so induce Britain to comply with his aims. The advance began on 16 December 1944, but was halted by the Allies after four days. Rejecting all persuasions to end the war – not least those of Field Marshal Rommel, who was compelled by the Nazis to commit suicide on 14 October – Hitler clung to the more and more illusory hope that a split in the enemy coalition would enable him to seize the initiative once more. But the Allies advanced progressively on all fronts. In February and March 1945 they conquered all of Germany west of the Rhine. American troops crossed the Rhine on 7 March at Remagen, and the British on 24 March at Wesel. The Americans and the First French Army moved into south Germany and also occupied Vorarlberg, the Tyrol as far as the Brenner Pass, the Salzkammergut, Upper Austria and western Bohemia as far as a line from Karlovy Vary (Karlsbad) to Budejovice (Budweis). The British in the north reached the Elbe at Lauenburg on 19 April, while American units in central Germany met the Russians at Torgau on the Elbe on 25 April. General Eisenhower, the Allied supreme commander, halted the advance for both political and military reasons, intending to use the bulk of his forces to subdue the 'Alpine Redoubt', a figment of Nazi propaganda which was taken seriously by the Allied governments.

In January–May eastern Germany was conquered by the Red Army, as millions of Germans sought to flee westward amid fearful suffering. On 13/14 February 1945 Dresden, which was full of refugees from Silesia, was savagely attacked and destroyed by Allied bombers. The number of dead has never been precisely known. Some estimates speak of 245,000 victims. Calculations of the Federal Statistical Office mention 60,000 dead, while Götz Bergander in his very thorough investigation *Dresden im Luftkrieg* (1977) gives a figure 'of the order' of 35,000 dead. The Dresden massacre marked the culmination of the Allied bombing campaign designed to destroy German civilian morale: the attacks demonstrated the Allies' air superiority and also gave Nazi propaganda a welcome opportunity to denounce Anglo-American 'terrorism' and appeal to the endurance of the German population.

Hitler committed suicide on 30 April, and the city of Berlin surrendered on 2 May. The successor government under Admiral Dönitz and Count Schwerin von Krosigk endeavoured to get as many German soldiers as possible out of the Soviet-occupied zone and into that of the Western powers. The idea of an alliance with those powers against Russia had prevailed in Hitler's mind towards the end of the war, and in that of most of the leading individuals and groups in Germany; it was now taken up by Dönitz's government, which declared that it was the mission of the Reich to keep Russia out of Central Europe. This attitude caused Stalin to take a stronger line against the new German government, which remained in the British zone and refused to move to Berlin.

On 7 May Colonel-General Jodl signed the instrument of surrender of the German armed forces at General Eisenhower's headquarters at Reims, the surrender being confirmed on 9 May by Field Marshal Keitel, Colonel-General Stumpff and Admiral von Friedeburg at the Soviet headquarters in Berlin-Karlshorst. The European war unleashed by Hitler was thus officially ended on 9 May at one minute past midnight. In a radio address on 8 May Dönitz described the situation of defeated Germany – the 'unconditional surrender' of which was an event of unique scope in modern history – in the words: 'With the occupation of Germany, power now rests with the occupying countries.'

2

Nazi Terror and German Resistance

In 1943–5, as Germany's military situation went from bad to worse, Nazi terror against the population increased steadily, as did the ideological 'penetration' of all aspects of public and private life. In order to 'develop all forces to the uttermost' and ensure 'final victory', a decree was issued on 27 January 1943 making all men from 16 to 65 and all women from 17 to 45 liable for compulsory labour duties. The Casablanca demand for 'unconditional surrender' was taken up by Goebbels, who opposed to it a demagogic call for 'totalitarian warfare'. In a speech on 30 January 1943, the tenth anniversary of the Nazi 'seizure of power' – the date coincided with the defeat of the German Sixth Army at Stalingrad – Goebbels spurned the idea of surrender and endeavoured to rouse the population to a state of fanaticism. In the celebrated meeting at the Berlin Sportpalast on 18 February 1943 he endeavoured to counter the despondent mood of the German people after the Stalingrad débâcle with a rhetorical appeal culminating in the question: 'Do you want total war? Do you want it, if it must be so, more total and more radical than we today can even imagine?' The audience screamed 'Yes', and Goebbels, treating their answer as a kind of plebiscite, continued: 'I have asked you and you have given me your answer. You are a part of the people, and the German people has declared itself through your lips.' No doubt Goebbel's main concern was to provide a propaganda counter to the shock of Stalingrad, but the applause of his audience must have confirmed the Allies in their belief that it was right to demand Germany's 'unconditional surrender'.

From this point of view, however, not only did the propaganda weapon have a real effect in prolonging the war, but so, to at least an equal extent, did the regime's use of terror. For instance, 'Operation Thunderstorm' on 22 August 1944 involved the arrest and detention of about 5,000 former ministers, mayors, deputies, officials of the Nazi Party and of the Weimar Republic, including Konrad Adenauer and Kurt Schumacher. The Nazi leaders, aware of coming defeat, were clearly determined to eliminate 'Germany's political reserve' (Haffner, 1979) so that they themselves might fight 'until five minutes past twelve' (ibid.). The complete control of the SS over the Reich was formally sealed on 24 August 1943, when Himmler, already Reichsführer SS, became Minister of the Interior as well. In an atmosphere of military defeat, even a cautious expression of doubt as to 'final victory' became a capital crime. Ulrich von Hassell's diary for 8 March 1944 records a macabre reflection of this in the Berlin joke: 'I'd rather believe in victory than run around with my head cut off.'

The last pockets of independence, for example, in the armed forces, were gradually mopped up, as may be seen from the introduction of 'National Socialist Leadership Officers' on 22 December 1943. The office of Reich defence commissioners was conferred on the Gauleiters so as to re-emphasise the party's priority over the *Wehrmacht*. A further step towards 'total war' was taken when in October 1944 all German men between 16 and 60 who were fit for military service were obliged to join the *Volkssturm* (militia), while on 12 February 1945 German women and girls were conscripted as auxiliaries to that force. A proclamation on 2 April 1945 announced the formation of the 'Werewolves', to fight as an underground army for 'final victory' after Germany had been conquered in regular warfare. This plan was never put into effect, however; it was taken seriously by no one but the Allies, resembling in this the fiction of an 'Alpine redoubt' in southern Germany (cf. p. 80 above).

Hitler's last directive of March 1945, and especially the 'Nero order' of 19 March – which called on retreating German troops to destroy the industrial plant and supply installations that were vital for the future existence of the German people – were disregarded by the *Wehrmacht*, in co-operation with responsible state and party officials and representatives of industry. Thus the dictator failed in both his alternative aims: he neither led Germany to world domination nor to complete ruin, though he came within sight of both objectives in 1940–1 and 1944–5 respectively. When military defeat was already in prospect, and especially after the attempt on his life on 20 July 1944, Hitler and the regime exercised power in Germany in a way that far exceeded what had gone before. This took such savage and partly atavistic forms as *Sippenhaft* – the punishment of a whole family for the misdeeds of one of its members – which was enacted on 1 August 1944 and put into practice against the relatives of those responsible for the attempt of 20 July. The importance of the coup is indeed shown by the ferocity of reprisals against members of the German resistance and their families. The scale of the regime's reaction threw serious doubt on the contention of both Nazi and Allied propaganda that Hitler was to be identified with the German people; and this was a fact of importance for the future of Germany.

There was no single, unified resistance movement in Nazi Germany, and partly for this reason it is difficult from a methodical and practical point of view to distinguish exactly what resistance there was, where it began and in what ways it operated. Not everyone who remained aloof from party organisations was a member of the resistance. Conversely, many members of those organisations gradually found their way into the resistance, and others joined the party ranks with the sole or principal object of carrying on the opposition. 'Private non-conformity, opposition-mindedness, active resistance, and direct conspiracy to overthrow Hitler' (Erdmann, 1976a): the transition between each of these and the next appears on examination to be fluid.

The communists, certainly, were determined on active resistance from the beginning. Although Hitler's seizure of power took them by surprise and they were unprepared either for open mass resistance or for underground operations, they at once concentrated on developing propaganda activity against the regime and setting up clandestine cells and groups. Their work was largely directed from abroad, and the German Communist Party was under the orders of the Executive Committee of the Communist International. It was weakened by Stalin's purges of the 1930s, to which, it is estimated, more German communists fell victim than to Nazi terror. A further setback was the Nazi-Soviet pact of 23 August 1939, which largely paralysed communist resistance in Germany. Only with the invasion of Russia was Soviet *raison d'état* again reconciled with German communist ideology. To some extent the German communists had gone on resisting between August 1939 and June 1941, but with the invasion they were more and more cut off from their masters abroad. About 20,000 of them paid for their resistance activity with their lives. This for a time gave them a certain independent status *vis-à-vis* Moscow, which however was soon corrected when the exiled party leaders returned from the Soviet Union after the war.

Linked with the communists was a resistance and espionage group known as the *Rote Kapelle* (Red Orchestra). This was headed by Arndt von Harnack, a senior official in the Reich Economic Ministry, and Harro Schulze-Boysen, a flying officer in the Air Ministry who was interested in socialist ideas. Some of the group's members transmitted information to the Soviet Union or speculated on a future German-Soviet partnership; they were, however, mostly artists and intellectuals and in no way considered themselves orthodox communists of the Moscow obedience. They were detected in August 1942 and put on trial; many were put to death.

The detection of the 'Schulze-Boysen group' led, for the first time since the 1930s, to attempts at co-operation between communists and socialists. This cautious *rapprochement* in the latter part of the war marked a new attempt, in the face of overwhelming Nazi strength, to mend relations between the two parties, which had always been difficult since Weimar days, oscillating between co-operation and hostility. The *Neubeginnen* ('new beginning') socialist group in Germany, unlike the Social Democratic Party leadership, sought at all times to co-operate with the communists, and in the second half of the war the Social Democrats Leber and Reichwein, who belonged to the Kreisau circle, also made contact with them. But of the SPD (Social Democratic Party) as such it can be said that in general it did not carry on underground activity or propaganda like the KPD (Communist Party), or give priority to the need to join the communists in fighting the regime, but concentrated on keeping its membership intact, a policy which stood it in good stead after 1945. The SPD also co-operated with bourgeois and aristocratic opponents of the regime in resistance groups such as the Kreisau circle, and thus laid a firm foundation for inter-party co-operation in the future.

Apart from the communists, the chief German resistance groups were the conservative notables including Goerdeler, Beck and von Hassell on the one hand, and the Kreisau circle, inspired more by Christian socialist ideas, whose leaders were Count Helmut James von Moltke and Yorck von Wartenburg, and who met at the former's estate of Kreisau in Silesia. From the turn of the year 1941/2 these two groups came closer together. Their objectives for the future, whether shared or divergent at different times, are difficult to formulate, as none of their plans were couched in definite form and there was no finality about aims expressed in different situations by various leaders of the resistance. However, it can be seen that the Kreisau circle for a long time shrank from the idea of using force against the tyrant, whereas Goerdeler from the beginning saw Hitler's removal as the precondition of a new order. The Kreisau circle came to agree with him, but Moltke, its leading spirit, continued also to believe that the reconstruction of Europe must be preceded by the total defeat of the Reich. As regards internal policy, the leaders of the Kreisau group thought in terms of a society organised from the bottom upwards, and in economic and social matters they held to an undogmatic form of socialism with Christian overtones. They believed in a new type of humanity superior to all forms of class antagonism, and in foreign affairs their ideal was a united Europe composed of small self-governing units with equal rights. This would at last put an end to centuries of fighting for hegemony and equilibrium, and in this framework a repentant Germany could join with the nations it had attacked and subjugated.

How far this ideal was compatible with world realities was repeatedly questioned by such conservative resistants as Goerdeler, the diplomat Ulrich von Hassell, and Popitz, the Prussian Finance Minister. Such men thought in terms of a strong and even authoritarian state in the Bismarckian tradition, but based on tolerance and the rule of law and conscious of its social obligations. As would be expected in view of the origins and background of this group, parliamentary democracy did not figure among their aims. In the international sphere, which was to them decisive, they took it for granted that Germany was the naturally predominant power with the main responsibility for European order. In view of the global antagonism between Britain and the Soviet Union, the extent of which they exaggerated, they trusted that Britain would see it as in her interest to leave Germany the leadership of Europe as a bulwark against the danger from the East. The conservative resistants scarcely realised that these ideas of hegemony in foreign affairs caused them to be regarded in Britain and America as not much different from Hitler – though in fact their ideas were far removed from his – and as more dangerous than the Soviet Union under Stalin.

However one may judge in retrospect the chances of the two groups of resisters and the failure of their attempts, their legitimacy did not derive from their plans for the future but from the action they took against Hitler and the sacrifice they made, which was ultimately based on ethical grounds irrespective of practical calculations. In discussions among conservative officers, too, ideas of military or political opportunism that had loomed large at the beginning eventually gave place to a sense of moral duty. One of the chief members of the military resistance, Hans-Henning von Tresckow, First General Staff Officer to Central Army Group and later chief of staff of the Second Army, expressed this view to Count Stauffenberg from the Eastern front in the summer of 1944: 'The assassination must be attempted at all costs. If it should fail, action must still be taken in Berlin. For it is no longer a question of the practical aim: it must be demonstrated to the world and to history that the German resistance has decided on a supreme throw. Nothing matters in comparison with this.'

The military resistance was best placed, as far as means went, to strike a decisive blow at the regime. To say this is not to belittle the action of other persons or groups, such as the brave deed of Georg Elser, who, on his own initiative, tried to assassinate Hitler on 8 November 1939 by planting a time-bomb in the Bürgerbräukeller, or the Munich students of the 'White Rose' group led by Hans and Sophie Scholl, who distributed anti-Nazi leaflets and were executed in 1943. But the action which came closest to overthrowing the regime was the attempted assassination of Hitler on 20 July 1944 by Count Claus von Stauffenberg, chief of staff to the commander of the Army Reserve. The prior history of this attempt goes back as far as 1938, showing that it was not primarily an act of desperation by a few officers faced with the prospect of Germany's military defeat.

In 1938 senior officers, diplomats and civil servants had tried to stage a rising and depose Hitler. Their motive was the realisation that his warlike policy would unite the whole world against Germany and end in her complete ruin. Attempts were made to persuade the British to take a firm line against Hitler and, by inflicting a setback on him, provide the resistance movement with some chance of successful action; but these aims were defeated by the interests and limitations of British policy. Prime Minister Chamberlain mistrusted the old-style Prussia from which the German conservative resistance was largely recruited at that time; he considered it in no way more trustworthy than Hitler, whom he recognised as the legitimate head of the German government. When the British government consented to the Munich agreement of 29 September 1938 it made a *coup d'état* impossible for the time being, as Hitler was borne aloft on a wave of popularity as victor and preserver of the peace. Later attempts by the military conspirators to avert the threat of war in summer 1939 were unsuccessful, as were similar moves to forestall the invasion of France in the winter of 1939/40. Hitler was to have been arrested while visiting one of the army headquarters, but the visit was cancelled at the last moment. This was one of several occasions between 1939 and 1944 when Hitler eluded the conspirators' plans as if by a miracle.

After the victorious campaign in the West there could be no question of action for some time to come. Despite the fact that conservatives such as Beck and Goerdeler were not dazzled by the success in France and at no time abandoned their opposition to Nazism, positive action against the regime could not again be considered until such time as Hitler's prestige was shaken by military reverses in the future. But this calculation itself pointed to the fearful dilemma of the German resistance movement, which distinguished it so basically from the resistants in other countries. In order that their country might be saved, the German conspirators had to hope that it would first be grievously defeated. From this point of view all their contacts with Allied governments – via Switzerland, the Vatican, or the Bishop of Chichester – were tainted with the odium that attached to treating with the enemy in wartime behind the backs of their own lawful authorities. In any case, even these controversial attempts and the vague hopes to which they gave rise were frustrated when the Allies at Casablanca adopted the formula of 'unconditional surrender' – in doing which they confirmed to some extent the tendency, as it has been called, for belligerents to take on each other's characteristics.

Resistance activity in Germany did not resume to any extent until the turn in the fortunes of war in 1943, which was clearly felt throughout the population. But all the plans and attempts were either not put into effect or failed owing to a chain of coincidences which seemed to favour Hitler to an amazing extent. This is true also of 20 July 1944, when Stauffenberg attempted to kill the dictator at his headquarters in East Prussia and also direct the *coup d'état* in Berlin. Stauffenberg, who had been appointed to the Army Reserve on account of his severe war injuries, enjoyed access to the briefing meetings in Hitler's head-quarters at Rastenburg; by this time he was also 'chief of staff' of the resistance. Action became imperative when the conspirators were in danger of being discovered owing to the arrest of Leber and Reichwein and the hue and cry for Goerdeler in July 1944. On 20 July Stauffenberg exploded a bomb concealed in a briefcase during one of Hitler's meetings, but once again the dictator was saved by circumstances that could scarcely have been foreseen. First, the conference was not held in Hitler's bunker but in a less solid building where the bomb could do less damage, and secondly, after Stauffenberg left the briefcase it was moved so that Hitler escaped the main force of the explosion. In addition, owing to a misunderstanding or a failure of communication between East Prussia and Berlin, the coup was not set in motion in the capital until Stauffenberg had returned there. Hitler received only slight injuries, and he and his headquarters soon resumed charge. The guard battalion in Berlin under Major Remer was supposed to cordon off and occupy the government quarter, but Goebbels put through a telephone call to Hitler, who personally ordered him to suppress the coup. During the afternoon and evening of 20 July it became increasingly clear in Berlin that Hitler was still alive, and the conspiracy collapsed.

In Paris the conspirators – led by General von Stülpnagel, the military governor of France – acted with determination and quickly seized the head-quarters of the police, Gestapo, SS and SD, but the coup was finally frustrated. Field Marshal von Kluge, commander-in-chief in the West, had been hesitant, but on learning that Hitler was still alive he cancelled all measures taken against the party and SS. This did not save him from the charge of sharing in responsibility for the conspiracy, and on 18 August he committed suicide.

For the inner circle of the resistance it was the deed itself which counted, and despite failure they mounted the scaffold convinced that they had done the right thing.

I do not consider Hitler only the arch-enemy of Germany [Tresckow declared], but also the arch-enemy of the whole world. In a few hours I shall stand before my God, responsible for my actions and for my omissions. I believe I shall be able to say with a clear conscience that I have done my best in the struggle against Hitler. God once promised Abraham to spare Sodom should there be ten just men in the city. He will, I hope, spare Germany because of what we have done, and not destroy her. None of us can complain of the death we are to die. Whoever joined the Resistance put on the shirt of Nessus. The worth of a man is certain only if he is prepared to sacrifice his life for what he believes.

The conspirators and their families were then subjected to an orgy of murders organised by the SS and the Reich Security Office under SS-Gruppenführer Kaltenbrunner. The Prussian nobility, which had led the conspiracy, paid a high price in blood. This class had already been affected by the egalitarian policies of the regime and the overrunning of its estates in eastern Germany by the Red Army. The death of the conspirators, and the approaching military collapse, contributed to the 'German revolution' which Nazism brought about, partly by design and probably to a greater extent by accident, and which was to become a key factor in the origin and development of the Federal Republic of Germany.

It was decisive in this connection that sections of the aristocracy which had joined with other groups to help Hitler attain power in 1933, only to realise afterwards that they enjoyed as few rights in the totalitarian state as the workers and peasants whom they had formerly combated, were prepared during the war to resist Hitler side by side with members of all classes, including socialists and communists, whose inaction or hostility had likewise helped to bring down the Weimar Republic. Conservative, bourgeois and socialist conspirators shared common experiences in the fight against Nazism. When the new dawn came in 1945, breaking down social barriers that had long been of doubtful utility and restoring the dignity of man that had been flouted during the Nazi years, there seemed, as Ernst Nolte put it (1968), to be a chance of immunising the bourgeoisie against totalitarian excesses and also suggesting to their communist opponents the possibility of changing their spots. In the Federal Republic, which came into being as a result of the Second World War and the 'cold war', and which was likewise shaped by the effects of the 'German catastrophe' and the 'German revolution', up to now only the first of these expectations has been realised, while the second seems to be an unattainable hope from the national or international point of view.

Summary

The following conclusions may be drawn from our account of the Third Reich between 1943 and 1945.

To observers in summer 1942 the war situation once more seemed to admit of victory, as the German armies, still fighting successfully against time, advanced to the Caucasus and into Egypt. The turning-point of the war had in fact come in December 1941, when the Germans failed to take Moscow, but this was not so evident as we now know it to have been. But after the Sixth Army surrendered at Stalingrad at the beginning of 1943 the German population came gradually to realise that Hitler was no longer the stronger party, 'overthrowing the weak and unprepared as the fancy took him'. In the long final phase of the war an unbroken series of defeats presented a counterpart to the successes of 1939–41, signifying this time, as Ernst Nolte put it (1965), 'not compromise and reconciliation, but total ruin'.

This was not only due to the advancing enemy armies, which, provoked by Hitler's attacks and Nazi terrorism and racism in the occupied territories, committed similar acts of inhumanity against German prisoners and the civil population, especially in eastern Germany. Hitler himself in these years repeatedly declared that in the event of defeat he would see to it 'that the German people does not outlive this shame'. At a time when his ambitious political and racial plans were collapsing, his feelings of contempt and hatred, derived from popular ideas of racial Darwinism, were directed against his own people, whom he condemned to destruction.

The end of the Third Reich was preceded by an intensification of terror which, especially in the second half of 1944, subjected the German people to Nazi dictatorship more firmly than ever. 'The more fearful the defeats on all fronts, the more victorious the Nazi party became' – thus Golo Mann (1961), commenting on the introduction of the 'Hitler salute' into the *Wehrmacht* on 23 June 1944 as a response to the attempt on Hitler's life three days earlier. The population groaned under the increasing terror of the police, SS and party organs, but it was fettered more and more firmly to the regime by universal fear of an uncertain future, by the terror inspired by the advancing Red Army in the East, and not least by impotent anger at the intensification of Allied bombing raids in the second half of the war. These raids sometimes degenerated into a senseless exercise in terror for its own sake. They were used by Nazi propaganda to strengthen morale, to distract the public from wartime hardships and to prevent them giving any thought to the racial extermination being carried out in the Eastern part of the Nazi realm.

But the German public, caught between the terror of Allied bombing and that of Nazism, and only vaguely aware of the regime's racial atrocities, was far from supporting or approving as a matter of course the activities of the German resistance, which revived again after 1943. The resistance leaders, caught in the fearful dilemma between war and civil war, were obliged to look beyond the external adversary and treat their own leaders as the enemy to be fought. 'Those who seemed to terrorise the whole of Europe themselves lived under the same terror' (Mann, 1961). To contemporaries the German resistance did not wear the appearance of a patriotic rising, but bore the stigma of high treason. Most of the German people could not see clearly, as we can, that a state founded on injustice, which had flouted the rule of law in both national and international concerns, had no longer any moral claim to be obeyed, and that resistance to it had long been a moral duty. As the enemy coalition began to threaten the frontiers of the Reich, there appeared to be almost insuperable objections to treating the authorities of one's own state as the enemy. While members of the resistance movements in the occupied countries found support among the population and were regarded as patriots, the position of the German resistance leaders was far more ambiguous: 'They went to the scaffold alone . . . reviled and cast out by the community' (Mann, 1961).

When the end came in May 1945 many Germans did not see it as the peoples of the occupied countries naturally did, as simply a liberation from the Nazi dictatorship – the less so as the countries of Central and South-Eastern Europe and the Soviet-occupied zone of Germany soon discovered the doubtful blessings of the 'democracy' thrust upon them by the USSR. Certainly in all sections of the German population there was widespread relief when the external threat, and the terror of the Nazi regime, both came to an end; and this was soon accompanied by horror as the crimes committed by the regime in the name of the German people became known. But neither the excitement of freedom nor dismay at the atrocities of Nazism could obscure the fact that the downfall of Nazism also meant the end of the *kleindeutsch* national state created by Bismarck in 1871, at a comparatively late moment in history. The title of F. Meinecke's book *Die deutsche Katastrophe* (1946) reflected the feeling of many sections of the public who were grateful for liberation from the dictator's yoke, but could not yet grasp the extent of the regime's racist crimes, and were thrown into disarray by the destruction of the national state.

With its destruction political freedom, which had been extinguished for twelve years, was restored and enabled to develop, at least in the Republic set up in the Western zones of occupation. A considerable part of the credit for this was due to the modernisation of society unwittingly brought about by the Third Reich and its history. In the catastrophe of 1945 it was not at first evident that the Nazi revolution had had important effects in fostering German democracy. Class differences had been to some extent ironed out by the *Volksgemeinschaft* (sense of national and racial unity) of the Third Reich; another important factor was the destruction of Prussia, the former nucleus of the German empire, as its leading elements were decimated or deprived of political power and driven out of the territory east of the Elbe, which was partly lost to the successor states of the Reich. The less than friendly attitude of the Prussian élite towards the Weimar Republic had led them to call in Hitler as a 'strong man' who would consolidate their power. Instead he became their destroyer, doing to death many of them who were active in the resistance movement, and bringing both Prussia and Germany to ruin. It was a long time before the Prussian leaders realised that Hitler was a revolutionary *par excellence* in both home and foreign affairs, and by then it was too late to escape the consequences. Hitler, however, became a revolutionary motive force of German (and European) history – one who, at the price of admittedly disproportionate sacrifices such as genocide and the destruction of the *kleindeutsch* national state, introduced or set in motion a political and social revolution whose effects were felt far outside Germany and are still active in our day.

CONCLUDING REMARKS: THE THIRD REICH IN GERMAN AND EUROPEAN HISTORY

The attempt of Hitler's Germany to make itself master of the old continent was a last display of European power politics in a style which already seemed anachronistic in view of the huge increase in the influence of the two peripheral powers, the US and the Soviet Union. The plan was to overrun Russia and make it a German colony, in readiness for what was seen as an inevitable struggle with the US. In addition Nazi Germany aimed to transform the nature of home and foreign policy by creating a worldwide racial utopia. This would alter the conditions of history once and for all; every social movement would find its termination in the biological myth of racial supremacy, and the greater Germanic Reich would eventually rule the world. The arrogance of this project, and the radical methods by which it was pursued, were sufficient to condemn it to failure.

At the same time, Hitler's ambitious attempt to carry out his programme contributed to an important extent – though partly without his intending it, and partly even against his will – to developments which had revolutionary consequences for Germany, Europe and world politics. The effect of Hitler's plan to pave the way for Germany to become master of the world was to destroy for an indefinite time, if not for ever, the possibility of Germany being a great power in the traditional sense implying full sovereignty. He wished to conquer the Soviet Union and defy the USA, and instead helped to bring about the present age in which those two powers dominate the world. He believed Europe to be still in control of the international system, yet he finally undermined Europe's predominance. He regarded the whole world, strictly speaking, as Germany's colonial empire, yet brought about the triumph of decolonisation. He attempted to annihilate the Jews, yet could not prevent the foundation of the state of Israel.

These are examples of the paradoxical effect on world affairs of the revolutionary policy of the Third Reich. In home and foreign affairs Hitler's state failed to achieve any of its global and totalitarian objectives, and often brought about the opposite of what it intended. Yet the results of its history, however paradoxical, are themselves of a revolutionary character. The failures of the Third Reich demonstrate that world history survived the 'Thousand-Year Reich' instead of being brought to a complete standstill by the fulfilment of Nazi policy with its universal racial utopia – even though the human, social and political costs were so high as probably to be without precedent.

The revolutionary policy of Nazi Germany failed in its aims and had far-reaching consequences that were contrary to its intentions. This points to the fact that the autonomy of the Third Reich was characterised by ambivalence in many respects, as it stood in relation to various ideological, social and political forces but served none of them. Nazism basically belonged neither to the right nor to the left in politics; it was neither simply revolutionary nor simply reactionary, but was a phenomenon *sui generis* with a historical weight of its own.

In this sense our review of its history may have shown that it is neither appropriate nor possible to describe the Third Reich concisely as 'traditional or revolutionary, counter-revolutionary or modernistic, improvised or systematic' (Bracher, 1976b). Its historical basis was ambiguous from the beginning. It achieved totalitarian dictatorship under the guise of a 'legal revolution' and amid the euphoria of a 'national revival'. For a long time it combined traditional revisionist aims with those of global expansion, in such a way that the difference was scarcely noticed. It fascinated contemporaries by making much of modern technology, yet at the same time upheld an ideal of romantic rusticity which it managed to combine with technical elements. It was hard to tell which was the end here and which the means, because the instruments of policy sometimes got the upper hand so that Nazi ideology was obscured by technical and economic developments and practical necessities. The basic doctrine of racial politics was intermixed with political calculation to produce a dynamic force which was both feared and admired, and which for many years characterised the regime's picture of itself and the way it was perceived by others. This impetus petered out at a comparatively late date, when the combination of power-political calculations and racial dogma came to grief and ideology was allowed to triumph over practical necessities.

The Third Reich in fact presented a combination of tradition and revolution, the two opposed forces which – since the transformations of the eighteenth century, the French and the industrial revolution – had kept European and German history in a state of motion and instability. The conflict between the 'old society and the new masses' (Meinecke, 1950) had brought about social maladjustments and political tensions which put an increasing strain on the ability of the old-fashioned state, or of the liberal parliamentary system, to resolve them by compromise. Large sections of the German population felt that in Nazism they had a force which was at last able to reconcile the two powerful, antagonistic trends of nineteenth-century history, namely, nationalism and socialism, and which seemed to offer a middle way into the future between liberal capitalism and Marxist communism. The attraction of the German experiment and its partial success in eliminating class differences in the 'national community' of the Third Reich, at least as far as politics and social psychology were concerned, for some time concealed the fact that the dominant motive force of Hitler's regime was racialism.

Nazi racial doctrine was both an instrument of political integration and an objective of the policy of annihilation. From time to time it appeared in either or both these aspects, and it was typical of the distinctive character of the novel ideology and practice of the Third Reich. It departed radically from the liberal idea of world civilisation and the Marxist belief in a state of deliverance to be attained through the class struggle. It also had nothing in common with the national state of modern times, which it radically rejected in favour of a Reich based on racial and biological principles. Colonel-General Beck expressed this well in a conversation with Meinecke about Hitler by saying: 'The man has no fatherland.' The historian Otto Hintze also noted the monstrous singularity of the Third Reich, which rejected all faith and all the ideologies of history, replacing them with Hitler's archaic and destructive hatred of tradition in every form. 'This fellow', he remarked (Meinecke, op. cit.), 'really does not belong to our race at all. There is something wholly foreign about him, something like an otherwise extinct primitive race that is still completely amoral in its nature.'

Only at a late stage, indeed almost at the last moment, did the powers which were so radically challenged by Nazism, the liberal Anglo-Americans and communist Russia, succeed in repelling and defeating the Third Reich's attempt at world domination. But the fact that Nazi Germany was able to become so strong and achieve such success was not only due to its exceptionally violent character or its ability to hoodwink its associates and adversaries at home and abroad: there were prior reasons in its favour. Its propaganda slogans of 'national community' and the 'aristocracy of labour' (even though these were at first more proclaimed than practised), its nostalgic idealisation of the peasantry, the institutions by which it enabled the individual to take part in community life – all these answered to deeply felt needs and desires of the German people, born of an obscure but widespread fear of the challenges of modern times. The Nazi movement promised a way of escape from these by simply turning its back on modernity. Meanwhile, however, Hitler made adroit use of modern techniques to further his all-or-nothing plan of conquering the world and regenerating it racially. In the end he achieved only the contrary of what he aimed at, while the history of the Third Reich stimulated a process of political, social and economic modernisation that became important to the development of parliamentary democracy in the Federal Republic of Germany.

How far was the ambivalence of the Third Reich, which makes it appear a historical phenomenon *sui generis*, a basic feature of the whole 'era of fascism'? Was Nazism primarily the German variant of a European phenomenon, or was it more radically different from the other forms of interwar fascism? The conflict between tradition and revolution, and the 'non-identical identity' of conservative and fascist elements in comparable movements and regimes from 1919 to 1945, responding to the challenge of communism and the 'crisis of the liberal system' (Nolte, 1968), may be regarded as containing a common nucleus of political manifestation, from which 'fascism' could be derived as a middle way between liberalism and Marxism. But on closer inspection there are far more differences than similarities – as regards causes, evolution, ideology and objectives – between the phenomena of interwar politics which are often lumped together under the term 'fascist'. This caveat applies not least to the two most developed forms of 'fascism', those of Mussolini's Italy and Hitler's Germany.

Certainly if we examine in the first instance the basis and (to some extent) the function and form of the 'fascist' dictatorships of Italy and Germany, there are many evident similarities. If, however, we consider their aims in racial and foreign policy, there are clearly major differences. Mussolini's aim of reviving the Roman *impero* and claiming the Mediterranean as *mare nostro* can hardly be seriously compared with Hitler's policy of conquest and racial purity or his objective of world dominion. There is a contrast here between what is historically familiar and a type of utopian policy aimed at overthrowing the whole course of history: or, as Meinecke (1950) put it in a different context, 'Now with Hitler came something new, not indeed absolutely new, but new in its consequences and its possibilities for the future'.

Over and above all the generalities of European history in the age of world wars and revolutions, which tend in some degree to explain the origin of fascism – the 'crisis of liberalism'; communism as a basic challenge to the hitherto more or less homogeneous social order of national states and the international system; specific economic hardships of the 1920s and early 1930s – we still have to consider the historical circumstances of individual countries in order to understand, for example, why the British parliamentary system kept its identity in response to the communist and fascist challenge, whereas the short-lived Weimar Republic failed to survive. In other words, we must glance at the course of Prussian-German history in the nineteenth and twentieth centuries in order to determine the historical place of the Third Reich in the history of the modern German national state.

Taking into account the dominant influence of the big landowners in Prussian Germany, and the effect of their norms of behaviour on modern German history and the origin of the Third Reich, we must in a sense agree with Hans Rothfels's thesis of a hidden thread of continuity leading from Bismarck to Hitler. This, it is true, only makes sense if one is thinking of the circumstances which made Hitler 'possible', and which to a considerable extent arose from matters of foreign relations, and not of his ultimate aims as formulated in the 1920s and displayed with increasing clarity from 1936–7 onwards. However, as far as the relation between home and foreign policy in German history between 1862 and 1945 is concerned, this distinction means that the policy of the Third Reich cannot be primarily understood as 'social imperialism', that is, a conservative-type strategy using foreign policy as a distraction from troubles at home. For the qualitative difference between Bismarck's and Hitler's policy is precisely that the former was concerned, after the creation of the empire, to keep Germany at peace with her neighbours and more or less maintain the existing order in home affairs, whereas Hitler's policy was aimed at warlike expansion and also at overturning the social hierarchy in Germany itself.

It becomes plausible to regard the seizure of power as an alliance between the new movement and the old establishment if we consider the revolutionary features of the new regime, as they had become evident by 1936–7, against the background of the long domination of the big landowning class in Germany and its frequent opposition to parliamentarianism. Only when the new regime had established itself firmly and began to use terrorist methods as a supplement to nationalism and the Führer principle did the conservatives who had helped to create the dictatorship perceive that they themselves were, or soon would be, victims of the Nazis.

In this context we should not forget, on the one hand, that attempts were made towards setting up a parliamentary regime in the 'Bismarck era' or during the Kaiser's reign; nor, on the other hand, should we idealise too strongly the normative developments in the Western countries, which went through crises of their own. It can hardly be disputed, for instance, that from the point of view of industrialisation Bismarck's Germany proved extremely efficient and relatively humane in comparison with Britain in the eighteenth and nineteenth centuries or the Soviet Union in the twentieth. We cannot here discuss in detail the reasons for the long predominance of the agrarian élite in Prussian Germany, or examine the degree to which it was historically and politically justified. But, if all the arguments briefly touched on here are properly considered, it must be conceded that the influence of the big landowners on the political and social behaviour of leading circles in the army, bureaucracy and economy was decisive in pointing the way towards Hitler.

It can therefore be said, apropos of an argument which has currently been revived, that the cause of Hitler's rise and the precondition of the success of Nazism was not capitalism as such but rather – to put it with slight exaggeration – the lack of capitalism in a non-parliamentary state which in important respects was still pre-modern. As John Weiss puts it, 'Fascism was not the "last gasp of monopoly capitalism"; if anything, it was the last gasp of conservatism'; and H. A. Winkler (1972) makes the point more specifically when he says: 'The success of fascist movements was not due to capitalism in the abstract but to its opportunities of reinsuring with supporters of a pre-industrial type' – a judgement which is certainly true of Nazism.

Hitler's policy – misunderstood as conservative, but in fact revolutionary – endeavoured to create a new type of humanity by means of global and racial conquest and eugenic methods, within the framework of a 'Greater Germanic Reich' organised on the basis of an agrarian economy; but it was that policy which in the end destroyed the social and political influence of the big landowners among the country's leaders. Prussian-German conservatism gave birth unawares to a revolutionary who pretended to be its servant but proved to be its murderer. The ruling classes in Germany had fought long and successfully against adapting themselves to the consequences of the industrial revolution; in Britain, by contrast, their opposite numbers had, within the parliamentary system, come to terms with a policy of cautious reform which, while by no means undisputed, was never rejected in principle. In Germany, anti-parliamentarianism led increasingly to a state of crisis which made itself felt in Bismarck's time and became acuter in the next two decades. In the last years of the Weimar Republic influential sections of the traditional leadership felt that only Hitler and his movement offered any hope of combating the threat – partly real, partly imaginary – to their political and social privileges. The date of 30 January 1933 marks both the culmination and the end of this conservative policy of specifically Prussian-German origin. The anti-parliamentarianism that had characterised Prussian Germany for decades before 1933 led, though it need not have done so, to the Nazi seizure of power and indirectly to the realisation of the full Nazi programme – race, foreign policy, totalitarianism, attempt at world domination – although the conservative German leaders did not foresee this and basically did not want it.

The aspects of Hitler's policy which involved a racial revolutionising of world history and the biological transformation of the human species can indeed hardly be viewed as historical consequences of Prussian-German development from Bismarck to Hitler. They were contrary to the intentions and remote from the imagination of those members of the élite who had clung for so long and so uncompromisingly to positions that were increasingly open to question, and had refused to accept or carry out political reforms that appear in the light of history to have been unavoidable. The attempt to flee from the demands of the modern world instead of meeting them led ultimately to the catastrophe of 1945. But, contrary to Hitler's wishes and objectives, that catastrophe contained within itself advantageous conditions for a revival of parliamentarianism in the future Federal Republic.

Our judgement on the Third Reich must be dictated primarily by the mean and monstrous crimes which at all times outweighed its more benevolent aspects. Thus it is hardly correct to treat it in general as the Jacobin phase of a long revolutionary process in Germany. We must rather conclude that the Third Reich was brought to grief by its radical revolt against the whole established order. This complete rejection deprived it of the chance of surviving as a living memory or a political tradition, since no historical necessity can justify the aims and means of its policy or the radicality of its principles and practice.

PART TWO

Basic Problems and Trends of Research

Introduction

The academic literature on the history of the Third Reich is already almost beyond the scope even of specialists. The following survey of the development of research can only outline and discuss some of the basic problems and tendencies.

The high quality of most of the research, and the fact that this period has become one of the most intensively studied themes in modern history altogether, is due to a considerable extent, though not solely, to non-academic motives, stimuli and conditions which have led historians to concentrate on the twelve years of Hitler's rule, their antecedents and consequences.

Research in general has proceeded from investigation into personal or collective guilt for the 'German catastrophe', via the question of its historical causes, to a methodical appraisal of the Third Reich and its place in history. It has been especially assisted by the fact that from the beginning of the 1960s the German archives, at least those of them which were captured by the Western Allies, have been fully at the disposal of historians. This has made it possible for recent German history to become a central theme of international historiography in the postwar period. At the outset, it is true, distortions of the history and problems of the Nazi period were almost inevitable: prior to 1960 the source basis was too narrow, while investigators were too close to the events they described and were in some cases still personally affected by them. Some errors were also due to understandable moral revulsion, leading to a general condemnation of the twelve dark years. The inadequacy or one-sidedness of many judgements, requiring completion or correction, was and still is to some extent due to the fact that researchers have not had full access to the archives of other states which dominated, or at least affected, international relations in the 1930s and 1940s. The British and US records, it is true, have been published by degrees since the early 1960s; but, for example, the French and Soviet archives, or those of neutral Sweden and Switzerland, are still closed or only partly accessible.

The abolition of the Prussian-German state in 1945 deprived German historians of the national criteria which basically still hold good in many other states in and outside Europe. In retrospective judgements of the Third Reich and modern German history, and to some extent also in judgements concerning the old Empire, the individual German lands, their rulers and estates, a less nationally prejudiced approach has become noticeable, leading to a complete and radical revision of traditional ideas of history.

This loss of the national-historical standard after 1945 was at times felt by the older generation of German historians as a painful disadvantage, depriving them of political and academic bearings, but by degrees its advantages became clear. German historical science suffered the loss of familiar judgements and categories, but this compelled it to seek new methods of research and exposition which at least led historians to transcend a national standpoint which was felt to be narrow and no longer appropriate. Scholars were thus presented with a new kind of freedom, affording both risks and opportunities. It sometimes led to very debatable results, but on the whole these were regularly corrected and adjusted in a process of lively debate which still goes on, as the 'other side' of each event and problem is investigated and presented. Our review of the state of research will show in detail this genuinely historical process of differentiation and may make it easier to understand, though perhaps not to accept as satisfactory, the fact that comprehensive accounts of the Nazi period continue to be few in number.

There is in fact a preponderance of learned, indispensable monographs over books on Hitler's policy and personality, or such general accounts as Bracher (1970) and Erdmann (1976a). In the same way the state of research tends to be reflected by bibliographies (such as F. Herre and H. Auerbach, *Bibliographie zur Zeitgeschichte und zum Zweiten Weltkrieg für die Jahre 1945–1950*, Munich, 1955, and that compiled by T. Vogelsang till his death in 1978, published as an appendix to the *Vierteljahreshefte für Zeitgeschichte*), and in the series of brief but informative reviews of current literature that have appeared in *Geschichte in Wissenschaft und Unterricht*, vol. 1 (1950) ff., *Historisches Jahrbuch der Görres-Gesellschaft*, vol. 70 (1951) ff., and *Neue Politische Literatur*, vol. 2 (1957) ff. There are also constant reviews of research into special problems of the Third Reich: for example, on the subject of Hitler, Jäckel (1977) and Hillgruber (1978). In addition, scientific monographs often begin with a résumé of the current state of research, extending beyond their immediate subject, so as to make clear the relevance and importance of the matter they are concerned with: for example, Hildebrand, 1969, pp. 13–25. More comprehensive accounts of the history of research concerning the Third Reich are infrequent and unfortunately are sometimes published in less accessible places.

This is not the case with H. Mommsen's article 'Nationalsozialismus' (1971), which unmistakably shows the author's indebtedness to a school of thought which has since the 1960s been engaged in a fundamental revision of previous judgements of Nazism and the Third Reich. At the same time, this writer gives plentiful information on the main trends of German and foreign research on Nazism.

A. Hillgruber's account (1973a) has unfortunately only been published in the series *Informationsdienst für die Auslandsvertretungen des Auswärtigen Amtes* (Information Bulletin for Foreign Service Officers Abroad). Like Mommsen's article, to which it is a useful counterpart, it covers the main problems and trends of current research on Nazism. It conforms more closely to the traditional pattern of political history, whereas Mommsen is more influenced by the methods and results of economic and social research and 'structural history'. In this way Mommsen to a large extent interprets Hitler's policies and personality as a reflection and function of processes transcending the individual – 'structural', as they are more precisely called – though of course he does not deny that there is an irreducible element of personal decision. Hillgruber (1973a), on the other hand, takes as his central theme 'what can be called the "problem of Hitler" ', though he does not overlook the question of 'what made Hitler possible' (Deuerlein) in terms of social history.

These two controversial approaches, which are characteristic of current research on Nazism and the Third Reich, were challenged by K. D. Bracher (1976b), in a volume of essays which in masterly fashion traces the main lines of the development of research and appraises their results, without however attempting to survey basic problems and tendencies on a scale comparable to Mommsen or Hillgruber. As Bracher showed in his pioneering and now standard work *Die Auflösung der Weimarer Republik* (1971) and his chapters of *Die nationalsocialistische Machtergreifung* (1962), he is concerned to avoid exaggerated structuralism on the one hand and overemphasis on Hitler's personality on the other. His judgement takes account of both general and personal, derivative and deliberate elements in Hitler's rule, and at the same time he rightly stresses that the history of Nazism and the Third Reich would be unthinkable without Hitler: 'This man and his intentions and actions will always be central to any history of National Socialism' (Bracher, 1976b, p. 85).

The task of compiling a fairly representative account of the history of research on our subject has been undertaken by W. Wippermann (1976) and W. Michalka (1978). The former addresses himself to the 'history of the interpretation of the Third Reich in postwar Germany' (covering also research into certain topics in other countries, especially the Soviet Union and Eastern Europe), and his title ' "German catastrophe" or "dictatorship of finance capital"?' leads into the current controversy as to the origin, development and collapse of the Third Reich. Starting with considerations on the general background of German and European history in the nineteenth and twentieth centuries, he proceeds to consider the peculiarities of the 'Hitler phenomenon'. Michalka, on the other hand, adopts a more or less opposite method: he traces the 'directions of Hitler research' which are to be treated fully in a thesis by Wolf-Rüdiger Hartmann, and in this 'provisional summary' he includes the general presuppositions of the history of Nazism and the Third Reich.

In the same fashion as the accounts mentioned above, but completing and varying them from a practical point of view – and perhaps also from the point of view of ideas – our own survey will first deal with contemporary assessments of Nazism and the Third Reich. The historian today, looking back over more than thirty years of research, is often amazed to see how clearly and comprehensively the problems of the time presented themselves to contemporaries, who nevertheless judged them in very different ways. It cannot be overlooked, for instance, that conflicting interpretations which are again at the centre of academic debate, and which connect the Third Reich with fascism or rather totalitarianism, were basically formulated as early as the interwar period and during the Second World War. Much the same is true of other sections of this account of the history of research: for example, that dealing with the problem, to which today widely differing answers are given, as to whether the origin and development of the Third Reich were due primarily to the 'Hitler phenomenon' or rather to a concept of fascism that held sway throughout Europe in the interwar period. Closely connected with this is the question of the relations between big business, the party and Hitler's dictatorship, which has been a subject of controversy since the 1930s and even the 1920s (in the context of Italian fascism): research on this subject continues to progress and to break fresh ground, and requires to be analysed. Whether the command structure of the Third Reich was firmly subordinate to the totalitarian will of its leader or was more of an administrative chaos is an old but still lively topic of controversy. Closely allied to it is the question whether Hitler himself determined the foreign and racial policy of the Third Reich on the basis of preconceived objectives and principles, or whether he was carried away by rival, centrifugal forces within the system of conflicting authorities and by opportunities of expansion which presented themselves from time to time and which he seized without any coherent purpose. This question naturally comes next in line and is discussed from the point of view of the 1930s and subsequently.

The sense of disorientation which we mentioned at the beginning, which is essentially political but has had useful results for historical discipline, will be illustrated by a glance at the history of research on the German resistance movement and the ever-repeated efforts to relate the Third Reich to the main course of modern history.

As regards genocide and the Nazi racial utopia, consciously designed and partially put into practice, the Third Reich is generally regarded today as unique in European history (though comparable past events in non-European countries have perhaps not been studied as thoroughly as they might be). This judgement can scarcely be disputed, even if we take account of the other totalitarian dictatorship of the twentieth century, which is no less radical and reprehensible in its principles and practice. It should be borne in mind that we are still inadequately informed of what may be comparable events in post-revolutionary Russia. Moreover, what we know of the Third Reich might be put in perspective – *horribile dictu* – by developments that still lie in an uncertain future. But conjectures of things to come, even if present-day tendencies make them seem likely, cannot be used by the historian as a criterion for judging the past events with which he is concerned. The history of the Nazi dictatorship has hitherto been studied by researchers with unusual energy and perseverance, and their conclusions and assessments are here described in the light of current knowledge and existing standards of judgement.

1

Contemporary Judgements of Nazism and the Third Reich

As pointed out in the above introduction, some of the main lines of interpretation of Nazism and the Third Reich were already suggested and discussed between the wars and during the Second World War. The current debate as to whether the notion of fascism or totalitarianism is more relevant (cf. Erdmann, 1976b, and Bracher, 1976b, pp. 13–32 and 33–61) is a revival of one which goes back to that period. So is the question whether Nazism and the Third Reich are primarily to be regarded as a product of the capitalist economy and social order, or whether they are historical and political phenomena in their own right.

In this connection the orthodox Marxist conception of fascism may be considered as the first attempt to explain national socialism. In it is rooted the 'Soviet formula' (Bracher) of 'German fascism' and the interpretation of Nazism and the Third Reich as a specific national variant of fascism, considered as a common factor of European history between the wars. As far as present-day Western research is concerned, this interpretation has by now more or less cut loose from its 'orthodox' origins. Especially since the 1960s, as Marxist ideas in general have enjoyed a revival in the Western world, and the conclusions of political historiography concerning the Nazi dictatorship have undergone critical revision from the standpoint of social and economic history and 'structuralism', the Marxist interpretation has contributed appreciably to the debate as to the nature and essential quality of national socialism.

Communist politicians and Marxist thinkers at the time of Italian fascism and German Nazism applied the question 'cui bono?' to relations between the business world, fascism and the state. They did so in an isolated fashion which prejudged the answer, and believed they had unmasked Italian and German fascism by reducing it to its supposed social function. This, they believed, consisted in the fascist movements acting as agents (hence the 'agent theory') of capitalist economic interests and their traditional representatives, in favour of social conservatism or reaction. According to this theory the fascists were paid by the ruling élite to protect it against the worldwide political, economic and social changes and crises due to the First World War and the Russian revolution. This is still the orthodox Marxist interpretation and holds the field in the historiography of the Soviet Union and the Eastern bloc, though, for example, in Poland and Hungary there have been cautious attempts to modify it. It was formulated by the executive committee of the Comintern in December 1933, which declared fascism to be a direct consequence of capitalism and nothing else: 'Fascism is the open, terrorist dictatorship of the most reactionary, most chauvinist and most imperialist elements of finance capital' (Jane Degras, ed., *The Communist International 1919–1943. Documents*, London, 1956 ff., vol. III, p. 296).

In connection with this explanation of Italian and German fascism, which more or less held sway in the Soviet Union and in the worldwide communist movement in the 1920s and early 1930s, we may note two interpretations of Nazism which, though related to it, are clearly different: one was immediately relevant in the political sphere, the other with some time-lag in the field of economics. In the first place, Zinovyev and Stalin evolved the concept of 'social fascism', a crudely unscientific version of the basic theory, which had effects of the greatest consequence in interwar history. On the other hand there appeared a more discriminating view which, instead of the 'agent theory', recognised the relative independence and novelty of the fascist and Nazi state and 'movements'; this view is associated with the names of more independent Marxist thinkers such as the German right-wing communist August Thalheimer or Otto Bauer, the theorist of Austro-Marxism.

The Soviet leaders believed it to be in their interest to identify fascism with social democracy. They therefore developed the theory of 'social fascism' and denounced social democracy as a 'wing of fascism', as Zinovyev expressed it at the Fifth Comintern Congress in June–July 1924. Not long afterwards Stalin described fascism and social democracy as 'twin brothers', and in 1928–9 the theory of 'social fascism' became part of the official ideology of the world communist movement; this was partly a reaction to the fact that Hermann Müller, representing the Western-oriented SPD (Social Democratic Party), became German Chancellor on 28 June 1928. Until Soviet policy switched to 'popular front' tactics in 1934–5 social democracy was stigmatised as a peculiarly dangerous variant of fascist tendencies, and Hitler's seizure of power was treated as a confirmation of its 'social fascist' character (W. Schieder, 1968, col. 457). Stalin and the Comintern were prevented by 'ideological blinkers' (T. Weingartner) from perceiving the essential difference between the Nazi party and the SPD, the distinctive nature of the 'brownshirt movement' and the Third Reich, and the fundamental differences between the Weimar parliamentary system, the authoritarian Cabinets of Brüning, Papen and Schleicher, and Hitler's totalitarian rule. This misconception, due to thinking in economic terms, played an important part in the downfall of the Weimar Republic and the establishment of the Nazi dictatorship. It also had momentous indirect effects on international relations in the 1930s and 1940s.

Marxists of more independent mind developed a much more differentiated view which rejected the 'agent theory' and recognised the novel and autonomous features of the fascist regimes. Since the revival of Marxist thinking in the

Western world in the 1960s this view has been taken up and further developed: cf. Dülffer's 'Bonapartism, fascism and National Socialism' (1967).

In 1930, shortly after he was expelled from the German Communist Party (KPD), August Thalheimer compared twentieth-century fascism with Bonapartism as analysed by Karl Marx in *The 18th Brumaire*. Thalheimer treated the differences between the two historical epochs as ultimately not of the first importance, but, following Marx's interpretation, saw the decisive similarity between the two movements in the fact that they were both 'a form of the overt dictatorship of capital' (Thalheimer in Abendroth, 1968, p. 28); he no longer spoke dogmatically of fascism as *the* overt dictatorship of the bourgeoisie, but merely as one of its forms (ibid.). Examining fascism more closely, he took note that the power of the state remained relatively autonomous as between the bourgeoisie and the workers; over and above the social function of the regime, he described its independent political role.

Thalheimer still adhered in principle to the 'basic Marxist pattern' (W. Schieder) which ultimately saw a causal connection between capitalism and fascism. In the same way Otto Bauer, who of all unorthodox Marxist theoreticians on this subject (besides Thalheimer and Bauer we may mention Franz Borkenau, Daniel Guérin, Ignazio Silone and Max Horkheimer) perhaps laid most emphasis on the development of state power under fascism, never abandoned the functional explanation. He reached the conclusion that fascism had a certain inherent dynamism of its own, by way of the belief that fascism was the result of an equilibrium, observable in his day, between the bourgeoisie and the working class. 'The weakness of both these classes', he argued, 'is the victory of fascism, which overthrows the working class in the service of capitalism but, although in the pay of capitalists, rises so much above their heads that in the end they have to give it absolute mastery over the whole people, including themselves' (O. Bauer, 1936, *Zwischen zwei Weltkriegen? Die Krise der Weltwirtschaft und des Sozialismus*, Bratislava, p. 129). But, on the lines of the 'basic Marxist pattern', Bauer continues: 'Although fascist dictatorship also rules over the capitalist class, it inevitably becomes an instrument of the needs, interests and intentions of that class.' In other words, in Bauer's opinion, given a partial split in the ranks of the bourgeoisie, it is basically possible only with the help of 'fascist counter-revolution' to precipitate the 'transition from class rule by the whole bourgeoisie, restricted by democratic institutions, to the unrestricted dictatorship of big industrialists and big landowners'.

The unorthodox Marxist theoreticians between the wars, like most of their followers today, emphasised the independent strength of fascism and Nazism but, in their assessment of the latter, never freed themselves from the 'basic Marxist pattern', which was in the last analysis out of perspective and too closely confined to the economic dimension. Still less were they capable of explaining the effect of Hitler's policies and personality, which were so decisive for German and European history. To orthodox Marxists Hitler was never more than a puppet, of no intrinsic importance, in the service of the established economic and political élite; while unorthodox Marxists as well as non-Marxist Western historians saw him as a more or less important 'residue' in the 'structural' context of the history of National Socialism.

The 'Hitler phenomenon' received little elucidation from the phenomeno-logical interpretation of fascism which, transcending the economic approach of the Marxist critique of capitalism, based itself on the history of ideas. This view was first developed in 1963 in Ernst Nolte's *Der Faschismus in seiner Epoche* (translation, *The Three Faces of Fascism*, 1965); however, it to some extent echoed contemporary thoughts such as those expressed by Thomas Mann (*Gesammelte Werke*, Frankfurt am Main, 1960, vol. 12, p. 831) on the 'massive tendencies of the time ... grouped under the name of "fascism" '. Shortly afterwards (ibid., p. 930) Mann spoke of the 'disease of the age, which is at home everywhere and from which no country is free'. Perceptive contemporary observers took this as referring to a political and intellectual trend in Europe which included Nazism but extended far beyond it. Its appearance, ideology and view of life gave the impression of something common to a whole era, so that even after the Second World War Thomas Mann spoke (op. cit., vol. 9, p. 702) of the 'fascist epoch of the West'. However, the theory, as we have said, was comparatively unhelpful to an understanding of the 'Hitler phenomenon', which contemporaries viewed with admiration or contempt but without fascination, and which they sought to have explained to them.

The totalitarian theory, which was foreshadowed by contemporaries and still holds the field today, is the scientific antithesis to the Marxist and non-Marxist conception of fascism. It regards Nazism not primarily as a political and social counter-revolution against the ideas and effects of the Russian revolution of 1917, but rather as an anti-democratic revolution against liberal parliamen-tarianism. On this view, while clearly Nazism was to some extent a child of capitalism, this is not its essential feature; on the contrary, it is akin to, if not identical with, the communist dictatorship in the Soviet Union. From the point of view of Western parliamentarianism and the constitutional development of the liberal democracies, the 'red' and the 'brown' tyranny are equally to be rejected and condemned.

The historian Friedrich Meinecke did not expressly use the concept of totalitarianism, but his approach clearly owed much to it and to the basic interpretation that it implies. As early as 1930 he wrote that the German democratic bourgeoisie felt simultaneously threatened by the onslaught of Bolshevism and Nazism (F. Meinecke, 1958, *Politische Schriften und Reden*, Darmstadt, p. 444). The dictatorships of Hitler and Stalin, who were in alliance from 23 August 1939 to 22 June 1941, and who had carried out the fourth partition of Poland in modern history, were a joint challenge to Western notions of constitutional freedom. At a 'Symposium on the Totalitarian State' in the USA in November 1939 the participants analysed resemblances between the regimes of Mussolini, Hitler and Stalin and gave an effective stimulus to the concept of totalitarianism, which was to undergo still more remarkable developments under the pressure of political events in the coming years.

The ideas of these predecessors were picked up in studies by Hannah Arendt (1951, revised 1958) and by Carl J. Friedrich and Z. Brzezinski (1956, revised 1965) on the idea of totalitarianism and the opposition between the free world on the one hand and Nazism and communism on the other. From observation of the principal actual types of totalitarian regimes, Friedrich deduced that the essential features common to communism and Nazism were 'a total ideology, a single mass party, a terroristic secret police, a monopoly of mass communication, a monopoly of weapons, and a centrally directed planned economy' (op. cit., 1956, p. 294).

Objections of principle can be raised against any attempts to compare historical phenomena of independent origin, and today there is broad agreement as to the uniqueness of Hitler's programme and especially the Nazi racial utopia; as already observed, we are not in a position to assess its comparability with the mass murders and terror of the Bolshevik regime in so far as we know them at present. Nevertheless, the most recent research holds fast to the utility of the concept of totalitarianism, and does so to great effect, as is shown not least by K. D. Bracher's major work (1976a) on 'Europe's crisis, 1917–1975'. At least the concept of totalitarianism seems at present more helpful than that of fascism as a means of describing and explaining twentieth-century history, in view of the more and more evident basic differences between the different European forms of fascism: cf., for instance, Turner (1972), pp. 157–82; de Felice (1975); and Bracher (1976b), pp. 13–32. However, both types of theory based on a comparison of regimes and applied to the history of Nazism and the Third Reich – viz., the 'fascist' theory, Marxist in origin but by now to a considerable extent divorced from Marxism in Western research, and the 'totalitarian' theory, which considered the dictatorships primarily in their character as a threat to Western parliamentary democracy – are equally inadequate when it comes to explaining the personality and policies of Hitler as a historical phenomenon exercising a relatively high degree of autonomy.

The importance of the 'Hitler factor' for the development of Nazism and the Third Reich was noted at an early date, for example by Theodor Heuss (1932) and the journalist Konrad Heiden, whose two-volume biography of Hitler dates from 1936–7 and 'in the boldness of its inquiry and the freedom of its judgement . . . remains exemplary to the present day' (Fest, 1974b, p. 767). Heiden's early work raised what is still a controversial question, namely, whether Hitler improvised or whether all his actions were premeditated. Heiden regarded unscrupulous opportunism as central to Hitler's personality, but recognised the systematic elements in the policy of the 'most world-shaking figure' (*der grösste Menschenerschütter*) in history (Heiden, 1936, vol. 1 of German edition, p. 6); he rightly pointed out that 'All Hitler's truly political acts derive from the programme set out in *Mein Kampf*' (op. cit., vol. 2, p. 259).

Heiden's somewhat indecisive conclusion as to the combination, at one and the same time, of purpose and improvisation in Hitler's ideas and policy contrasts with the view of another contemporary, Hermann Rauschning (1939a). In his thoughtful and penetrating work, written from a conservative standpoint, Rauschning inclines to regard Hitler as an out-and-out Machiavellian hastening to his own destruction. At the same time it can no longer be overlooked that, as Theodor Schieder showed in his work of 1972, Rauschning was well aware of the elements of continuity in Hitler's ideas and policy.

Recent research strongly emphasises the ambivalence of the Third Reich, which was both modern and anti-modern, traditional and revolutionary, derivative and independent, skilfully planned and improvised, monolithic and polycratic. All these features were plain to contemporaries as well. This may be seen from the title of Ernst Fraenkel's *The Dual State* (1941), which described the gulf between state and party in Nazi Germany, the contrast between traditional 'standards' and terroristic 'measures', with a clarity that has probably never been surpassed. At the same time Fraenkel foresaw the progressive 'decay of standards in a repressive system, a process directed by ideology but ultimately uncontrolled' (Schulz, 1974). The dualism of state and party, the contradiction between the internal anarchy of the Third Reich and the totalitarian claims of its propaganda, became, partly thanks to Fraenkel's work, a leitmotiv of revisionist accounts of the Nazi regime from the 1960s onwards. The picture of the 'Führer state' with its monolithic organisation was more and more replaced – sometimes without justification – by that of 'authoritarian anarchy' (W. Petwaidic) and administrative chaos raised to the level of an institution. Often in a one-sided and exaggerated form, this approach came to predominate in academic studies of Nazism.

From this point of view the 'revisionists' (cf., for example, Hillgruber, 1978, p. 612, and Bracher, 1977, p. 640) were supported not only by Fraenkel's study but by Franz Neumann's work (1944) on the 'Structure and practice of National Socialism'. Neumann regarded the Nazi system as a form of 'totalitarian monopoly capitalism' characterised by 'vertical pluralism', with the state resting on four independent sources of power: the party, the army, the bureaucracy and industry. In the last resort, Neumann believed, the sole victors of this permanent competition must be the party and the army.

Both Fraenkel and Neumann strongly emphasised the inner coherence of the Third Reich and the importance of its socio-economic foundations. Their conclusions, adopted after some delay in the 1960s, have been developed into a theory of the (supposedly) polycratic nature of the Nazi system.

Contemporaries of the Third Reich also repeatedly attempted to place it in a continuum of German history. Today we dismiss as politically and scientifically untenable the attempts of Nazi propaganda and Nazi historians to present the Third Reich as the legitimate heir of Bismarck's Germany and the Prussia of Frederick the Great, or even in some degree of Luther and the medieval emperors. This 'pedigree of Germany's greatness' (K. O. von Aretin) was viewed with disfavour by those contemporaries who saw it as recalling Germany's fatal involvement in wars and catastrophes throughout the ages – a mirror-image, in fact, of the propaganda which represented German history as a tale of continuous progress. Among wartime utterances the most drastic expression of the anti-German view was no doubt contained in the 'Black Record' broadcasts by Lord Vansittart (1941), formerly permanent under-secretary at the Foreign Office. Their travesty of history, which in a sense parallels the anxiety of the Third Reich leaders to find themselves ancestors, must be considered, largely but not solely, as hostile propaganda inspired by the war. Against the background of this denunciation of the Third Reich as the alleged culmination of a logical historical process, the question of the proper place of Nazism in modern German history was raised immediately after the war: it is a question which still receives different answers and was given fresh actuality by the 'Fischer controversy' in the 1960s (see Section 7, pp. 159 f. below). Was the Third Reich a necessary, likely, or accidental result of the development of Germany especially in the nineteenth and twentieth centuries, or is it rather to be seen as a transnational phenomenon, an extreme embodiment of European fascism? This problem is an important element in the history of the Third Reich, as a background to interpretations involving the 'Hitler phenomenon' on the one hand and the existence and nature of European fascism on the other.

2

The 'Hitler Phenomenon' and European Fascism

Two opposite yet interdependent types of interpretation at present hold the field as regards our understanding of the Third Reich. On the one hand is the traditional biographical method, which has been practised with success particularly in recent years. This takes as its starting-point Hitler's personality and policy, and advances to a general estimate of the history of his time. The value of a biographical approach to the history of Nazism and the Third Reich was pointed out by Waldemar Besson as early as 1961, when he expressed the opinion that Bullock's life of Hitler gave the best comprehensive account of Nazism for a long time (Besson, 1961, 'Zeitgeschichte', in *Geschichte. Fischer Lexikon 24*, Frankfurt am Main, p. 344). Even today, when there is an unmistakable trend towards social, economic and 'structural' history, there can scarcely be any serious doubt of the value and justification of the biographical approach to the history of Nazism. For, after all, Hitler represented and shaped his 'movement' and his state to an exceptional and decisive extent. His policy and personality, which stamped the general history of the interwar period, have not yet been adequately or even approximately explained by any general theory of fascism or totalitarianism.

On the other hand, concentration on Hitler himself, which is the essence of the biographical method but has also at times dominated monographic studies, has aroused a certain degree of uneasiness, in so far as it takes too little account of general economic and social conditions which certainly play a part in explaining what 'made Hitler possible' and why his policy and conduct of the war took the form they did. Especially since the 1960s, a more 'structural' trend in contemporary research has sought to remedy this defect. Nazism has thus been viewed more and more in a transnational and comparative light, as an aspect of 'European fascism', a concept that used to be encountered only 'occasionally' (Besson, op. cit., p. 340). If the 'Hitler factor' has till now scarcely been adequately recognised in this context, this may to some extent be a transient state of affairs, to be remedied as the state of knowledge improves. On the other hand, an overemphasis on the structural method, and the acceptance of its results to the exclusion of others, have certainly led to underestimating Hitler's unique and decisive role in the history of the Third Reich and the context of his time, so that he has been too easily considered as 'replaceable' and in some ways even a 'weak dictator' (H. Mommsen, 1971).

The two rival approaches and their variants are no doubt more indebted to and dependent on each other than might be suggested by the current debate between them, which has at times been conducted in a distinctly polemical spirit: cf., for example, K. Hildebrand, 'Nationalsozialismus oder Hitlerismus?' and H. Mommsen's article with the same title in M. Bosch (ed.) (1977), *Persönlichkeit und Struktur in der Geschichte*, Düsseldorf, pp. 55–61 and 62–71. At the present time both schools of thought are intensively developing their position with, on the whole, fruitful results. The advocates of the 'fascist' theory are still concerned to investigate the existence of the phenomenon and the validity of the concept of fascism, so as to confirm or reject the view of national socialism as a variant of European fascism. The school of research which focuses on Hitler himself is currently enlarging its study of his personality and policy to include interdisciplinary co-operation with psychology. In addition it still has the important task of presenting a coherent account of Hitler's racial policy – that is, not only the 'Jewish question' (cf. Section 5, pp. 141 ff. below) but also the euthanasia programme and attempts to breed a 'new race of mankind' in the Third Reich – so as to present a proper picture of something that had no precedent in European history and constituted the essential feature of national socialism.

There is no need to insist on the fact that both schools of thought are equally important in themselves and to each other. This being so, bold assertions that a biography is 'easier' to write than structural history are neither true nor plausible. To begin with, there can hardly be a more difficult task in the field of humane studies than to explore the many facets of a human personality, with its hidden depths and frequent inconsistencies, and, secondly, the biographical genre which is still the classic form of historiography involves not only the quest for an individual but also a 'supra-personal' element (W. Besson). At the same time, as biography sets out to present the individual in the general framework of events which are formed by him on the one hand and which sustain and limit his activities on the other, it is constantly faced with what is perhaps the most difficult problem of historical science, namely, that of recognising and making intelligible the interrelation of freedom and necessity in the political and personal acts of human beings. No one concerned with any of the component disciplines of historical science can convincingly dispute the legitimate claims of biography as a fundamental and specific method of presenting history.

The great majority of researchers (cf. Section 4, pp. 136 ff. below) recognise the dominant importance of Hitler as the representative and creator of national socialism. Norman Rich, one of the chief authorities on modern German history, expresses it in the concise phrase 'Hitler was master in the Third Reich' (Rich, 1973, vol. 1, p. 11). It is thus natural to examine the interpretations that treat the Third Reich as a variant of European fascism in order to discover whether they account adequately for 'Hitler and his programme' (Erdmann, 1976a) or whether they fail to explain the 'residual' Hitler who determined the character of national socialism and the history of the Third Reich.

Within the general theory of fascism, there are four types of explanation that receive particular attention at the present time and should be of a nature to demonstrate the validity of this approach. They are: (1) The heteronomistic interpretation offered by Marxists of every stamp. This is basically as old as fascism itself; it claims to solve the problem according to the maxim 'cui bono?' and postulates a far-reaching if not complete identity between economics and politics. (2) Ernst Nolte's attempt to treat fascism as 'non-identical identity' and as a rebellion against every kind of human transcendence. (3) What we have called the structural-functional theory of a school of historians that places itself beyond historicism and interprets fascism as a phenomenon, relatively independent politically, having as its background specific organisational forms and developments of industrial capitalism. (4) The view that sets out to treat fascism in connection with the problem of modernisation.

(1)   Marxist interpretations of fascism, however different they may appear from one another, all break down in as much as the multiplicity of political forms of articulation on the same basis of a capitalist economy makes it absurd to identify capitalism with fascism. None of the Marxist theories can explain, for instance, why, when the world economic crisis of the twentieth century was causing comparable economic and social shocks in all countries, Britain held fast to its parliamentary tradition while the Weimar Republic failed to stand the test. In other words, these theories scarcely give sufficient weight to the background of national history which transcends the economic and social dimension and gives its specific character to English history on the one hand and German on the other (cf. Section 3, pp. 124 ff. below). The range of Marxist interpretations in East and West extends from the orthodox 'agency theory' to attempts which attribute a somewhat higher degree of importance to the independent executive authority within a conservative-fascist power cartel. But all these theories suffer from the defect that they underrate the 'Hitler factor' in national socialism: they regard Hitler's policy, which determined the course of history in the 1930s and 1940s, as more or less 'exchangeable', not least in the international field, and so underestimate his autonomy. This has been pointed out by H. A. Winkler (1978) in his 'Critique of neo-Marxist theories of national socialism', in which he subjects to thorough examination the attitude to fascism of the 'new Left' in the Federal Republic of Germany. In short, by postulating too close a relationship between capitalism and fascism, Marxist interpretations ignore the former's capacity to assume a multiplicity of political forms. In consequence, the Marxists are too prone to overlook the 'absolute primacy of political objectives' (Bracher) in the Third Reich. To quote a comparatively undogmatic Marxist, the British social historian Timothy Mason, 'A policy determined by ideology once more triumphed over economic calculation' (Mason, 1966, p. 492). Indeed, there is unmistakable evidence that Nazism in its advanced stage developed more and more towards what Axel Kuhn forcefully called 'the very opposite of capitalism' (Kuhn, 1973, p. 31). At the same time Nazism was 'an offspring of the capitalist

system', as Henry A. Turner once expressed it, in exactly the same way as 'every other political movement originating in modern Europe, whether liberal democracy or communism' (Turner, 1972, p. 32).

(2) Ernst Nolte's phenomenological observations on 'fascism in its day' lead to the conception of fascism as a trans-political phenomenon and a revolt against transcendence. In accordance with the dual aspect of fascism, Nolte interprets it as a revolt against the two trends of philosophical thought and political action which have hitherto dominated European history. In his view fascism is equally opposed to both the theoretical and the practical transcendence of mankind: that is to say, it rejects any theological or philosophical expectation of salvation in the beyond, in the same way as it combats the idea of an immanent emancipation striving to redeem humanity in this life. To put it more concretely, Nolte sees in fascism the 'third way' of European history, which is in the most far-reaching sense anti-traditional as well as anti-modern; or, more specifically, fascism is no less a challenge to bourgeois society than to Marxism. Such considerations support the conception of the autonomy of fascism, its 'non-identical identity' and its characteristic ambivalence. But we are left with the unsolved problem that Nolte's analysis of fascism in the light of intellectual history assumes the very point which is in debate, that fascism exists as the ruling phenomenon of an age and in a conceptually identifiable form. True, the phenomenological approach makes it possible to describe and compare the manifestations, varying greatly in intensity, of similar forms of political rule and organisation in Europe that can be called 'fascist', but this does not prove that the phenomenon exists as such. Since parliamentarianism and communism exist simultaneously and carry no less weight than fascism, it is hard to accept Nolte's thesis that fascism is the characteristic feature of the age.

(3) What is here called the 'structural-functional' theory considers fascism or its several varieties as 'a particular form of rule in societies which are going through a critical phase of social transformation into the industrial state, and which are at the same time threatened, either objectively or in the eyes of their ruling classes, with a communist revolution' (W. J. Mommsen, 1975, 'Gesellschaftliche Bedingtheit und gesellschaftliche Relevanz historischer Aussagen', in E. Jäckel and E. Weymar, *Die Funktion der Geschichte in unserer Zeit*, Stuttgart, p. 219). This interpretation ascribes to fascism a specific political function against the background of a particular historical 'structure'. It accordingly regards fascism as 'a particular stage of social development in the transition from a bourgeois to a pluralistic industrial society, and attributes its 'enormous political impact . . . above all to the resistance of residual élites to the egalitarian tendencies of that society' (ibid., p. 220).

This theory takes account of the researches of Ernst Nolte, Martin Broszat, Hans Mommsen and Peter Diehl-Thiele, and is largely derived from an examination of national socialism, which it regards as 'a form of fascist rule' (ibid., p. 219). Its value is limited by two main objections:

(*a*)   The 'enormous impact' of fascism is mainly ascribed to the resistance of 'residual élites'. In the case of Germany this clearly does too little justice to the effect of Hitler. True, as we have shown in the historical part of this work, Hitler's rise to power and the violent character of the Nazi state were due in an important degree to the obstinate refusal of the traditional ruling classes of Prussian Germany to accept the modern age. However, the 'impact' of the Third Reich with Hitler at its head must certainly be explained by quite other historical circumstances. Indeed, a great deal of its dynamism came at the outset from co-operation between the Nazis and the conservative élite. Apart from this the motive force and direction of the movement, its objectives and its lack of moderation, were basically derived from Hitler's 'desperado' mentality, the psychology of a man who was partly governed by the influences of his time and partly intensified them to a radical degree. This aspect, and the difficulty of assessing it, were in effect pointed out some time ago by Alfred Weber (*Der dritte oder der vierte Mensch. Vom Sinn des geschichtlichen Daseins*, Munich, 1963 (1st edition 1953), p. 43). But the political aims of the Third Reich possessed such a degree of historical autonomy that they are to be considered as a phenomenon *sui generis*, which still requires investigation especially as regards its origins. These political aims, which constituted the essence of the Third Reich, to a great extent resist explanation by the structural-functional theory, because their intentionality is only loosely connected with the (original) functions of the dictatorship, and because the effects of Nazi policy that were not foreseeable but became apparent in the functioning of the regime were decisive as to the course of history in Hitler's state and 'Hitler's Europe' (A. Toynbee).

(*b*)   The question arises as to which states in the interwar period answer the description of being in a state of transition from a bourgeois to a pluralistic industrial society. Germany may be one such, but it was precisely here that fascism did not take a 'normal' form: that of performing a political function in response to 'structural' demands, that is, preserving the traditional social structure and keeping the workers in subjection. On the contrary, Nazism soon divested itself of its 'functional' character and developed an autonomy and dynamism almost without precedent; it destroyed or at least seriously damaged the traditional social fabric in Germany and eventually abroad as well, and kept the world of German business and industry under a permanent threat of nationalisation (cf. Section 3, pp. 124 ff. below). Hitler's conservative opponents in the later 1930s, who disapproved of the policy of rearmament and war for economic and social reasons as well as on grounds of foreign relations, would have liked to see an Italian-style government, possibly headed by Göring and composed of conservatives and moderate Nazis, to which the description of 'normal fascism' might be applied. The structural-functional theory is well able to account for such trends, but it is inadequate to explain the history of the Third Reich as it in fact developed. To repeat our question: which European states were then evolving from a bourgeois to a pluralistic industrial society? Was this true of Italy, and does it explain the rise of fascism in that country? How does it apply to Spain and Portugal, which were still largely agrarian? The theory will hardly explain fascism in countries of Southern Europe, where industrial society had not begun to develop at all: on this whole subject cf. Thamer and Wippermann (1977).

(4)   Connected to some extent with what is here called the structural-functional theory is the attempt to interpret fascism in terms of modernisation. According to this view modern history 'consists in a single process, the displacement of the traditional fabric of society by a process of transformation more penetrating and rapid than any before – one which is basically the same everywhere and comprises industrialisation, urbanisation, secularisation and rationalisation' (Turner, 1972, p. 159).

If, however – leaving out of account for the time being the effects of modernisation which were not a matter of conscious decision, but began to make themselves felt after the collapse of Nazism and Italian fascism – we follow the method of inquiring into the aims of the respective leading groups and representatives of fascist states and movements, according to whether they attempted to further the process of modernisation or to arrest or reverse it, the conclusion we arrive at is as follows. It can hardly be doubted that it was the aim of the Third Reich to use the means provided by the modern age to move towards a pre-modern or anti-modern utopia. This is true despite the fact that under the spell of anti-modernism, and with the very object of achieving their ideological aim, the Nazi leaders brought about a partial modernisation in some spheres and at certain times. This never became an independent or dominant aspect of their policy, but, as we have said, it was to play an important part in the development of the Federal Republic after 1945. The political aims of the Nazi dictatorship are thus to be understood as a revolution against modernity. But is this anti-modernism an essential characteristic of the essence of other states that are called fascist, so that a general equation could be made between fascism and anti-modernism? Was utopian anti-modernism, for instance, a feature of Mussolini's Italy? This question (which implicitly revives the old problem of fascism as a dictatorship of development) is still a subject of dispute and uncertainty (cf. also Thamer, 1977, pp. 19–35). Some scholars, such as E. Nolte and W. Sauer, emphasise the anti-modern aspect of Italian fascism, while others (for example, R. Sarti, A. J. Gregor and E. R. Tannenbaum) refer to fascist attempts at modernisation. It would be necessary to consider other states known as fascist before deciding whether anti-modernism could be the distinguishing theoretical mark of a concept of fascism valid for the whole of Europe.

But, apart from the question of modernisation, a comparison between Nazism and Italian fascism leads to inescapable doubts as to the meaning and usefulness of a supranational concept of fascism. In this connection reference has frequently been made (especially by Renzo de Felice for Mussolini's foreign policy and A. Hillgruber for Hitler's) to the relatively well researched field of foreign relations; here, when Italy and Germany are viewed comparatively, the concept of fascism breaks down in the context of international politics, which were decisive for the history of the time.

If, for instance, we regard anti-Semitism and eugenics, the racial dogma in Hitler's mind and policy, as the essential factor in Nazi foreign policy and aims, the basis of comparison with Italian fascism seems to disappear. Mussolini's aspirations to a fascist *impero Romano*, the *mare nostro* and colonial rule, together with his policy of holding the balance of power, are in the last analysis not to be compared with Hitler's aims of warlike conquest and worldwide racial domination. The difference is surely rather between an imperialist foreign policy of the traditional kind and Hitler's new type of policy based on war and genocide, and here common features are outweighed by the qualitative difference. Mussolini still thought in familiar historical categories, whereas Hitler's ideas burst the bounds of tradition: they were intended to precipitate the course of history and finally bring it to a standstill in a biological utopia. In the field of international politics, that was of such decisive importance for Europe and the world, it is hardly possible to speak of a uniform concept of fascism that would fit both Germany and Italy. Some time ago Henry A. Turner recommended that it be considered whether the term 'fascism', which purports also to apply to Nazism, really contributes to clarity of definition or is more liable to cause confusion. In the present state of research it can hardly be overlooked that, while the term 'fascism' is used frequently and with effect as a political slogan, it is lacking in sharpness of definition as a scientific concept.

This observation could be supported by pointing out many other differences between the various forms of fascism: cf. K. Hildebrand, 'Hitlerism or national socialism? The "Hitler phenomenon" and European fascism', MS of lecture delivered at Harvard University on 9 February 1977. This being so, a number of scholars such as H. A. Turner, R. de Felice and K. D. Bracher are inclined to use differential terms to describe the German dictatorship in the 1930s and 1940s. In Bracher's view (1976b, p. 32), we can hardly treat Nazism as a variant of European fascism and call it 'German fascism' or 'Hitlerian fascism' without palliating its totalitarian character and by implication demonising the capitalistic economic and social system in Europe at that time. But, leaving out of account those who use the idea of fascism as a political weapon and use the specious term 'anti-fascism' to divert attention from the totalitarian quality of (Soviet) communism, it cannot be overlooked that many scholars still advance weighty arguments in defence of the concept of fascism. In accordance with the observations, studies and anthologies of Ernst Nolte, Eugene Weber, Walter Laqueur, George L. Mosse, Stuart Woolf and Wolfgang Schieder, in quite recent times Karl Dietrich Erdmann, Hans-Ulrich Thamer and Wolfgang Wippermann have expressed the view that the different forms of fascism have enough in common for the generic term to be applied to them all.

At the same time there seems to be a tendency to review the applicability of the concept to a closer comparison between Germany and Italy. This tendency implies a restriction, quite understandable for working purposes, of the originally much wider concept of European fascism. It may to some extent be a response to K. D. Bracher's warning that the 'inflationary' use of the concept of fascism is 'essentially a trivialisation of totalitarian dictatorship, as it lumps everything under the one head: military regimes, dictatorships in developing countries or Latin American oligarchies, or even Western democracies which it is convenient to label "Fascist" when they go through periods of crisis' (Bracher, 1973, p. 551).

K. D. Erdmann, who also sees clear differences between Nazism and fascism, none the less holds fast to the latter as a significant term, as he considers the differences to be 'modifications, or different degrees of intensity, of common structural elements. These modifications and degrees of intensity are what determines the historical individuality of the respective movements. The common basic pattern, on the other hand, makes it possible, contrary to Bracher's view, to assign them to a common type and use "fascism" as a generic term despite the above reservations' (Erdmann, 1976b, p. 459). Similarly H.-U. Thamer recognises 'differences in the political and social preconditions, the emphasising and importance of particular ideological components, and the speed and intensity with which fascist aims were put into practice'. At the same time, he perceives a 'common nucleus of all forms of fascism' in the 'non-identical identity of conservative-authoritarian and fascist forces, the heterogeneity of principle, the alliance between them and the compromise as to the leadership, as well as the ambivalence of tradition and revolution in fascism as a response to a specific situation of crisis', and this vindicates the 'legitimacy of a generic concept of fascism' (Thamer, 1977, p. 35).

In this connection Erdmann ascribes much greater importance to the historical individuality of Nazism within European fascism than is suggested by the ambiguous formula of 'German fascism', and he parts company with Nolte by firmly rejecting the idea of fascism as characteristic of the age in general. At the same time, when he suggests that the idea of fascism should be regarded as generally valid for the interwar period in Europe, it must be objected that Nazism remains in a category by itself by virtue of the utopian racial programme of Hitler and the SS; and it was this dogma which became the dominant characteristic of the Third Reich, with apocalyptic consequences that are still felt at the present day. While Nazism and Italian fascism present many similar features, Renzo de Felice, for instance (1975, *passim*), emphasises the differences rather than the similarities in their basis, functions and purposes. In any case the essence of Nazism hardly corresponds to that of the other forms of fascism, and the unity of the concept remains problematical.

In the present state of research, at all events, the reservations expressed by Turner, de Felice and Bracher would seem to be justified in so far as they suggest that Hitler's movement and the state he created should be referred to by the term 'national socialism' and not 'German fascism'. For the idea of a supranational fascism still seems questionable, while Hitler's dictatorship appears *sui generis* in the light of present-day research.

In the context of whether the 'Hitler phenomenon' is or is not to be equated with European fascism, and in the light of discussions of fascism in recent years, we may recall H. A. Turner's advice that in order to define the overall phenomenon of fascism we should examine the intentions and objectives of the respective leading groups in Italy and Germany (Turner, 1972, p. 161). Without demonising Hitler 'personalistically' (a fashionable reproach, often levelled over-hastily), it cannot be overlooked that the historical impact of his personality and policies has so far invalidated generalising theories of Nazism. It can hardly be sufficiently emphasised that, as Norman Rich reiterates in his great work on Hitler's war aims, he 'undoubtedly possessed one of the most forceful leadership personalities in recorded history . . . and was indeed the Führer' (Rich, vol. 1, 1973, pp. 76–7). In view of all we know of Hitler's dictatorship this view is more convincing than Hans Mommsen's statement (1971, col. 702) that Hitler was in some ways a 'weak dictator'. As Besson rightly pointed out in 1961, 'a biography of Hitler is the greatest, most important task in the historiography of national socialism' (W. Besson, 1961, 'Neuere Literatur zur Geschichte des National-sozialismus', *VfZg*, vol. 9, p. 329).

However, this is no longer such a gap as it was at the time of Besson's article. Independently of superficial political or commercial interests, which contributed to the 'Hitler wave' of the 1970s, we now possess two major studies of Hitler, each valid in its own way. The first, already known to Besson, is Alan Bullock's *Hitler: A Study in Tyranny*, first published in 1952 and fully revised in 1962; the second, by Joachim Fest, was published in German in 1973 and in English in 1974. The latter, based on many years' intensive research, is in some respects an advance on Bullock's work, which however is still by no means superfluous. While Fest deals in a more reflective style, and with much literary skill, with the circumstances of the time and the extraordinary features of Hitler's personality, Bullock's work is valuable as a copious and lucid record of the facts, which to some extent speak for themselves and show the reader 'what actually happened'.

Bullock originally saw Hitler as an opportunist devoid of principle, who was at no time guided by a plan or design of political rule but exploited circumstances whenever he could in order to gain power. Subsequently Bullock modified this view to some extent, partly under the influence of his compatriot Trevor-Roper, who emphasised the element of purpose in Hitler's programme (cf. Section 5, p. 143 below). Despite this adaptation to the development of research, or perhaps because of it, Bullock's work held the field without serious competition until the appearance of Fest's biography, as scholars unanimously considered it superior to such works as those by Heiber (*Adolf Hitler. Eine Biographie*, Berlin, 1960), Gisevius (*Adolf Hitler. Versuch einer Deutung*, Munich, 1963), or

Deuerlein (*Hitler. Eine politische Biographie*, Munich, 1969) – to name only a few out of a larger number.

The same is true of Werner Maser's work (1973), which indeed is not a biography in its basic structure. Its value lies in the new information it provides about Hitler's youth, while the dictator's political career is not treated chronologically but according to subject. This also applies, *mutatis mutandis*, to David Irving's *Hitler's War* (New York, 1977), first published in German in 1975 as *Hitler und seine Feldherren* (Hitler and his Generals). Articles by Eberhard Jäckel (1977) and Andreas Hillgruber (1978) give details of the differences between the German and English versions of this work. Irving's sensational view, which attracted most attention, that Hitler knew nothing of the extermination of Jews until 1943 and that the Nazi programme of genocide was really Himmler's work, has been unanimously rejected by researchers in all countries (cf. Section 5 below).

Fest's biography (1974a) will undoubtedly remain the definitive account for a considerable time, despite certain weaknesses of detail. The 'Interpolations' which periodically break the chronological sequence portray Hitler both as a child of his age and as one who took part in determining its course – a unique, autonomous and evil figure. Certainly exception has been taken here and there to Fest's hostility towards the revolutionary idea. His comments on the modernising implications and effects of Nazism – on the lines of Dahrendorf (1961), pp. 260–99, and Schoenbaum (1966) – need to be considered in greater depth to provide a more definite answer to the question how far Hitler's ideologically utopian policy of the 'brown revolution' intentionally or accidentally produced modernising effects in Germany, and how far his negative qualities brought about positive results, exorbitant though the price undoubtedly was.

In the wake of Fest's biography there appeared in the 1970s several further studies of Hitler, of which we may mention here the detailed portrait by John Toland. Information about others can be found in various bibliographies: for example, A. Bullock, 'The Schicklgruber story', *New York Review of Books*, 7 July 1977; Jäckel (1977); Hillgruber (1978); and Hildebrand (1976). Sebastian Haffner's *The Meaning of Hitler* (London, 1979) presents a convincing picture and may serve as a kind of provisional résumé of all these works. It does not set out to be a miniature biography, but offers a thoughtful discussion of decisive phases and problems in Hitler's life and the career of a dictator who 'made politics by the yardstick of his personal biography' (p. 163). Haffner is concerned throughout with historical understanding and comparisons, but at no point falls into the danger of 'comparative trivialisation' (Peter Gay) of Hitler's rule. Indeed, it is precisely the comparative element in his remarks and assessment of Hitler's 'Life', 'Achievements', 'Successes', 'Misconceptions', 'Mistakes', 'Crimes' and 'Betrayal' that brings out the negative uniqueness of the Nazi leader. Haffner's analysis not only sets out recognised conclusions of research but also presents a number of new and stimulating interpretations which will no doubt occupy the attention of future historians (cf. also Sections 4 and 5 below).

John Toland's above-mentioned biography attempts a psychological explanation of Hitler's hatred of the Jews. In this he is indebted to one of the most eminent of psycho-historians, Rudolph Binion, who has enriched our knowledge of Hitler and Nazism in recent years. For a long time historians concentrated, sometimes very one-sidedly, on the general social conditions which gave rise to Nazism, and dealt at the same time with its socio-psychological background; but recently due attention has also been paid to Hitler's personal psychology, of which previously comparatively little was known. Among the various studies, details of which can be found, for example, in Michalka (1978), special attention should be drawn to Binion's *Hitler among the Germans* (1976). This attempts to relate Hitler's hatred of Jews to the time he spent in the military hospital at Pasewalk in the autumn of 1918, under the crushing effect of the German defeat, his own injuries due to gassing, and also the trauma dating from 1907, when the Jewish Dr Bloch gave an overdose of iodoform (at her son's insistence) to Hitler's mother, who died soon afterwards of cancer of the breast. According to Binion's well-documented account, from 1918 onwards Hitler considered it his mission to avenge his mother and Germany, while the German people for its part suffered from an obsessional urge to repeat Ludendorff's policy of eastward expansion in another war.

Time will show whether the psychological school of history can succeed in overcoming the scepticism as regards its methods and conclusions which is unmistakably felt by historians in general, and is typically expressed by A. Bullock in 'The Schicklgruber story'.

In general, however, it can be observed with reference to the 'Hitler phenomenon' and European fascism that the pendulum of scientific interest oscillates sharply between the extremes of 'Hitlerocentrism' and the theory of fascism; between undue personalisation and the urge to depersonalise history, between demonising and underrating the policy of Hitler and the Third Reich. But there is wide agreement that Hitler's personality is on no account to be treated as indifferent, despite occasional speculation to the contrary. Hitler gave a stamp to his age and imposed his will on it, with an autonomy and a limitless power that have seldom been equalled. He never merged into the general context, and has resisted every attempt to reduce him to a purely 'functional' status: it was he who gave a decisive shape to his surroundings, admittedly in a destructive sense.

The question whether Hitler was a 'great man', which constantly recurs in this connection, has been answered by K. D. Erdmann in terms which represent the current view fairly closely: 'Can one attribute historical greatness to a man who described conscience as a Jewish invention? It was Hegel's conviction that the supreme personalities of world history could not be judged by normal standards, and Burckhardt claimed that historical greatness was exempt from the ordinary laws of morality. But neither of them had conceived the possibility of such appalling crimes as Hitler committed against the Jews and other nations, not least the German people itself. This fact should not indeed be allowed to conceal from us that Hitler embodied what Burckhardt regards as the attribute of historical greatness, viz. "the concentration of a world movement in a single individual" ... Hitler's greatness was diabolical: it was that of a world figure who confused the minds of men, who rose rapidly to power in a few years, then set the world ablaze and dragged down his own nation with him' (Erdmann, 1976a, pp. 340–1).

It may be objected that such a judgement introduces criteria of moral philosophy in order to personalise the problem of fascism, which is properly a social one. But this objection is scarcely more justified, and perhaps even less so, than the criticism levelled with emphasis at 'structural history' that it constructs history instead of simply presenting it. The 'Hitlerocentric' and the structural approach ought perhaps to take more account of each other than they have done hitherto. The investigation of fascism, which at present experiments in a theoretical and empirical fashion, will for its own advantage have to admit that its general insight into European fascism and Nazism must constantly be appraised for its compatibility with the 'Hitler phenomenon', which will be an essential yardstick of the validity of any theory of fascism. This applies not least to research into the relations between big business, the Nazi Party and the Third Reich, which has been carried on intensively in recent years.

3

The Third Reich and
the Business World

The relationship between German industry and commerce on the one hand and the Nazi regime on the other is a subject which has received, relatively speaking, the most intensive study in recent years. This is partly connected with the general tendency of historians to concern themselves more than previously with economic and social problems. Another aspect is that, not least owing to the revival of Marxist thinking in the Western world, the subject has been, and still is, largely confined to a study of relations between 'capitalism and fascism'. The course and intensity of the economic debate are unmistakably affected by the feeling that insight into this problem will furnish a verdict as to the legitimacy of the liberalistic political and social order of the West. As Turner concisely puts it: 'If there is truth in the widespread view that fascism is a product of modern capitalism, then that system can hardly be defended. But if this view is false, then so is the presumption on which many people in the East and West base their attitude towards the capitalist system' (Turner, 1972, p. 7).

While the subject claims attention in view of its political importance, current interest in it should not lead us to take a sectional view of the past. We should not concentrate on the economic and social aspects and functions of Nazi policy to the exclusion of the ideological dimension and the regime's racial policy, which were the ultimately decisive factor. It may be connected with the present state of research, in which controversial and (as yet) scarcely compatible positions are taken up, that recent Western studies have consisted of contributions debating particular issues (for example, Stegmann, 1973, and Turner, 1975) rather than comprehensive works. However, the existence of some wider studies should not be overlooked. Among them are Wolfram Fischer (1968) on German economic policy from 1918 to 1945, and Charles Bettelheim's Marxist interpretation of the German economy under Nazism, published in French in 1946; also Arthur Schweitzer's *Big Business in the Third Reich* (Bloomington, Ind., 1965) and more recently Dietmar Petzina's monograph (1977) summing up the state of research on the German business world between the wars.

In addition to these attempts at a general synthesis, the current state of research is no less typically represented by Eike Hennig's 'Theses' (1973) on German social and economic history from 1933 to 1938. Within the framework of an enlarged account of existing research, this work principally records judgements on 'German fascism', emanating from the political left (of all shades), which often strike the unprejudiced reader as sectarian. With zeal and thoroughness Hennig describes sympathetically the almost infinitely numerous trends within orthodox and especially unorthodox Marxism and their judgements of Nazism and the Third Reich. These trends need not be discussed in detail here. For Marxist interpretations of the relationship between the business world and national socialism will only become of interest to non-Marxist research if – in the development of the Marxist approach based on the theory of Bonapartism, cf. Section 1, pp. 106–7 above – a frank and open-minded discussion can take place on the subjection of the economic community to the state, the autonomy of state power and its effect on the relationship between politics and economics under the Nazi dictatorship. Such a discussion would parallel the way in which non-Marxist research has for a long time acknowledged the suggestions and results of Marxist thinking.

For the present, however, there are two sharply opposed views as to relations between the business world, the Nazi Party and the Third Reich. The orthodox Marxist interpretation of Nazism, following Dimitrov's definition of fascism, still maintains the dogma of the 'primacy of economics over politics', the former term signifying in particular heavy industry and the big landowners. This also applies, with considerable variations of emphasis, to a good many contributions to the discussion of fascism in the West, which in recent years, consciously or otherwise, have been strongly influenced by an unmistakable hostility to capitalism and parliamentary democracy.

As against this, the theory of the 'primacy of politics' takes up a contrary position to the economic interpretation of Nazism and the Third Reich. Its advocates have for some time developed and refined the postwar concept of totalitarianism, which also applies to relations between economic and political factors, in as much as they examine without prejudice, and take critically into account, the effect of the economic community on the political sphere. (It should not be overlooked, however, that the same scientific approach was observed, for example, in the large standard work by Bracher, Sauer and Schulz, 1962, on the Nazi seizure of power.) These authors' maintenance of the view that politics played a primary part in relations between the business world and the Third Reich is a long way from the defensive accounts of industrial circles that were published in the 1940s and 1950s (for example, L. P. Lochner, 1955, *Die Mächtigen und der Tyrann. Die deutsche Industrie von Hitler bis Adenauer*, Darmstadt). As regards quantity of material and depth of analysis, subsequent research has in a sense outdistanced studies such as that by Wilhelm Treue (1966) on the attitude of German industrialists to Hitler's foreign policy; but such works are still valid in so far as they rightly emphasise the 'conception of Hitler's commanding role *vis-à-vis* the economic community' (Hillgruber, 1973a, pp. 6–7).

The advance of knowledge, reflected in the differentiation of judgements, is probably due to the fact that the charges levelled against heavy industry immediately after the war were soon dropped, for political and academic reasons which will be further discussed. The simplistic arraignment of 'wicked capitalists' as the henchmen or masters of the Nazi dictatorship is no longer altogether typical even of communist historiography in the GDR: cf., for example, Eichholtz's history of the German war economy, 1969.

While the two basic theses as to the primacy of politics and economics respectively have each been revised and refined, it would be a mistake, and might be detrimental to future research, to adopt the view (Volkmann, introduction to Forstmeier and Volkmann, 1975, p. 13) that the two opposite views have 'merged together' and can be regarded as simply interdependent. G. Myrdal's maxim that the distinction between economic and non-economic factors is methodologically useless and meaningless is problematical in itself and seems especially inappropriate to the Third Reich, as it obscures instead of revealing the political and ideological motives and aims of the regime and its Führer, which were crucial for German and European history. On the other hand, the scientific analysis of both types of explanation might take as its starting-point the insight, itself achieved from several directions, into the fact of the autonomy of the national socialist state. This might lead to further conclusions as to the relationship between politics and economics in the Third Reich, and would at the same time make it possible for Western research to assess more appropriately a problem which was originally perhaps neglected in academic studies and is today often given undue prominence: namely, the relative importance of economics as compared with ideological, political, anthropological and psychological (social or individual) aspects of the history of the Nazi dictatorship.

Reviewing the research of the past three decades and the continuing discussion, the opposing theses of the primacy of politics or economics may be basically reduced to two lines of inquiry which are still intensively pursued and are still to a large extent controversial.

(1)   The first relates to the general question how far leading German circles, and particularly industrialists, influenced and aided Hitler's seizure of power and were therefore responsible for it. This leads immediately to the connected question, how far the idea of Hitler being 'used' by the big capitalists was compatible with the demands and promises associated with the 'middle-class' Nazi movement, which was hostile to 'faceless capitalism' as well as to egalitarian socialism.

(2)   The second line of inquiry relates to the development of relations between the political and the economic world of the Third Reich. Paying due attention to the time factor, the question is to ascertain, as between the representatives of the state and the economy, who was in charge at any given time, which made demands on the other and how far they were complied with.

As to (1): On 'zero day' at the end of the Second World War the victors, and many defeated Germans, were largely in agreement that the blame for Hitler's seizure of power rested on all responsible classes in Germany, especially capitalists and the money power. This conviction was reflected in the trials for war crimes, in which industrialists were arraigned as well as others. It also represented the ideological credo of the communists and the Soviet Union, and the feelings of many in Germany. In this respect, as E. Nolte once remarked, the victorious coalition of the Allies survived the war for a short time. The widely held view no doubt also had much to do with the basic postwar mood of anti-capitalism, and met the understandable desire for an explanation of the past twelve years. It was only too easy to look for guilty men among the rich and powerful in commerce, industry and the financial world. Ordinary envy played its part, as did horror at the atrocities perpetrated by Nazi Germany, as they gradually became known. Another factor was the persistent effect of Nazi ideology with its anti-capitalist slogans, and perhaps a tendency, very characteristic of modern German history, also came again to the fore, namely, that of regarding the state as superior to the economy. Many traditional and plausible prejudices were gratified by the idea that the capitalists had 'bought' Hitler and his movement for their own purposes.

But this wholesale judgement in the immediate postwar period was more and more abandoned as research progressed. Politically, as the 'cold war' began in earnest, the Americans took a more flexible line over denazification and were less interested in condemning German industrialists, as their attention and energies were taken up by the challenge of Soviet totalitarianism. It was thus not only because of reactionary forces in the Federal Republic (as so frequently asserted) that researchers came to differentiate more and more in their judgement of relations between the Nazis and the business world.

While Wilhelm Treue's references to opposition groups in German industrial circles (Treue, 1966, p. 504) still require more detailed analysis, research into the origins of the Nazi dictatorship has tended increasingly to qualify the judgement of the immediate postwar period. Ernst Nolte pointed out, for instance, that not only the workers were oppressed by the state and party in the Third Reich: to some extent the capitalists were also deprived of power, and their property subjected to the political will of the regime (E. Nolte, 1970, 'Hitlers Aufstieg und die Grossindustrie', in his *Der Nationalsozialismus*, Frankfurt am Main, p. 193). Apart from this, non-Marxist research has come largely to agree that other sections of the traditional ruling class, with a pre-modern orientation, played a more important and more decisive part than the industrialists and bankers in enabling Hitler to achieve power (cf. Hildebrand, 1973, for the historical perspective). The American historian Henry A. Turner has done valuable service by his painstaking and detailed investigation of the many assertions and conjectures concerning financial help allegedly given to Hitler in the 1920s and the run-up to the seizure of power: this is usually supposed to have been considerable, but Turner's research (1972) has reduced it to a relatively small scale. On the basis of empirical evidence Turner formulated his doubts as to the thesis that Hitler was bought by the money of the rich, showing instead that before 1933 the bankers and industrialists gave crucial support not to Hitler's movement but to other authoritarian politicians: 'If money had been able to buy political power, the Republic would have been followed by Papen's "new state" and not by Hitler's "Third Reich" ' (op. cit., p. 19). One way and another, Max Horkheimer's often quoted maxim that 'Anyone who won't talk about capitalism should keep silent about fascism' carried less conviction as the connection between industrialists and the Nazi Party was shown to have been more and more complex in the context of relations between ruling social circles and the Nazi movement. Meanwhile research has progressed beyond such unenlightening and highly disputable commonplaces to a much more exact and detailed knowledge of the part played by political and economic factors in Hitler's seizure of power.

This process was assisted by a type of interpretation which linked the specific problem of relations between the Nazi regime and the business world with questions of the social basis and function and political aims of Hitler's movement. The fact that Nazism was largely a movement representing the 'middle class' (that is, smaller traders and business men) already appears from the contemporary researches of Theodor Geiger, although his view that the 'panic' of that class in Germany was a spontaneous reaction to the effects of the world economic crisis has been modified by later research, and its behaviour under the Weimar Republic has been analysed as 'the result of a long historical process' (Winkler, 1972, p. 17). Leaving aside the question of motives, for a long time Marxist and non-Marxist historians agreed that the Nazis were a 'catch-all party of the middle class' (K. D. Bracher) and that the parties of the bourgeois centre had lost to the Nazis their electoral support among the middle class and the peasantry (Hillgruber, 1973a, p. 4). It was also unanimously agreed by Marxists and non-Marxists alike that accretions to the Nazi Party 'certainly did not come from the working class or the proletariat, which voted for the SDP or KPD until the bitter end in 1933' (ibid.).

This conclusion is basically still valid, but recent studies have modified it to some extent. The Nazi Party did include a comparatively high proportion of 'middle-class or petty bourgeois social and occupational groups' (Broszat, 1981, p. 30), but it also showed the 'highest percentage of workers' of any non-Marxist party in the Weimar Republic (Erdmann, 1976a, p. 354). It was in fact a party of a modern type, transcending traditional barriers of class and status. H. Mommsen described it as a 'negative People's Party'; Winkler (1976, p. 112) as an 'openly anti-democratic, . . . (in Sigmund Neumann's sense) "absolutist" or "totalitarian" People's Party'. None the less, it could not divest itself of its origin as a 'middle-class' party, a fact which showed to some extent in the provenance of its ideology.

Although it has hitherto been accepted that the workers took up a uniform attitude during the final phase of the Weimar Republic, this view has been criticised, for example in Kele (1972) and Fischer's contribution to Stachura (1978), pp. 131–59. The quantitative investigations that have been pursued more intensively in recent years with respect, *inter alia*, to the history of the Nazi Party may be of a nature either to confirm or to modify the present state of research on this point. This has been summarised by Gerhard Schulz, who, however, is understandably influenced by new advances in knowledge and perhaps underrates the extent to which the party was rooted in the middle class. He writes (Schulz, 1975, p. 552): 'The reservoirs from which the NSDAP was recruited are such that it cannot be described merely as a party of the bourgeois middle class . . . but rather as a party integrating all sections of the population.' For 'bearing in mind that probably less than ten per cent of the ten million industrial workers (out of 67 million Germans) were organised politically, it can be seen that the NSDAP was one of the largest of such parties to represent the working class and make it politically conscious. In this it stood alongside the SPD, the KPD and the [Catholic] Centre, and was wider in its appeal than the two latter' (ibid., p. 551).

However, the decisive factor in the breakthrough of the middle-class people's party (to use H. A. Winkler's term) or the 'universal ersatz party', as Wolfgang Schieder calls it, was that its seizure of power had the necessary support of the pre-modern élite classes of Prussian Germany. As Winkler has shown, 'what determined the success of fascist movements was not capitalism in the abstract', but to some extent 'the possibility of reinsurance with pre-industrial sources of support' (Winkler, 1972, p. 162). As far as the Nazi movement is concerned John Weiss has brought out this fact and set in its correct perspective the part played by 'capital', which is too often treated as an autonomous force: 'Fascism was not the "last gasp of monopoly capitalism". If anything, it was the last gasp of conservatism' (J. Weiss, 1967, *The Fascist Tradition. Radical Right-Wing Extremism in Modern Europe*, New York, p. 5). It should be added that this conservatism was of a specifically Prussian-German stamp, lacking to a great extent the parliamentary and reformist dimension of English Toryism: cf. 'Concluding Remarks' to Part One, pp. 96 ff. above.

Although many of the independent ideological aims of the 'military desperados' of the Third Reich are related to their middle-class origin by present-day research (Winkler, 1976, p. 113), Hitler's programme in the 1930s and 1940s involved an economic policy contrary to the anti-capitalist ideas of this class, who became more and more 'expendable' (Winkler, 1977). The NSDAP did not act as the servant of its members and those who had helped it to power, whether they belonged to the middle class or to other social groups. The functional modernisation that was necessary to achieve Hitler's aims confirmed a process, which had long been going on, whereby the middle class was weakened and its interests neglected: for the time being Nazi policy was confined to the economic and financial sphere and served the interests of big business.

Is the final conclusion, then, that Hitler was an instrument of the industrialists and that they were responsible for his accession to power? Orthodox Marxist research has never doubted this, as may be seen from Fritz Klein's article of 1953 ('Zur Vorbereitung der faschistischen Diktatur durch die deutsche Gross-bourgeoisie 1929', *Zeitschrift für Geschichtswissenschaft*) or Eberhard Czichon's *Wer half Hitler zur Macht?* (Cologne, 1967), or again the documentary work by Wolfgang Schumann and Ludwig Nestler (1975) on German imperialist plans for world domination from 1900 to 1945. The consistent view of these writers is that 'Hitler became Chancellor thanks to the organisation and determination of a majority group of German industrialists, bankers and big landowners' (Czichon, op. cit., p. 54). As against this, in non-Marxist and to some extent in Western Marxist research there is some degree of unanimity on the point that Hitler was not simply bought by capitalist gold. For example, the Marxist sociologist Eike Hennig takes the view that the Nazi seizure of power cannot be regarded as a 'monocausal act of purchase' (E. Hennig, 1969, 'Industrie und Faschismus. Anmerkungen zur sowjetmarxistischen Interpretation', *NPL*, vol. 14, p. 439). However, acceptance of this conclusion does not exclude a subtler (but scarcely provable) interpretation: within the general framework of Marxist thinking, it is quite possible to argue from the 'socio-economic regularity of the class conflict' (Mason, 1977, p. 41) that the link between capitalism and fascism is forged by the mighty, anonymous and objective process of history, operating through individuals but advancing independently of them.

On the other hand H. A. Turner, without disputing that the German industrialists were to some extent responsible for Hitler's accession to power, has shown that 'the great majority of big business men in Germany neither desired Hitler's triumph nor contributed materially to it' (Turner, 1972, p. 30). Dirk Stegmann has criticised Turner's conclusions, taking the view that the big industrialists were largely responsible for Hitler's seizure of power, that 'German fascism' was a 'particular technique of traditional authoritarian rule' (Stegmann, 1973, p. 441), and that up to 1936 the 'political rule of the Führer's party, combined with the social predominance of big business' was 'the specifically German form of fascism': see Stegmann (1976), 'Kapitalismus und Faschismus in Deutschland 1929–1934. Thesen und Materialien zur Restituierung des Primats der Grossindustrie zwischen Weltwirtschaftskrise und beginnender Rüstungskonjunktur', in *Gesellschaft. Beiträge zur Marxschen Theorie*, No. 6, Frankfurt am Main, p. 68. This opinion is on the whole convincingly rebutted by Turner (1975), and Erdmann expresses the measured view that Stegmann's thesis 'will not do as it stands' (Erdmann, 1976a, p. 359). Erdmann, whose attitude is representative of Western scholars who are open-minded towards the conclusions of Marxist research, is as far from whitewashing the industrialists as from accepting the charge that Hitler was merely their agent. He sums up our views, based on present knowledge, as follows: 'It would be wrong to lay the direct responsibility for Hitler becoming Chancellor on the employer class as a whole, or even on the greater or economically more important part of that class. It was, however, indirectly responsible in as much as it refused to support the last attempt to bar Hitler's road to power.' Indeed, 'the fact that a situation could arise in which Germany's fate depended so completely on the court intrigues surrounding the Reich president, who was politically not equal to his task, was the result of a chain of events in which big business did not adopt a neutral, wait-and-see policy but played a part, along with others, in destroying the foundations of the Weimar Republic' (Erdmann, op. cit., p. 358).

The trade unions, though with quite different motives to the industrialists, behaved in a manner that was in some ways comparable, so that from the beginning of 1930 there no longer existed a compromise, such as is vital to parliamentary democracy, between key social groups and political parties (cf. A. Hillgruber (MS), *Die Parteien der Mitte und der Untergang der Weimarer Republik*). Hence the general trend of serious research today concerning the relationship between political and economic factors in bringing about the Nazi seizure of power is, having regard to the historical complexity of the time and weighing all relevant aspects, to avoid oversimplified judgements and, while still attributing the main role to politics, to do so with perhaps more qualification than previously.

Turning to the second field of inquiry mentioned above: it appears from an examination of the relationship between politics and economics in the history of the Third Reich that other sections of the economy were subject to interference from the regime to a greater extent than industry, which has so far received more attention in academic discussion. For instance, Arthur Schweitzer has pointed out that, for ideological reasons that are not far to seek, German agriculture was already in a state approaching 'peasant socialism', whereas industry was able to preserve a much higher degree of independence.

In assessing the relationship between the big industrialists and the state, which varied as time went on, scholars today distinguish different phases, which were suggested at a relatively early stage by A. Schweitzer and have since been criticised and supplemented by Dietmar Petzina, Alan S. Milward, Timothy Mason and others.

(1)   In the period of 'partial fascism' (Schweitzer) from 1933 to 1936 industry was largely able to remain independent of the regime, though from the beginning of the Third Reich it had to conform to Hitler's established aims. In particular, 'from a very early date, virtually from the moment of the seizure of power, rearmament was given undisputed priority and the whole of economic policy, including foreign trade, was subordinated to it' (W. Fischer in Forstmeier and Volkmann, eds, 1975, p. 132).

(2)   Coming to the phase of 'full fascism' (Schweitzer) from 1936 onwards, the frequently discussed question whether the economic system of the Third Reich is to be regarded as a state-directed or a private economy appears retrospectively to be easier to answer from one point of view and more difficult

from another. Thanks in particular to D. Petzina's study of the Four-Year Plan (1968) and T. Mason's article on the 'primacy of politics' (1966), we can on the one hand clearly recognise how firmly the private sector was subordinated to the state's rearmament programme. True, the factories remained in their owners' hands, and the latter no doubt did well out of the armaments boom; but, as the demand for arms increased and autarky became the watchword under Göring's orders, less and less account was taken of the capitalist principle of economic efficiency and the relation of means to ends. Moreover industrialists were constantly under threat from the party and state, knowing that if they failed to deliver the goods their remaining rights would be taken away from them. Apart from this, both Göring and the SS had ideas of establishing industries of their own in competition with private enterprise: Enno Georg described this as regards the SS, as early as 1963. On the other hand there was a degree of interconnection that makes it difficult in some cases to draw the line between the state and the private sphere: for example, as M. Broszat pointed out, between the Four-Year Plan organisation and IG Farben, though the latter's role within the Nazi rearmament programme was not exactly typical. For within the Nazi 'war economy in time of peace' (Erbe, 1958, p. 177), 'in these semi-official, semi-private co-ordination and planning staffs the principles of the Führer state already imposed on the traditional state apparatus blended with the apparatus of leadership and co-ordination of industry in a virtually indistinguishable whole' (Broszat, 1981, p. 303).

In this connection, as Wolfram Fischer has remarked (in Forstmeier and Volkmann, eds, 1975, p. 135), we still know far too little about any discussion in state and party circles of possible alternatives to the economic policy that was actually followed. This would, for example, throw more light on the evolution of Hjalmar Schacht's attitude: originally a collaborator with the regime, he came to regard its principles and practice as economically wrong and pernicious, and ended up as a member of the opposition to Hitler. It could be equally instructive to examine Göring's political and economic ideas and activities more closely. On the one hand he appears as the exponent of the ruinous rearmament policy of the Nazi state, with war as its *ultima ratio* and with the prospect of wiping out debts by the atavistic method of plundering one's enemies; but on the other hand there is reason to think that he was politically somewhat sceptical towards Hitler's war policy. From this point of view it sometimes appears that Göring, perhaps without fully realising it, was closer to meeting the demands of a rational economic and foreign policy such as that advocated by his rival Schacht; and it is possible that policies of this sort were discussed in the offices of the Four-Year Plan and the various ministries, as alternatives to Hitler's road to premeditated war.

(3)   The peacetime preparation for *Blitzkrieg* has also been studied from the point of view of economic policy. Alan S. Milward has shown why, in the debate between Hitler and General Thomas as to whether rearmament should be 'in

width' or 'in depth', the former alternative was chosen as appropriate to the intended *Blitzkrieg* strategy. Among the reasons were Germany's limited economic resources and Hitler's preferred method of striking a quick, decisive blow against an isolated opponent. But, as Milward points out, 'rearmament in width' was also suited in every way to the 'diplomatic situation of the German government. It suited the political position of the Nazi regime, its method of administration and the structure of Nazi society' (A. Milward, 1975, in Forstmeier and Volkmann, eds, op. cit., p. 191). For all these reasons the conception of *Blitzkrieg* commended itself to Hitler and his regime as a limited involvement of the economy in war (op. cit., p. 194).

(4)　Only after the *Blitzkrieg* strategy proved a failure in 1941–2 was Albert Speer given a free hand to adopt measures more or less similar to those of the Western democracies so as to create a long-term war economy and armaments industry giving more scope to private producers and limiting the output of consumer goods. Finally (5) the 'Speer era' came to an end in 1944–5, when Speer's ideological opponents, especially Gauleiter Sauckel, once more insisted on closer control of the economy by the state and party.

Western research has so far produced no account of all the problems outlined here concerning the relationship between politics, economics and strategy, comparable, for example, to Dietrich Eichholtz's history of the German war economy (two volumes planned; the one published in 1969 covers 1939–41) or the four projected volumes (two published in 1974–5) by a group of GDR authors on 'Germany in the Second World War': both these works expressly concentrate on relations between the economy and the state. GDR historians continue to take the view that economic factors had a decisive effect on the war aims of the Third Reich: their conclusions are summarised, for example, in W. Schumann (ed.), 'Die Kriegsziele Hitlerdeutschlands im zweiten Weltkrieg und die Ursachen ihres Scheiterns. Diskussionsmaterial für das internationale Historiker-Kolloquium in Weimar vom 26. bis 31. Mai 1975', n.p., 1975. Western historians, on the other hand, are broadly agreed that the reverse was the case, and that Hitler's political and strategic aims at all times prevailed over economic considerations. The primacy of politics in Hitler's Nazi dictatorship excluded the possibility of economic interest groups influencing the formulation of political aims as they had, for example, in the First World War (cf. Section 5, p. 141 below).

An interesting variant of the 'primacy of politics' thesis, still rejected by orthodox Marxist historians, was put forward by Timothy Mason in the introduction to his documentary volume of 1975. Though Mason regards himself as a Marxist, he put forward this theory at a fairly early stage, in a controversy that aroused much attention: see Mason (1966), Czichon (1968), Mason's rejoinder (1968), and Eichholtz and Gossweiler (1968). In his later work Mason still maintained the same view. He starts from the observation that the Reich's resources were more and more strained by the economic requirements of its foreign policy and war aims. This state of affairs was aggravated to a decisive degree by the fact that Hitler, fearing a repetition of the 1918 revolution, insisted on simultaneously increased civilian consumption, so as not to alienate the working class. In this way, according to Mason (who probably exaggerates the workers' disaffection and acts of hostility to the regime), Hitler's political aims led to an increasingly acute economic and social 'crisis' which obliged the regime in the late summer of 1939 to 'retreat forwards' by attacking Poland.

Mason's book, especially its documentary part, provides us with many new facts and details of economic and social history. However, his main thesis of the 'crisis' compelling the Third Reich to 'retreat forwards' has so far been received rather critically: cf. especially H. A. Winkler (1977), 'Vom Mythos der Volksgemeinschaft', *Arch. f. SozG*, vol. XVII, pp. 488–9. In the first place, the supposed economic compulsions remain secondary *vis-à-vis* Hitler's politically autonomous aims. They did not run counter to his policy and strategy, but were initiated by the latter; they then intensified and served them, and found an appropriate political and economic strategy in the form of the *Blitzkrieg*. Secondly, Mason overestimates the scope and intensity of the economic and social 'crisis' of the Third Reich. As Ernst Nolte once pointed out in a different context, 'An economic crisis can only lead to radicalisation if it works itself out in the framework of a parliamentary system' (E. Nolte, 1970, 'Hitlers Aufstieg und die Grossindustrie', in his *Der Nationalsozialismus*, Frankfurt am Main, p. 193). The so-called crisis did not have a decisive effect on Hitler's thoughts and decisions: he could always in the last resort have mastered it by force and terror. It must not be overlooked that Hitler's political successes down to the summer of 1939 had made him popular with the German people, including the workers. His decision for war was based purely on political motives and was timed in accordance with the march of international events. Economic and social factors were secondary and were used by him partly as a pretext, for example, to persuade hesitant members of the conservative élite that economic reasons made it necessary to go to war (cf. Section B1, p. 38 above). At no time in the history of the Third Reich did crises of themselves dictate the regime's political course. Rather did they serve to confirm Hitler's policy, and they were not even decisive as regards the timing of the war. The pact with Stalin, which was concluded for political reasons and was so vital to the German war economy until 1941 (cf. Birkenfeld, 1964), was far more decisive in fixing the date of the invasion of Poland than the internal and social considerations which Mason describes, acutely but with exaggeration. The most penetrating criticism of Mason's 'untenable thesis' at the present time is probably that of H. A. Winkler:

> Mason does not differentiate enough when he ascribes the decline in labour discipline to basically political motives, as if it was part of a conscious struggle against fascism. In reality much of what took place in conditions of full employment in Germany was not specifically due to Nazism. In Britain

too, after the outbreak of war, when the country first achieved full employment, there were many cases of indiscipline. It is understandable to wish to see the working class as an active opponent to fascism and war, but we should not paint an ideal picture of its political awareness and behaviour in a totalitarian society. If Nazi rule was not directly and fundamentally threatened by the workers, we must be sceptical of Mason's theory of a political crisis of the Third Reich in 1936–9 and of his thesis that the social, economic and political crisis more or less compelled the country's leaders to make a 'dash for freedom' and unleash the war.

As the foregoing analysis may have shown, all attempts to treat Hitler and 'German fascism' in the widest sense as exponents and derivatives of the crises of capitalism and its problems of exploitation, and to represent the Third Reich as subservient to economic aims, leave two basic questions unsolved. The first is: why did such things happen in Germany and not, for instance, in Britain or the USA? Here, as with the problem of the seizure of power (cf. 'Concluding Remarks' to Part One, pp. 93–8 above), recourse is had to arguments beyond the economic sphere, extending into the realm of political culture in its historical perspective; it may even be suggested that Germany, with its tradition of a powerful state and its pre-modern leadership, suffered from a specific lack of capitalism, and that this shaped the development of the Prussian-German national state rather than any domination of economic over political factors or even an equality between them. The second unsolved problem is: how could the principles of capitalist efficiency be reconciled with Nazi racialism? The primacy of racial doctrine in the regime's policy was unquestioned, and was scarcely compatible in any respect with the needs of a capitalist economy. It may be, and must be left to future research to discover, that members of the regime who opposed Hitler's war policy – such as Schacht and, occasionally and in certain ways, perhaps even Göring – envisaged the possibility of modifying the totalitarian character of the regime and strengthening the influence of economic factors *vis-à-vis* the state. As it is, we may conclude with Norman Rich that 'The Nazi use of economic assets was never characterized by efficiency . . . for almost all Nazi leaders, if not to the same extreme extent as Himmler, regarded the economy primarily as a means to an end. It was therefore hardly surprising that the Nazi operation of the economy was almost exclusively determined by political and ideological considerations' (Rich, 1973, vol. 1, p. 58).

4

The Structure of the Leadership

At the end of the Second World War most contemporaries, and especially those who had been persecuted by the regime or had opposed it, were firmly convinced that the Third Reich was 'a rationally organised and highly perfected system of terrorist rule' (H. Mommsen, 1971, col. 702). Gradually historical research showed this idea to be in need of modification. While it was more or less true as regards Hitler's all-powerful personality and his integrating role as a leader, a different picture was presented by the multiplicity of overlapping bureaucracies and authorities in the Nazi state.

This typical ambivalence of monocratic and polycratic elements in the Third Reich, dominated in principle at all times by Hitler's personality and policy, was described by Karl Dietrich Bracher as far back as 1956 and in several subsequent works on the history of the Nazi period. Basically his account still holds good: 'The antagonisms of power were only resolved in the key position of the omnipotent Führer. This state of affairs, and not the efficient functioning of the state as such, was the ultimate object of the co-ordination (*Gleichschaltung*) of authority, which was by no means perfect. For the dictator held a key position precisely because of the confusion of conflicting power groups and personal connections. These intricacies were also the basis of the ever-increasing importance of supervisory and coercive bodies in the totalitarian police state' (K. D. Bracher, 1956, 'Stufen totalitärer Gleichschaltung: Die Befestigung der nationalsozialistischen Herrschaft 1933/34', *VfZg*, vol. 4, p. 42).

Against the background of this summing-up of the characteristic features of structure and organisation of the Nazi dictatorship, we have to consider the debate of subsequent years in which researchers joined issue with the view expressed by Bracher and others. The discussion, which still continues, lays less emphasis on monocratic features and more on polycratic or pluralistic ones in 'Hitler's exercise of power' (M. Kater). It throws doubt on the inner rationality of the regime and the element of planning in Hitler's actions, and regards the self-destructive tendency of the Third Reich as an inbuilt necessity of the dictatorship, prone by its very nature to crises and final ruin. If the two views of the Nazi system are compared, we may first of all note this: the 'older' view, emphasising the totalitarian aspect, recognised and analysed with scientific exactitude 'the discrepancy between the claim to monolithic rule on the one hand

and, on the other, dualistic or polycratic structures of leadership based on an anarchistic confusion of powers and "organised chaos" ' (Bracher, 1976b, p. 64). As Bracher also points out (ibid.), 'in the search for a completely new approach' this insight has, understandably perhaps, been too frequently underrated. The works of Bracher himself, and also, for example, those of Gerhard Schulz, concentrate on the problem of the 'administrative inefficiency and arbitrariness of the Führer system in its relation to the totalitarian claim of the Führer's dictatorship' (ibid.). At the same time they regard the element of chaos and improvisation more as a precondition of the Führer's absolutism, without succumbing to the risk of demonising Hitler's personality and policies.

However – not least in the light of documents on the history of Nazism which have been restored to the Federal Republic and made available to scholars – the previously accepted picture of the Third Reich has been more and more questioned and experimentally revised in the direction of an 'authoritarian anarchy', as Walter Petwaidic suggested as early as 1948. On the basis of individual, empirical findings – not always undisputed, as shown, for example, by the continuing controversy over responsibility for the Reichstag fire (cf. Tobias, 1964; H. Mommsen, 1972a; Hofer *et al.*, eds, 1972; Hofer and Graf, 1976) – Hans Mommsen has sharply criticised 'over-rational' judgements of the Third Reich. Following Broszat's picture of the inner workings of the Nazi state, a leading work in this field, Mommsen depicts 'an unparalleled institutional anarchy and increasing divorce from practical reality in the process of decision at all levels,' the system being 'held together externally by the Führer myth' (H. Mommsen, 1971, col. 702). Hitler himself, in Mommsen's opinion, was 'reluctant to take decisions, often uncertain, concerned only to maintain his own prestige and personal authority, and strongly subject to the influence of his environment for the time being – in fact, in many ways a weak dictator' (ibid.). This was an emphatic statement of 'the limits of Hitler's power' (E. N. Peterson), which fundamentally questioned what had till then been the accepted view of the dictator's almost absolute authority.

Some historians (for example, Bollmus, 1970, and W. J. Mommsen, 1970/1) apply this qualification of Hitler's position primarily to internal affairs, and continue to speak of Hitler's 'personal rule' (W. J. Mommsen) where foreign relations were concerned. Others apply the 'revisionist' view to foreign affairs as well. This is the case, for example, with Hans Mommsen (1976, pp. 30–45), Martin Broszat (1970, pp. 392–409) and, to an extent not fully determined here, Wolfgang Schieder (1976, pp. 162–90): cf., in more detail, Section 5, pp. 141–51 below. According to these interpretations Hitler appears as a more or less important but not basically an autonomous figure: more of an executive, a representative, or a dependent agent, moved by events instead of moving them. In this way he is seen not primarily as a political creator but rather as a social medium. Thus H. Mommsen argues for a 'normalisation' of the dictator, who he thinks has been unduly demonised. In Mommsen's view (H. Mommsen, 1972b,

p. 1) Hitler is merely a representative of 'fascism in Germany', whose origin he sets out to explain in terms of 'structural' links between the later phase of the Weimar Republic and the 'phase of the [Nazi] conquest of power'.

This revisionist view of the Nazi state as a polycratic chaos in both home and foreign affairs has been challenged, for example, by Bracher (1976b, esp. pp. 62–78) and Hillgruber (1978). Bracher (op. cit., p. 64) objects that 'the polycratic, often anarchic character' attributed to Nazi internal policy was not essential to the regime but related more to inadequacies of 'execution', though he does not dispute that ambivalence in this field too was a characteristic of Nazism. Such ambivalence, in Bracher's view, lay 'in the very nature of a programme which was laid down as unalterable, or rather an ideological fixation, which unquestionably included contradictory elements, without however desisting from the aim of radical implementation'; it was not to be understood merely 'in the sense, and as the consequence, of Machiavellian adroitness on Hitler's part' (op. cit., p. 65). This aspect of the relationship between Hitler's dictatorship and the polycratic system has recently been re-emphasised by Sebastian Haffner, who describes the chaos of the Third Reich as 'Hitler's creation'.

> [Hitler] deliberately destroyed the state's ability to function in favour of his personal omnipotence and irreplaceability, and he did so right from the start ... [He] brought about a state of affairs in which the most various autonomous authorities were ranged alongside and against one another, without defined boundaries, in competition, and overlapping – and only he himself was at the head of all of them ... For he had the entirely proper understanding that ... absolute rule was not possible in an intact state organism but only amidst controlled chaos. That was why, from the outset, he replaced the state by chaos – and one has to hand it to him that, while he was alive, he knew how to control it. (Haffner, 1979, pp. 43–4)

This vivid description of the system of government in the Third Reich may be criticised as over-rational. But, taking due account of both intentional and derivative aspects of Hitler's state, we may at least establish the following conclusion. While the coexistence of monocratic and polycratic elements in the Nazi state enables us to discover and describe much that was antagonistic and almost irreconcilable, the existence of a chaos of competence in the regime does not affect the fact that 'Hitler's wishes and policy were finally decisive and self-consistent in terms of final aims' (Bracher, 1976b, p. 65).

The 'revisionists' (for this term cf. p. 110 above) hold that the traditional view is in danger of over-rationalising the Third Reich and demonising Hitler. This criticism has been most firmly combated by K. D. Bracher, who rejects not only the ' "new Left" and Marxist dogmatism of a whole-sale, undifferentiated interpretation of fascism' but also the 'more recent revisionist interpretation': both of these 'abandon the "old-fashioned liberal" approach to totalitarianism in favour of a more relative interpretation stressing the element of improvisation in Nazi rule. The revisionists seek to bypass the question of guilt and responsibility in favour of what they claim to be a more up-to-date and realistic analysis; but in so doing they run the risk of once again underrating and trivialising the national socialist movement itself, just as the left wing does in a different way with its clichés of fascism and reaction' (Bracher, op. cit., p. 62). Without intending it, the 'revisionists' may indeed be in danger of diminishing and ignoring the ideological and totalitarian dimension of Nazism, thus overlooking the essential feature of the history of the Third Reich and encouraging an interpretation that tends to exonerate totalitarian dictatorship and do less than justice to Western liberal ideas of society and political organisation. In attempting to present a 'normal' picture of the Third Reich and to explain the ambivalence of Nazism mainly as due to the continued presence or influence of traditional 'structures', the 'revisionists' relativise the autonomy of Hitler's dictatorship and its historical aims.

Whether the policy of the Third Reich was bound in the long run to bring it to destruction, by inner necessity and without any outside pressure, is a much controverted question and is probably difficult of solution. The more recent tendency, as described by Wolfram Fischer in a different connection, is to regard the matter less from the standpoint of the actual history and collapse of the Nazi dictatorship and rather to inquire in a more 'open' fashion into inherent features of the system that might have produced 'alternatives to what actually happened' (Fischer, in Forstmeier and Volkmann, eds, 1975, p. 135). In this connection Norman Rich notably observes: 'Had Hitler died soon after naming Göring as his successor, German policy during the Second World War might have been very different' (Rich, 1973, vol. 1, p. 75).

While the 'revisionists' take the line that Hitler was basically dependent on the polycratic nature of the Nazi regime and that his acts were dictated by it, Alan S. Milward has expressed the opposite view in a kind of parallel to Haffner's remarks. According to him, it was the Führer principle and the primacy of the Nazi ideology in Hitler's mind which to some extent made the creation of administrative chaos necessary, and it was the apparent diffusion of authority which in reality made Hitler all-powerful. For the Nazi Party was 'fiercely suspicious of all administrative machinery not under its own supervision and imbued with its own world-outlook ... It became a regular part of National Socialist practice, when important administrative tasks needed to be done, to appoint a new administrative machine to do the job.' The Führer principle was designed to put a stop to the indecision and slowness of the Weimar bureaucrats and naturally also to ensure that the Führer's personal decisions were promptly transmitted through the administrative hierarchy. 'Usually the responsibility of the head of a new machine was to a very high leader, sometimes only to the Führer himself' (Milward, 1975, in Forstmeier and Volkmann, eds, op. cit.,

p. 197; cf. his *War, Economy and Society 1939–1945,* London, 1977, p. 27).

Those historians who, since the 1960s, have set out to differentiate and 'revise' accepted views as to the monolithic or pluralistic, monocratic or polycratic nature of the Nazi system have done valuable service by pointing out the dangers and limitations of a 'Hitlerocentric' approach and devoting more attention to the 'other side' of the Nazi 'dual state'. In some cases they have overshot the mark, however, so that researchers now have to address themselves to 'revisionist' conclusions that appear equally one-sided. This was pointed out by A. Hillgruber (1978), who endeavoured to do justice to the revisionist contribution to the history of the Third Reich while leaving no doubt that he regarded the 'polycratic' thesis as marginal and derivative in character. In this respect – leaving aside, for example, Geoffrey Barraclough's views expressed in 1972 in the *New York Review of Books* ('Mandarins and Nazis', 19 October, and 'The Liberals and German history', 2 November) – Hillgruber is in line with a highly representative tendency of international research. The views of historians such as Alan Bullock, Norman Rich, Renzo de Felice and Eberhard Jäckel may be summed up in the judgement expressed by H. R. Trevor-Roper more than thirty years ago, which seems no less true and pertinent today:

> Liberal refugees, theoretical Marxists, despairing reactionaries have pretended, or persuaded themselves, that Hitler was himself only a pawn in a game which not he but some other politicians, or some more cosmic forces, were playing. It is a fundamental delusion. Whatever independent forces he may have used, whatever incidental support he may have borrowed, Hitler remained to the end the sole master of the movement which he had himself inspired and founded, and which he was himself, by his personal leadership, to ruin. (Trevor-Roper, 1947, p. 43)

Research into all other aspects of the history of the Third Reich is at present influenced, consciously or unconsciously, by the debate as to whether the regime was monocratic or polycratic, whether its policies were autonomous or dictated by events. This is of course additional to the study devoted to each subject as a historical theme in its own right. On such traditional questions as, for example, the relationship between the army and the Nazi state we have for some time been relatively well informed (Messerschmidt, 1969, and K.-J. Müller, 1969). At present increased interest is being shown in sociological aspects, for example, the position of women in the Third Reich (Stephenson, 1975). The treatment of 'classical' themes has scarcely lost any of its popularity, as shown, for instance, by the strong public interest aroused, within a few weeks of its appearance in 1977, by the first volume of K. Scholder's work (1977) on the churches in the Third Reich. As already mentioned, some of the principal 'revisionists' apply their theory to the foreign and racial policy of the regime as well as to home affairs, and the controversy concerning this is still in progress.

5

Foreign and Racial Policy

Orthodox Marxist historians, in accordance with their theory of the state-monopolistic character of the Third Reich, interpret the foreign policy of Hitler and his regime as a function, directly or indirectly, of the basic necessities of the capitalist system and its leading economic and political groups and representatives. This view was expressed by GDR scholars in a representative volume of 1975 (Schumann and Nestler, eds) on German imperialist plans from 1900 to 1945. In the West it has frequently been disputed (cf. summary in Hildebrand, 1974) on two main grounds: (1) It ignores the primacy of the political factor (cf. Section 3, pp. 124 ff. above), which characterised Hitler's dictatorship especially in the field of strategy and foreign affairs, and which did not apply to such an extent, for example, in imperial Germany; and (2) it fails to take account (cf. Section 2, pp. 114–15 above) of the multiplicity of forms assumed by different political cultures which share the same background of a capitalist economic system.

Further specific objections can be raised to the Marxist interpretation: (1) It overlooks the fact that Hitler's ideas on foreign and racial policy, embodied as points in his 'programme', were framed long before he came to power or had any contact with industry. Hitler's programme was developed and pursued more or less independently of economic motives. (2) Not a single document exists to show that business circles took any initiative to make demands on Hitler in the field of foreign policy, which might have led him to alter or supplement his programme. Both in 1933–9 and especially during the Second World War the initiatives as to economic policy, for instance in occupied territories, always came from the state, the party or the army, and not from economic groups. In this respect too the history of the Third Reich was basically different from that of the Kaiser's Germany, where the Chancellor, von Bethmann Hollweg, had to pay more attention to representations from 'pressure groups' at the beginning of the First World War than Hitler ever did.

Hitler's systematic foreign policy was not in the first instance a complex of economic aims transferred into the political sphere – this is clear from a glance at its origins. Its roots lie in the latter years of the First World War, when there was a basic movement of political thought among the military leaders of Prussian Germany concerning problems of future warfare and peacetime organisation (cf. Hillgruber, 1967, pp. 58–67). Finally (3) Hitler's attitude to the Jews, which was decisive for the history of the Third Reich (cf. Section C2, pp. 69 ff. above), was at the very roots of his foreign policy, and was in principle diametrically opposed to any capitalist considerations of profit. Orthodox Marxist history has so far treated the persecution of the Jews in a purely 'functional' light, thus failing to understand and, in a sense, whitewashing it. If, however, it is viewed in its true character, the 'absolute priority of political aims' (Bracher) in the Nazi system becomes scarcely disputable.

The 'Jewish question' is equally a refutation of any explanations which, while not attempting to produce direct and personal evidence of economic influence on political events, postulate some anonymous historical process as the basis of a more or less complete identity of principle between politics and economics. According to such explanations, every policy is dictated by a capitalist 'structure' that is thought of as more or less omnipotent, operating as it were behind the backs of the ostensible agents and determining all they do. As against such views, Hitler's Jewish policy demonstrates the dominance of a racial doctrine over economic and rational considerations. Indeed, it can clearly be seen in the foreign policy, racial policy and strategy of the Third Reich that economic substance and political power were more and more divorced from each other. This was the intensification of a tendency which – apart from the Weimar years – was to some extent typical of modern German history, and which may help to explain the social and constitutional distortions in Prussian Germany that were part of the background to the Third Reich.

The subjection, postulated in Marxist theory, of Nazi foreign policy to the economic interests and social requirements of the traditional ruling classes of Prussian Germany did not in fact exist, either in the form of intentional acts that can be documented or as an empirically observable 'structural process'. In non-Marxist research the primacy of Hitler's foreign policy, and its high degree of autonomy, are universally emphasised, though with variations as to the exact degree of its independence.

While Marxist history over the years has only modified the emphasis, and not the substance, of its interpretation of Nazi foreign policy, in Western research there has been a lively debate and a corresponding development of knowledge in this area.

In the aftermath of the Nuremberg trials it was once supposed that .Nazi foreign policy consisted of a revisionist phase until 1937 and an expansionist period thereafter. This view has long been abandoned, however. As Hillgruber writes: 'On the basis of the evidence produced in the trial of major war criminals at Nuremberg, where particular key documents were for juridical reasons given more than their due historical weight, until about 1960 the Hossbach memorandum of the conference on 5 November 1937 with the service chiefs and the Reich Foreign Minister, at which Hitler revealed his intention to pursue a war policy, was treated as a turning-point between a peaceable phase which was essentially the continuation of the revisionist policy of the Weimar Republic, and a phase of warlike expansion on a major scale' (Hillgruber, 1973a, p. 8).

Another interpretation which can no longer be considered representative is that originally put forward by Alan Bullock (cf. Section 2, p. 120 above) and endorsed by, for example, the Swiss historian Walther Hofer (1955), according to which Hitler's foreign policy and strategy were those of a Machiavellian opportunist who treated war as an end in itself and took whatever fortune offered him at any given moment. The trend of historical science in this field was basically set by Hugh Trevor-Roper in his article on 'Hitler's war aims' (1960), which emphasised the consistency of Hitler's ideas on foreign policy ever since the 1920s, with the basic purpose of conquering *Lebensraum* in European Russia. This view has been largely accepted by subsequent research, with one or two exceptions such as Aigner (1978) and Michalka (1976a), and has meanwhile been developed in two directions. Eberhard Jäckel (1969) accepted Trevor-Roper's basic thesis, confirmed it in principle and elaborated it in detail. Hitler's foreign policy and plans for an alliance were reconstructed in this framework, and Jäckel also concentrated attention on the anti-Semitic doctrine which lay at the roots of his foreign-political and strategic ideas. The ultimate objectives, according to Jäckel, were the conquest of *Lebensraum* in Eastern Europe and the racial regeneration of the national socialist empire.

Other historians consider Hitler's foreign policy as involving essentially wider aims, beyond the borders of continental Europe. This is on the whole the conclusion of Milan Hauner's summary of the evidence (1978). As far back as 1937 Konrad Heiden described Hitler's ultimate aim as 'the re-creation of an Aryan élite which is to rule the world' (Heiden, 1937 (vol. 2 of German original), p. 239). In the postwar period this view was launched by Günther Moltmann in his article of 1961 on 'Hitler's ideas of world domination'. Andreas Hillgruber made a decisive contribution to the discussion with his post-doctoral thesis at Marburg University on Hitler's strategy, published in 1965, and later works, including his book on German policy prior to the two world wars (1967) and articles on 'the American factor in Hitler's strategy, 1938–41' (1965b) and 'the "final solution" and the German Empire in the East' (1972). He regards Hitler's policy in this respect as one of advancing by stages (Hillgruber, 1973a, p. 9), and explains that his 'globalistic' conclusions are 'based initially on Trevor-Roper's approach, but placed in a wider perspective by the much more abundant source material that has since become available'. He maintains that Hitler's programme 'did not end with the planned conquest of additional living space in the East, but was of a worldwide character. After the creation of a European continental empire buttressed by the conquest of Russia, a second stage of imperial expansion was to follow with the acquisition of complementary territory in Central Africa and a system of bases to support a strong surface fleet in the Atlantic and the Indian Ocean. Germany, in alliance with Japan and if possible also Britain, would in the first place isolate the USA and confine it to the Western hemisphere. Then, in the next generation, there would be a "battle of continents" in which the "Germanic empire of the German nation" would fight America for world supremacy' (ibid.).

The 'continental' and the 'global' theories of Hitler's ambitions have this in common, that they regard the conquest of *Lebensraum* and racial supremacy as basic to his philosophy and policy. Thus Norman Rich in his great work *Hitler's War Aims* describes racialism as 'the very rock on which the Nazi church was built' (1973, vol. 1, p. 4). Rich regards Hitler's continental aims, especially in Eastern Europe and the Soviet Union, as decisive: he describes them in detail, but also refers to those aspects of Hitler's foreign policy which looked beyond Europe. After the appearance of Rich's work, which presented a very full picture of the state of research, Jochen Thiess in 1976 published his thesis on Hitler's aims: this supported Hillgruber's view with a variety of documents, some already known but others new (not least those relating to Nazi architectural plans), which lent much force to the contention that Hitler indeed envisaged world domination.

The idea of a 'gradual plan' (*Stufenplan*), introduced by Hillgruber as a heuristic device, is still disputed by some, but has been described by K. D. Erdmann (1976a, p. 342) as 'in any case a fruitful suggestion'. Admittedly such terms as 'gradual plan' and 'programme' can at times be criticised as implying too systematic a design on Hitler's part. However, it must be borne in mind that they are not meant to suggest a 'timetable for world conquest'. They are rather intended to cover the essential motives and immutable central aims of Hitler's foreign policy – namely, the conquest of *Lebensraum*, racial supremacy and world power – without losing sight of the dictator's 'improvisations' (Erdmann) and his highly developed tactical versatility.

The historiographical results that are here outlined have deprived of scientific force the highly unorthodox or apologetic interpretations of Hitler's policy expressed in A. J. P. Taylor, *The Origins of the Second World War* (London), and David L. Hoggan, *Der erzwungene Krieg. Die Ursachen und Urheber des 2. Weltkrieges* (Tübingen), both published in 1961. No doubt in a spirit of opposition to the generally accepted view of Hitler's guilt, Taylor ('perhaps the most eccentric demythologiser of Hitler' – Hauner, 1978, p. 17) argues that the dictator was basically a 'revisionist' politician whose policy did not differ in essentials from that of Stresemann. Thus the Second World War was merely an accident for which all the states involved were responsible, a link in the long chain of European wars. In arguing thus, Taylor has been repeatedly criticised (cf., for example, Jasper, 1962) for ignoring fundamental differences between Stresemann's peaceful revisionist policy and Hitler's warlike expansionism, as well as the racial ideology by which Nazi foreign policy was inspired. As for David Hoggan's politically coloured interpretation, which represents the war as 'imposed' on Germany and lays the blame on Lord Halifax, the British Foreign Secretary, it has never been taken seriously by competent scholars (cf. Jasper, op. cit.).

Today a different controversy stands in the foreground of academic discussion of the problems of Nazi foreign policy. Believing that it is not sufficient to treat the foreign policy of the Third Reich solely or primarily from the standpoint of Hitler, Hans-Adolf Jacobsen in his large work (1968) attempted to describe the 'structure' of that policy and the multiplicity of agencies and institutions that were concerned with it. In so doing he left no doubt, however, that Hitler's programme was finally valid and that he had the last word. As against this, many contemporary German historians of the 'revisionist' school (cf. Section 4, pp. 138 ff. above) at present tend to regard Hitler's foreign policy as the 'ideological accentuation of dynamic social forces' (Schieder, 1976, p. 18). Taking issue with the 'programmologists' (Schieder, op. cit., p. 163), members of this school seek to relativise Hitler's omnipotence in foreign as well as home affairs, maintaining that 'the polycratic power structures of the so-called Führer state' (op. cit., p. 166) apply to this field as well. Probably the most thoughtful attempt to show 'that the polycratic internal system of the Nazi state . . . also affected foreign policy' (op. cit., p. 169) is that by Martin Broszat (1970). Broszat attempts to set off against each other the Nazi power system and Hitler's foreign policy in terms of 'ideological metaphor'. He regards Hitler's ultimate aims as symbols intended to justify ever-fresh activity on the part of the regime, whose basic principle was incessant motion and change for its own sake.

The idea that Hitler's foreign policy and strategy were not primarily independent phenomena but functions of a complex social process has hitherto been received rather coolly by foreign scholars, some of whom – for example, Norman Rich (1973–4) – opposed it with more or less indirect arguments. In West Germany, on the other hand, it has led to a continuing controversy, in which the chief opponents of the revisionist view have been K. D. Bracher, A. Hillgruber and the present author. Their main objections (summarised in Hildebrand, 1974, pp. 645–7) are as follows:

(1)   The revisionist interpretation of Nazi foreign policy overlooks the high degree of autonomy of Hitler's programme, the aims of which were formulated and implemented by the dictator. To ascribe to them too much of a 'functional' or derivative character also ignores the fact that Hitler was basically concerned not to perpetuate the existing political and social structure system in Germany but to overthrow it.

(2)   To treat the aims dictated by Hitler's *Weltanschauung* as a mere ideological outcome of social processes hardly accounts for the fact that, for example, the dictator's anti-Semitism and anti-Bolshevism are to be regarded not solely or even mainly as 'functional' but as primary, independent political aims.

(3)   In this sense the 'revisionists' are in danger of raising undoubted effects and consequences of Hitler's policy to the status of primary aims, and failing to distinguish properly between what is essential and what is derivative.

(4)   As the explicit, autonomous objectives of Hitler's programme were achieved one by one, it became harder and harder for Hitler to control the

dynamism of his own system. But this never forced him to adopt basic alternatives against his will. It did not affect the formulation of the aims that he set for himself and the German people, but rather reinforced them as intentions, although at times making them more difficult of achievement.

This criticism, however, should not prevent our appreciating the merits of the 'revisionist' interpretation and the possibilities it opens up. In the light of these, the position may perhaps be seen as follows:

(1)   The new approach is a clear warning against the danger, which has been recognised in the past, of ascribing too much regularity and coherence to Hitler's foreign policy and neglecting the activities of other persons and institutions. It is true that the 'revisionists' in their zeal overlook the fact that these alternatives are not so new as they suppose, but can already be found in the works of 'programmologists' and 'traditionalists'.

(2)   The 'revisionist' critique rightly draws attention to trends and effects which are part of the history of the regime's foreign policy. The reservations of this school against unduly 'Hitlerocentric' interpretations may be regarded as convincing in so far as they do not lead to the error of considering the dictator as a mere instrument of social processes.

(3)   The 'revisionist' thesis may have brought out more clearly than before the need for the type of study undertaken by W. Michalka in his thesis (1976b) on 'Ribbentrop and German policy towards Britain, 1933–40', drawing attention to 'the discussion of concepts of foreign policy in the Third Reich' and assessing the relative importance of monocratic and polycratic elements.

On the whole, apart from the 'revisionist' critique there is widespread agreement in international research that Hitler exercised 'personal rule' (W. J. Mommsen) in foreign affairs, and that his policy was not 'metaphorical' or symbolic, as M. Broszat suggests, but was genuinely intended to be carried out. It was not basically a means of achieving integration on the home front, but was directed towards expansion and racial domination. It was not a product of social dynamics but had a relatively high degree of autonomy; the dynamics of the Nazi regime derived from it, not vice versa, though admittedly they often tended to achieve an independence of their own.

In connection with the debate as to how far the foreign policy of the Third Reich was autonomous or 'functional', another controversy arises concerning Hitler's racial policy, which was essentially linked with it: namely, whether the Nazi extermination of Jews is to be regarded as a matter of deliberate intention or improvisation. In view of the fact that no document from Hitler's hand ordering the mass murder of the Jews has yet been found, traditional research has generally assumed that he issued a secret order to this effect as part of the preparation for the attack on Russia, which was the kernel of his ideological and political programme, and that this order, which first applied to captured Soviet territory, was afterwards extended to the whole of occupied Europe. Eberhard Jäckel dates the decision to the summer of 1940, while Helmut Krausnick places it in March 1941. Hans-Günther Seraphim believes it took place at the beginning of July 1941, shortly before Operation Barbarossa (cf. Hillgruber, 1977, p. 35, n. 43). In a further legal opinion of 1978 Hillgruber expresses the view that 'Hitler's oral instruction to Himmler or Heydrich to have all Jews in Russia shot was communicated orally by Heydrich, head of the RSHA, the SIPO and the SD, to the heads of the *Einsatzgruppen* and *Einsatzkommandos* [special extermination squads] at the end of May 1941, that is, some weeks before the attack on Russia, at the school for frontier police at Pretzsch near Wittenberg' (op. cit., p. 9). These writers leave no doubt as to the leading part played by Hitler in this matter, his personal and decisive action and his direct and absolute responsibility.

The most recent comprehensive account of the treatment of Jews in the Third Reich is L. Dawidowicz's *The War against the Jews* (1975). This does not entirely follow the line of K. A. Schleunes's *The Twisted Road to Auschwitz* (1970), but stresses the consistency of Nazi racial policy during the years of peace as well as the Second World War. Uwe Dietrich Adam (1972), on the other hand, takes a distinctly different view, the main effect of which is to relativise Hitler's role in the Jewish policy of the Third Reich. While admitting that the dictator played a part of some importance in the treatment of the Jews and the extermination process (op. cit., p. 360), he considers that in the last resort it was the institutional structure of the Third Reich which resulted in the order being given for the holocaust. His argument is that the chaos caused in the occupied Eastern territories by the arrival of trainloads of Jews had intensified the disorder typical of Nazi arrangements. When the German advance in Russia was brought to a halt in November–December 1941 there was still less room for deported Jews, and, as it seemed unlikely that more territory would be conquered, the organisational incompetence of the regime forced Hitler to improvise the solution of killing off the Jews. 'Certainly Hitler's order to have millions of people killed was his own personal decision; but the dynamic development of his state was not the result of ingenious calculation but was an inner development that in no small measure constrained Hitler himself' (ibid.). This conclusion was recently paraphrased by H. Mommsen: 'It cannot be proved, for instance, that Hitler himself gave the order for the final solution, though this does not mean that he did not approve the policy. That the solution was put into effect is by no means to be ascribed to Hitler alone, but to the complexity of the decision-taking process in the Third Reich, which brought about a progressive and cumulative radicalisation' (H. Mommsen, 1977, 'Nazionalsozialismus oder Hitlerismus?' in M. Bosch, ed., *Persönlichkeit und Struktur in der Geschichte*, Düsseldorf, p. 66).

This view has been amplified by Martin Broszat (1977) in a well-argued and perceptive article on 'Hitler and the genesis of the final solution'. The same article convincingly refutes the opinion put forward by David Irving in *Hitler's War* that Himmler organised the killing of Jews on his own authority and that

Hitler did not learn of it till 1943. Irving's view was also rebutted by H. Trevor-Roper (*Sunday Times*, 12 June 1977), A. Bullock (*New York Review of Books*, 7 July 1977) and E. Jäckel (*Frankfurter Allgemeine Zeitung*, 25 August 1977 and 22 June 1978).

Apart from this, however, Broszat takes the view that Hitler probably gave no specific order for the extermination of Jews, and that the dictator's decision was due to a combination of ideological dogma and pathological improvisation. Broszat considers that anti-Semitism was so strong a factor in Hitler's foreign policy that the desire to strike a blow at the Jews may have been one reason why he took the risk of war in September 1939. On the whole, however, Broszat believes that the destruction of European Jewry was not basically due to conscious planning on Hitler's part but to the uncontrolled dynamism of the regime, with its tendency towards improvisation and, in consequence, the ever-increasing radicalisation that finally defeated its own object. Broszat does not deny that Nazi ideology was in principle ready at all times for the most radical solution of the 'Jewish question'; but he believes that the actual historical situation determined acts of policy towards the Jews, which took place without co-ordination and in separate stages. According to Broszat it was the holding-up of the advance in Russia, the impossible situation created by the deportations to the Eastern territories, and the independent initiatives of local authorities, which increasingly compelled the top leaders to seek a desperate way out by putting into effect what became the 'final solution'.

> Hitler probably saw no reason to call off the plan for the wholesale deportation of Jews merely because the military difficulties and commitments in the East proved greater than had been expected in the summer of 1941. In the light of the situation in autumn of that year it seems that the original deportation plans were slowed up and reduced in scale, and that it was decided to do away with at least some of the deported Jews 'in a different way', that is, by systematic executions. The extermination of Jews came about, it would seem, not only because of the professed intention to destroy them but also as the way out of an impasse into which the regime had manoeuvred itself. However, once the process of liquidation had begun and was systematised, it became a dominant factor and finally led to an actual comprehensive 'programme'. (op. cit., pp. 752–3)

However, this new approach does not lead Broszat to dispute Hitler's responsibility in any way. 'If our interpretation is based on the view that the extermination of the Jews was an improvised solution, not something planned long before and put into effect by a single secret order, this indeed implies that responsibility for the initiative was not confined to Hitler, Himmler, or Heydrich; but it in no way exonerates Hitler' (op. cit., p. 756). However, Broszat clearly opposes the traditional view of Hitler's Jewish policy as an action specifically planned at an early stage. 'It is certain that Hitler's dogmatic ideological anti-Semitism was not independent of time and actuality. It did not develop according to a timetable but in a pathological fashion; at different times it was more or less highly charged, and this degree of intensity played at least as great a part as the unchanging dogma itself in determining Hitler's decisions and actions. This applies in particular to the persecution and annihilation of the Jews, which was not a steady, planned operation but was of a more improvised and fitful character, carried out by intensified *ad hoc* measures from time to time' (op. cit., p. 770).

Broszat's suggested interpretation will no doubt raise objections, among which the following may be mentioned: (1) The fact that no written order by Hitler for the killing of Jews has been found by no means proves that there was no such order, written or oral. To accept it as probable that there was such an order has nothing to do with any 'conspiracy theory' on the part of traditional historians, based on 'idealistic intentionalism': for there is ample documentary evidence that secrecy as to the Führer's intentions was a basic feature of politics in the Third Reich. As against this, the validity of the thesis that the regime was characterised by improvisation is still subject to question.

(2)   The executions of Jews in Russia were co-ordinated with the German advance and took place regardless of personal rank, position, or activity, on the mere ground that the victims were Jews. Broszat's interpretation in 'situational' and derivative terms does not adequately account for this policy, which must surely have been ordered by Hitler and carried out on a planned basis. In qualitative terms the executions by shooting were no different from the technically more efficient accomplishment of the 'physical final solution' by gassing, to which they were a prelude.

(3)   Even if one is prepared to ascribe a relatively high degree of importance to the historical situation in bringing about the Nazi extermination of Jews, it must not be overlooked that the genesis of the 'final solution' lay much further back in time, in Hitler's account of his own programme, and that the destruction of European Jewry was based on the racial dogma contained in the Nazi ideology. But for that ideology, the alleged spur-of-the-moment action would have had nothing to base itself on. Hitler's racial dogma was the root cause of Nazi genocide. That dogma may have brought about situations that called urgently for the radical application of a solution which had long been envisaged as a practical possibility. In other words, the situational element in the regime's attitude to the Jews may have contributed secondarily to the implementation of the racial dogma, but certainly did not create the latter as a new and essential feature of Nazi policy.

(4)   While historical situations may have served to reinforce original intentions and plans that had already been set on foot for pathological reasons, Hitler's programmatic ideas of destroying the Jews and establishing racial supremacy remain the prime cause and essential goal of the 'Jewish policy' of the

Third Reich. They constituted the dynamic impetus of the regime, which modified and accelerated Hitler's plans but at no time rushed him into solutions that he had not long envisaged and wanted.

Addressing himself to the problem of the treatment of Jews during the Second World War from a different standpoint to the 'revisionists', Sebastian Haffner has recently sought to explain the adoption in December 1941 of the policy of physical extermination by a technically perfected method, which from 1942 onwards was extended to the whole of Europe under German occupation or influence. Haffner believes that Hitler's calculations were the sole determining factor as regards the inception, development and planning of the extermination policy. 'So long as Hitler was still hoping to achieve in Russia a similarly rapid victory as a year before in France, he was also hoping that Britain would come to terms, since in Russia she would have lost her last "continental sword".' But for that purpose he must present himself as an acceptable party to negotiations with Britain. For this reason

> the systematic murder of the Jews had been confined to Poland and Russia, and its cumbersome method had been mass shooting . . . What he was doing in Poland and Russia could, so he had reason to hope, be kept secret from the outside world at least while the war was on; but mass murder in France, Holland, Belgium, Luxemburg, Denmark, Norway and even Germany itself would become immediately known in Britain and would make Hitler totally unacceptable there – which is what actually happened . . . In other words, Hitler would only be able to fulfil his long-cherished wish to exterminate the Jews from the whole of Europe if he abandoned all hope of a negotiated peace with Britain (and the associated hope of preventing America from joining the war). And that he only did after 5 December 1941, the day when the Russian offensive before Moscow rudely awakened him from his dreams of victory in Russia. (Haffner, 1979, p. 142)

Haffner thus sees no qualitative difference between the mass shootings of East European Jews on Polish and Soviet territory up to December 1941 and the subsequent gas-chamber operations (prepared as far back as June–July 1941) involving Jews from all over Europe. He regards both these as long-planned phases of Hitler's Jewish policy, separately put into effect in direct accordance with his ideological and strategic decisions. Future research will show whether Haffner's interpretation, based on penetrating conjecture, can be attested by sufficient first-hand evidence to make it generally acceptable to scholars.

Reviewing the present state of research concerning the foreign and racial policy of the Nazi regime, it appears desirable that historians should turn their attention to the following questions in particular:

(1)   It would be timely to investigate and present in a comprehensive manner the ideological aspect of Hitler's foreign policy and conduct of the war: for this

was closely linked with his plans for world power, and contributed in a high degree, though not decisively, to undermining and destroying them. Historical science urgently needs an account of the Nazi regime's policy towards the Jews, together with its euthanasia and eugenic programmes; all these were part of Hitler's ideology and complemented one another.

(2)   The history of Nazi foreign policy has already been more thoroughly researched, but it must be set in the historical context of international politics in the 1930s and 1940s, so as to establish how far Hitler was able to influence the course of world affairs during the twelve years of his rule, and how far international circumstances enabled him to carry out his plans or forced him to limit or modify them.

(3)   Continuing and developing the studies by A. Hillgruber (1965a) on Hitler's strategy, B. Martin (1976) on peace initiatives and W. Michalka (1976b) on Ribbentrop, it would be useful to devote attention to the existence of variants in the foreign policy (and foreign trade policy) of the Third Reich, whether intrinsic to the system or involving a modification of it, such as were envisaged, for example, by Hjalmar Schacht and perhaps even by Göring. This would throw light, *inter alia*, on the possibilities and limitations of the activity of opposition groups in the Third Reich, and would illustrate more clearly than before how fluid the transition between co-operation and resistance often was under the Nazi dictatorship.

6

The German Resistance

Both in the Federal Republic and in the GDR, academic studies of the history of the German resistance have served political ends to an unmistakable extent. In this respect the two German states scarcely differ from most other nations in Western and Eastern Europe. The depiction of the immediate past years of the Second World War, during which patriots of all parties and walks of life had fought against the German forces of occupation, enabled Germany's former victims to 'recover their sense of national identity and to develop the idea of European union; it also helped to foster the cult of communist heroes and the communist system' (Bracher, 1976a, p. 217).

As we saw in Section D2, the resistance in Germany differed from that in the occupied countries to an important if not a fundamental extent. The orthodox Marxist view is that 'only the communist resistance consistently fought against fascist rule from 1933 to 1945, and furnished the largest number of victims' (Hillgruber, 1973a, p. 11). Among the non-communist resisters Marxist historians pay tribute to only a few individuals. Count Stauffenberg, for instance, is credited with being a 'progressive' patriot, a judgement not echoed in non-Marxist accounts of that leading member of the German resistance, as may be seen from the large biography by C. Müller (1970, pp. 18–20). Clearly the ideological interpretation of the German resistance served to fortify the claim of the GDR to consider itself a state and to derive legitimacy from the legend of the communist resistance against the Third Reich, represented as the only important section of the resistance movement.

Studies of the German resistance by Western historians developed on much less systematic and unvarying lines. However, West German historians have shown similar concern to emphasise the historical continuity of the Federal Republic and to enhance its power of political integration by their accounts of the German resistance to Hitler, which are to some extent idealising and one-sided.

In the work of Anglo-American historians the dominant view was initially the same as the Nazi one, namely, that 'Hitler is Germany and Germany is Hitler'. (This appears paradoxical, but is an instance of the fact that in modern wars the two sides tend to share each other's misapprehensions.) Hitler's notorious statement on 20 July 1944 that the attempt on his life was the work of a 'small clique of ambitious officers' was echoed by such historians as J. Wheeler-

Bennett and Lewis Namier, who regarded 'the men of 20 July as militarists whose politics differed only in degree from those of the Nazis', and who hoped 'by sacrificing one victim to secure a negotiated peace which would rescue German militarism in its hour of need and deprive the Allies of a full-scale victory' (Plum, 1972, col. 962). In the course of time this interpretation gave place to a more balanced one, just as serious research offered no support to 'its extreme contrary, the view that Germany was the "first occupied country" and that all Germans had more or less actively resisted a small clique of usurpers' (Hillgruber, 1973a, p. 11).

The first efforts to correct prejudices were made in books published in Switzerland in 1946–7 by former members of the resistance such as Fabian von Schlabrendorff (*Offiziere gegen Hitler*, Zurich, 1946; translated as *Revolt against Hitler*, London, 1948), Hans Bernd Gisevius (*Bis zum bitteren Ende*, 2 vols, Zurich, 1946, translated as *To the Bitter End*, London, 1948) and Rudolf Pechel (*Deutscher Widerstand*, Erlenbach-Zurich, 1947). Ulrich von Hassell's posthumous diaries for 1938–44 (*Vom andern Deutschland*, 1947, translated as *The von Hassell Diaries*, New York and London, 1947), were also first published in Switzerland. Particularly effective was the publication in English, in 1948, of Hans Rothfels's *The German Opposition to Hitler* (Chicago), which contributed especially in the USA to producing a fairly comprehensive, historically reliable and balanced estimate. In the following year it was published in translation in Germany. It was largely owing to this book that historians at first concentrated with unmistakable one-sidedness on the activity of conservative forces in the resistance; their 'exaggerations and omissions' (Hillgruber) could also be put down partly to the 'cold war' and partly to the strong position of the universities and churches in Federal Germany. According to the assessment then prevalent, it was first and foremost the conservative and bourgeois members of the resistance who were responsible for the uprising of 20 July 1944; however, the fact that they had co-operated with social democrats was not overlooked, and they were represented as enjoying support among the German people, though the extent of this was never defined in detail.

The next major study which set the trend of Western research was Gerhard Ritter's account published in Germany in 1955 (translated as *The German Resistance. Carl Goerdeler's Struggle against Tyranny*, London, 1958). Ritter, like Rothfels, neglected the role of the communist and left-wing socialist resistance and stigmatised the activities of the 'Red orchestra' as treasonable. Writers of this school consciously or unconsciously used the German resistance to establish a tradition and fortify national self-awareness; in particular, the conspirators' plans for the future internal order of Germany were represented as prefiguring what came to be understood as 'liberal democracy' in the Federal Republic (Ehlers, 1964, p. 16). In a similar way there were efforts to show a direct link between the resisters' ideas on foreign policy and the concept of a 'United States of Europe' (W. Ritter von Schramm, 1954, 'Erhebung 1944', in

Politische Studien, p. 170). Meanwhile publications concerning the communist and left-wing socialist resistance, represented in the 1940s and 1950s by Hermann Brill (*Gegen den Strom*, Offenbach, 1946) and Günther Weisenborn (*Der lautlose Aufstand*, first published Weisenborn, 1953), were for the time being decidedly in the minority.

The 'conservative' writers, as already mentioned, were inspired by the desire to create a historical tradition and sense of identity in the newly established Federal Republic. The studies of such men as Goerdeler and Beck, and also of the 'Kreisau circle' (Ger van Roon, *Neuordnung im Widerstand*, 1967; translated as *German Resistance to Hitler: Count von Moltke and the Kreisau Circle*, London, 1971), laid emphasis on the moral motivation of the resistance leaders, an approach which was increasingly questioned from the beginning of the 1960s. The counter-movement which gained ground among researchers was fostered by opposition to those trends in Federal Germany which were believed to favour a restoration of the old order, and was symptomatic of a developing change in the intellectual and political climate of West Germany.

The reaction against previous views began with a more critical look at the part played by the universities and churches *vis-à-vis* the Third Reich. It was no longer accepted that they had at least practised passive resistance. 'Many highly placed persons were arraigned for opportunism and conformity' – thus the new trend was graphically described – 'and the attack was directed against conservatives who had co-operated with the regime rather than against avowed Nazis, of whom there had also been plenty' (Hillgruber, 1973a, p. 12). Two essays by Hans Mommsen ('Social views and constitutional plans of the resistance') and Hermann Graml ('Resistance thinking on foreign policy'), published in 1966 in W. Schmitthenner and H. Buchheim (eds), *Der deutsche Widerstand* (translated as *The German Resistance to Hitler*, London, 1970), played an important part in bringing about a revised view of the activity and ideas of the different resistance groups, and for some time imparted new directions to research. Mommsen's trenchant study showed that the views of the conservative resisters on the future constitution of Germany had little in common with the requirements of 'parliamentary democracy in conditions imposed by a world of technological and industrial labour' (Broszat, 1981, p. 146), but instead looked back to the authoritarianism of the Kaiser's Germany or even more absolutist models. Similarly Graml pointed out that as regards foreign affairs these representatives of the conservative resistance thought in terms of a national state and the direct or indirect domination of Central Europe by Germany – in other words, German hegemony in Europe after the old imperial style.

The effect of concentrating on conservative opposition to the regime was, as Hans Mommsen pithily described it, to produce a picture of 'resistance without a rank and file' (*Widerstand ohne Volk*). In contrast to this, stronger attention was now devoted to resistance by social democrats, communists and trade union members. The powerful impulse in this direction is still effective and tends for the present to dominate research. Less emphasis is now placed on resistance by the old conservative élites, and many regional studies and other accounts of the left-wing opposition have been published. Together with studies of local and industrial resistance groups, which are a favourite subject of study in the GDR, these works form a new picture which partly supplements and partly supersedes the criteria and conclusions that were accepted down to the 1960s.

In this new framework the men of the conservative resistance no longer appeared primarily as the 'other', better Germany standing up against Hitler's tyranny. Instead, their nostalgia for the past was stressed and they were criticised for the sterility of their ideas on home and foreign affairs. Thus the men of the conservative resistance could not be regarded as having been the right people to introduce or catch up with the process of modernisation in Germany which is regarded as historically necessary, and which is conceived as an adaptation of political and social institutions to the needs of an industrial society. An important expression of this new attitude towards the conservative resistance, as it developed in the 1960s, was Ralf Dahrendorf's essay (1961) on 'Democracy and social structure in Germany', which criticised the 'pre-industrial Prussian upper class' (p. 292) that had blocked Germany's path towards modernisation from Bismarck's time to 1933. In an interpretation which no doubt startled political opinion at the time, Dahrendorf expressed a highly sceptical view of the political ideas of the Prussian-German conservatives, including the men of 20 July 1944, while fully recognising their moral qualities. At the same time he spoke of the consequences that the Nazi regime had 'unintentionally' brought about, not least by the 'almost complete physical elimination of the old Prussian upper class' (op. cit., p. 293), and which had a modernising effect on the postwar development of West German society.

To sum up: (1) the present emphasis of historical research concerning the German resistance is almost precisely the opposite of what it was in the 1950s. At that time disproportionate stress was laid on the conservative resistance, while today interest is concentrated on non-élite and left-wing elements.

(2)   Whereas in the 1950s the trend was to neglect and overlook the left-wing socialist and communist resistance, today there is at least a strong tendency to discount the conservative resistance. Admittedly there is no reason why the conservatives of those days should have accepted as their own the values, standards and objectives of a parliamentary democracy like the Federal Republic of Germany; to reproach them for not doing so is to pass judgement on their political mentality by standards which they were not bound to recognise and which were probably foreign to German political thought at that time. The present author has referred elsewhere to this aspect and to the risk of blurring fundamental differences between, on the one hand, the ideas of the conservative resistance on home and foreign affairs and, on the other, Hitler's totalitarian dictatorship and racialist expansionism (Hildebrand, 1978).

(3)   The new interpretation of the opposition to Hitler tends to appraise it

purely from the political point of view and to underrate the ethical motivation of the resistance fighters and the moral example set by them, which is a phenomenon *sui generis* over and above all considerations of practical effectiveness. Karl Dietrich Erdmann has placed these aspects in a balanced frame of reference which attempts to do justice to the political and moral deserts of all the resistance groups: 'It is the legacy of the 20th of July that conservative, bourgeois and socialist conspirators sacrificed their lives in the revolt against the oppressor, overcoming the old antagonisms that destroyed the Weimar Republic. In an undogmatic spirit, seeking new ways, they strove to bring about a political order governed once more by standards of human dignity' (Erdmann, 1976a, p. 578).

(4)   There is a need for a differentiating treatment of the resistance, especially difficult problems of definition – as pointed out by P. Hüttenberger (1977) – and the bewildering multiplicity of its forms. This need is not well satisfied by the formula of 'anti-fascism' that has been used more and more frequently in recent years, sometimes by design but often quite unreflectingly. This reversion to the polemical slogans of the interwar period is apt dangerously to underrate important differences between political systems sharing a similar background of economic organisation and experience. It tendentiously identifies Nazism, crudely defined as 'German fascism', with the capitalist order, and suggests that communist or left-wing socialist elements predominated in the fight against Hitler's dictatorship, or even had a monopoly of resistance.

(5)   In the context of European history, the notions of 'collaboration' and 'resistance' are on the one hand opposed and on the other complementary to each other. From this point of view, research should not treat 'resistance' as something given *a priori* once and for all. In a way wholly appropriate to the structure of the Third Reich, it presents itself as an ambiguous phenomenon oscillating between adaptation to the regime and resistance to it. ' "Compliance" and resistance are not completely opposite entities, but must be carefully differentiated from the point of view of time and degree' (Hillgruber, 1973a): this has been shown, for instance, by Saul Friedländer, *Kurt Gerstein oder die Zwiespältigkeit des Guten* (Gütersloh, 1968) and Weizsäcker's papers in the edition by Leonidas E. Hill (1974).

There is still no comprehensive account of the German resistance covering all groups and avoiding condemnation on the one hand and special pleading on the other. We shall certainly not come near to understanding it until it is treated not only as the diametrical opposition to Hitler's dictatorship but also as part of the story of the Third Reich and of its place in modern German history.

7

The Verdict of Historians
on the Third Reich

After the collapse of Hitler's dictatorship, as the full extent of the 'German catastrophe' became apparent, the need to explain it was probably felt even more strongly than during the Nazi period itself. Discussion soon centred on the question whether the Third Reich was to be regarded as the outcome of German history or a break with its traditions.

Broadly in agreement with the crude slogans of Allied war propaganda, early postwar interpretations by foreign authors who treated Hitler's state as a more or less consistent result of the (faulty) development of the German nation: 'from Luther to Hitler', as William Montgomery McGovern put it (*The History of Fascist-Nazi Philosophy*, Boston, Mass., 1941). William L. Schirer in *The Rise and Fall of the Third Reich* (New York, 1959; London, 1960) likewise took the view that Nazism was basically the inevitable outcome of German history in the nineteenth and twentieth centuries. In 1953–4 the French historian Edmond Vermeil in his two-volume work *L'Allemagne contemporaine 1890–1950* (Paris) attributed the rise and development of Nazi Germany to authoritarian and imperialistic traditions which he traced back to the medieval empire. The quest for a discreditable pedigree was not confined to Anglo-American and French authors. As Wolfgang Wippermann has pointed out, Soviet and Polish historians in the immediate postwar period – 'in clear contrast to Marxist theory' – put forward similar interpretations in terms of national history and nationalism, linking the medieval *Drang nach Osten* with the ambitions of 'imperialist Junkerdom'.

While constructions of this sort have long ceased to appear to us tenable or worthy of discussion, their challenging and provocative nature caused them to be intensively debated by German historians as late as the 1950s.

The view of German history as a straight path to catastrophe was strongly opposed by Gerhard Ritter, probably at that time the most highly reputed German historian of the modern period (for example, in *Europa und die deutsche Frage*, Munich, 1948). Ritter was a conservative who had been in touch with the wartime resistance and had been persecuted after the coup of 20 July 1944. He drew a sharp line between Hitler's Third Reich and the rest of German and Prussian history, seeking the roots of Nazism rather in the democratic Jacobinism of European development since the French Revolution. In addition he repeatedly emphasised the demonic quality of Hitler's personality as a decisive factor in determining the course of German and international affairs from 1933 to 1945.

Another group of historians, belonging to the *grossdeutsch* tradition, rejected the superficial schema of an essential continuity stretching back indefinitely into the past, but at the same time opposed Ritter's tendency to treat the Third Reich as an isolated phenomenon in German history. Their views were expressed, for example, by Franz Schnabel (1949), 'Das Problem Bismarck', in L. Gall (ed.) (1971), *Das Bismarck-Problem in der Geschichtsschreibung nach 1945*, Cologne/Berlin, pp. 97–118, and Heinrich Ritter von Srbik (1950), 'Die Bismarck-Kontroverse. Zur Revision des deutschen Geschichtsbildes', ibid., pp. 138–53. These scholars took a critical view of the foundation of the *kleindeutsch* national state, which they saw as having set German history on a fatal course, though they did not draw an unduly close parallel between Bismarck and Hitler. But this view was out of harmony with the then prevailing trend of German historiography, as may be seen, for example, from Gerhard Ritter's firm rebuttal ('Das Bismarckproblem', ibid., pp. 119–37, and 'Zur "grossdeutschen" Frage', ibid., pp. 154–6).

In *Gleichgewicht oder Hegemonie*, first published in 1948, the Marburg historian Ludwig Dehio made an extremely influential attempt at interpretation which consistently projected the continuity of Prussian history into the European framework of international power politics. Dehio had not been led to this critical view of our national history by the catastrophe of 1945, but by his earlier years of 'internal exile' under the Third Reich. In his penetrating observations on 'equilibrium or hegemony' and in his essay of 1961 on Prussian-German history from 1640 to 1945, Dehio considered each different phase from Frederick William I to Hitler, evaluating events in the field of international politics as ultimately decisive for the history of the German nation. In so doing he diagnosed resemblances and factors of continuity in the development of Prussian and German power, emphasising the trend towards coercion in internal affairs and an expansionist foreign policy as typical of the history of Prussia and the Reich. Once again it was Gerhard Ritter who most vigorously opposed Dehio's view: cf. G. Ritter (1965), *Staatskunst und Kriegshandwerk. Das Problem des Militarismus in Deutschland*, 3rd edn, Munich, vol. I, p. 398. Ritter was supported by Eberhard Kessel, whose article of 1961 on 'Hitler and the betrayal of Prussiandom' joined issue with Dehio's trenchant analysis, stressing the differences and breaches of continuity between old Prussia, the empire of Bismarck and Wilhelm II, and Hitler's dictatorship.

Long before these controversies in the 1950s and early 1960s, Friedrich Meinecke in his 'reflections and recollections' entitled *Die deutsche Katastrophe*, first published in 1946 (translated as *The German Catastrophe*, Cambridge, Mass., and London, 1950), had taken a basically more comprehensive view of past events. While respecting the merits of the two rival schools of thought,

Meinecke's essay did not attempt to harmonise them or effect a compromise, but was remarkably critical in tone. True, he agreed in emphasising the European background of national socialism, viz. the 'age of the masses' which had its beginning in the nineteenth century, and at the same time he categorised Hitler's personality as fraught with evil historical consequences. But in terms of German historiography Meinecke referred unequivocally, at a surprisingly early stage, to the harbingers of Nazism in imperial Germany, when he wrote:

In domestic politics the harsh attitude of the master and employer (*Herrennatur*) opposed all suggestions and possibilities for reforming in a free and humane spirit the existing power structure as between employees, employers and the state, or the state's treatment of the Poles in the eastern provinces and the Danes in North Schleswig. The Hakatists [anti-Polish chauvinists] in Posen [Poznań] and West Prussia, the bullies (*Scharfmacher*) in big business, and the Junker bureaucrats in the ministries and the provincial governments were all agents of this domestic power system, which was complemented by the Pan-German movement in foreign affairs. However strongly one may emphasize the differences between the unsocial 'master' psychology of those times and Hitler's move-ment, the former was, if looked at as part of the whole development, a step towards national socialism. (op. cit., US edition, p. 22; the above translation is revised)

Hans Rothfels expressed a similar view, though with more restraint, in an essay on the 'problems of a biography of Bismarck', written, he informs us, during the war and first published in English in 1947: 'However long and tortuous the way "from Bismarck to Hitler" may have been, the founder of the Second Reich appears as responsible for a change of direction (*Wendung*), or at least for the legitimising of such a change, the fatal culmination of which is all too visible in our own day.' As Rothfels pointed out when the work was republished in German in 1970 (*Bismarck. Vorträge und Abhandlungen*, Stuttgart), his judgement was 'full of reservations' (p. 11) and his main point had been to emphasise 'that the Bismarckian empire was in sharp contrast to everything the Third Reich did or tried to do' (p. 12). None the less, the judgements by him and Meinecke have constantly been quoted and discussed as part of the argument concerning the continuity of German history in home and foreign affairs from Bismarck to Hitler.

In 1961 the discussion was again stirred up by a work of permanent influence by the Hamburg historian Fritz Fischer: *Griff nach der Weltmacht*, translated as *Germany's Aims in the First World War* (London, 1967). The author's Foreword remarked that the book 'contains pointers to fields wider than its own, for it indicates certain mental attitudes and aspirations which were active in German policy during the First World War and remained operative later. Seen from this angle, it may serve as a contribution towards the problem of the continuity of German policy from the First World War to the Second' (English edition, pp. ix–x). At the end of his impressive analysis Fischer laid stress on the identity of the German leading groups and the similarity of their political aims from imperial times to those of the Weimar Republic and the Third Reich. In 1968 he delivered a lecture at Sussex University pointing out the resemblance between German aims in the two wars, though perhaps underemphasising the difference between Hitler's ideological motivation and the political ambitions of the leaders of imperial Germany. 'The similarity in the directions, even if not in the essence of German aims in the two world wars is striking' (extract from lecture in Röhl, 1970, p. 146).

Fischer's powerful contribution gave rise to a lively and sometimes heated discussion of the problem of historical continuity in the Prussian-German state during the seventy-five years of its existence. Two main schools of thought emerged, both concerned in the first instance with the national-historical aspect of German development rather than its European bearings. Andreas Hillgruber continued Dehio's line of thought and took issue with Fischer's view of Prussian-German aims in foreign policy: among his various studies attention should be drawn to his inaugural lecture delivered at Freiburg University in 1969, and many times reprinted, on 'continuity and discontinuity in German foreign policy'. Hillgruber retrospectively expressed its conclusion as follows: 'The "ultimate" objective of Hitler's "programme" was undoubtedly "revolutionary", comprising world domination on a racial basis and a biologically created élite of masters (*Herrenmenschen*) . . . Although these "ultimate aims" included essential elements that were quite alien to the German tradition, Hitler's foreign political aims in the narrower sense, for the short and middle term as it were, had remarkably many features in common with the calculations and aspirations of the Wilhelmine period' (Hillgruber, 1973a, p. 14).

Continuity is also stressed in several works by Hans-Ulrich Wehler, who pays more attention to the internal development of Prussian Germany, treating its foreign policy as a resultant of internal processes. He interprets the development of Germany from the 'Bismarck era' to the Third Reich in terms of a theory of 'social imperialism', representing foreign policy as a series of moves designed to meet internal crises, to relieve social tensions and to maintain the social power structure. On this basis he postulates a continuous line extending from Bismarck to Hitler by way of Miquel, Bülow and Tirpitz. He describes Nazi policy as an 'extreme form of social imperialism, the object of which was to "break through to the East" in order once again to hold up internal progress and distract attention from the lack of freedom at home – Hitler too being in thrall to a conservative utopia' (H.-U. Wehler, 1970, *Krisenherde des Kaiserreichs 1871–1918. Studien zur deutschen Sozial- und Verfassungsgeschichte*, Göttingen, p. 161). The weaknesses of this 'functionalist' approach have been pointed out by Theodor

Schieder (1970, p. 446) as regards Bismarck's policy, and by the present author (1974, pp. 640–1) as regards the Third Reich.

What may be considered the first representative summary of the debate, especially as regards Prussian-German foreign policy within the international system, was contained in Schieder's essay on 'The German Reich in its national and universal relations, 1871–1945' (op. cit., 1970). There he cautiously weighed the elements of continuity and discontinuity in Prussian-German history, emphasising that over and above the national frame of reference 'the German question' continues to be 'part of a world problem from the political, social and ideological points of view'. A further attempt to balance the discussion was made by the present author in his article of 1973 on 'Hitler's place in the history of the Prussian-German national state', which endeavoured to relate internal and external policies to one another and also to take account of the results of socio-historical research. In this connection stress was laid on the decisive effect of the 'alliance between the old leading groups and the Nazi movement' in bringing about the Third Reich, while on the other hand the novel motives and objectives of Hitler's policy were treated as falling outside the bounds of German tradition. It was emphasised that 1933 constituted a new beginning, as became unmistakably clear from 1936–7 onwards, yet one which had among its causes the long anti-parliamentarian tradition of the German Reich. The article also discussed the problem of the modernisation of German society which the Third Reich brought about, probably more accidentally than consciously, and which became so important after the war. It was pointed out that as a result of Hitler's policy and strategy the Federal Republic of Germany was 'free from many of the handicaps that had affected the development of Prussian Germany down to 1933 or 1945', and could set up 'new standards of success for the second attempt at parliamentarianism in German history'.

These considerations and conclusions are by now fairly generally accepted by researchers, but have been criticised by some in the interests of differentiation and categorisation.

(1)   From this point of view it will be necessary once again to investigate thoroughly how far the modernisation due to the history of the Third Reich – which has already been pointed out by Ralf Dahrendorf (1961) and discussed more fully by David Schoenbaum (1966) – was a deliberate aim of Nazi foreign policy or rather a secondary, unintended expression of its historical effects and consequences. Following on Timothy Mason's studies, H. A. Winkler drew attention once more to the need for an ideologically critical attitude towards the claims and propaganda formulae of the Third Reich as regards the modernising and egalitarian effect of its revolutionary policy. As Winkler observes, 'the gradual erosion of the big estates and the closing down of inefficient small firms can no doubt be regarded as a partial modernisation of German society, but hardly as a social revolution'. Criticising the view that national socialism eliminated social differences, he continues: 'The term "social revolution" is still

less appropriate to conditions in the industrial field, where national socialism did not resolve class differences but only obscured them for a time.' On the other hand, Winkler emphasises the unintended effects of Nazism in the direction of modernisation. 'It was by its collapse that national socialism brought about a great social breach with the past. But for Germany's military defeat the economic power of the big landowners would scarcely have been radically broken, as it was in the Soviet occupation zone. The mass migration caused by the advance of the Red Army was also a source of irreversible social change . . . The relics of a pre-industrial age, who gave German society its distinctive stamp until 1945, are now largely relegated to the past. This is a fact of far wider historical range than any change in German society that took place during the Nazi period itself' (H. A. Winkler, 1977, 'Vom Mythos der Volksgemeinschaft', *Arch. f. SozG*, vol. XVII, p. 490).

(2)   Discussion continues, however, to a perhaps still more important extent than before, as to the categories by which the Third Reich is to be assessed in respect of its origin and its place in the history of the Prussian-German national state. Weighty arguments are used to challenge the assumption, which is often made explicitly or unconsciously, that the British road towards an industrial state and a parliamentary system is a parameter by which German history should be judged. In this connection it would certainly be legitimate to consider whether the concepts of 'Germany's separate way' and the 'belated nation' should not be reversed so as to emphasise their exceptional character in relation to the course of events in Britain, which were influenced by no historical precedent. Ernst Nolte, for instance, has forcefully expressed one aspect of this problem of historical judgement by the following observations, which are no doubt intended to present one side of the case rather than to sum up: 'Some recent accounts of the history of the Bismarckian Reich give the impression that the author is displeased by the fact that Bismarck wanted to preserve the power of the pre-industrial leaders, and that the forces of the *status quo* were opposed to the dynamism of the industrial world and the social changes it brought about. But one must once again step outside the German perspective with its implicit assumptions and put the question: In what European country did the "pre-industrial ruling class", that is, the nobility, ever relinquish its privileged position, voluntarily and *in toto* – but again, in what European country did that class ever intend or manage to call a halt to the "dynamics of industry"? . . . The right historical question and the correct perspective are rather: Did the social structure of the Bismarckian Reich essentially hinder the process of industrialisation, the fundamental importance and universality of which was not generally recognised at that time, and did the process entail comparatively great or small sacrifices? . . . There is probably no country in the world in which what we must now call the early process of industrialisation was accomplished so successfully and with so few sacrifices as in the German Empire between 1871 and 1914 . . . Thus the humanitarian argument fails to convince, and one might

be driven unexpectedly to the opposite conclusion, that the Empire failed because it did not industrialise completely or ruthlessly enough' (E. Nolte, 1977, 'Ideologie, Engagement, Perspektive', in his *Marxismus, Faschismus. Kalter Krieg. Vorträge und Aufsätze 1964–1976*, Stuttgart, p. 271).

No doubt it would not be difficult to raise objections to these remarks, which are necessarily couched in summary terms. For instance, it could be pointed out that the British and German élites reacted in a decisively different way to the claims of the modern age, despite undeniable similarities in the political and social history of the two countries. But what cannot be disputed is that the question of categories is a problem of the first rank in this connection. Together with it there must be a thorough re-examination of the question, still not answered empirically, of the importance in German history of the 'feudalisation of capitalism' and the argument concerning the long, or over-long, predominance of the landed aristocracy with its large estates. Meanwhile we may accept Fritz Stern's observation that the political cost of the domination of the big landowners was 'indeed staggering and included the disastrous ineptitude of Germany's diplomacy before 1914, the fatality of her wartime policies, the frenzied failure of Weimar, and her self-destruction under Hitler' (F. Stern, 1977, 'Prussia', in D. Spring, ed., *European Landed Elites in the 19th Century*, Baltimore, Md., and London, p. 64).

While the discussion of these methodical and practical problems is still in progress, the present state of research as regards the historical judgement to be passed on Hitler's Third Reich – a phenomenon *sui generis* between tradition and revolution, reaction and modernity – may be more or less summarised in K. D. Bracher's words. Although the European background and conditions of the Nazi dictatorship must never be lost sight of, 'Hitler is a German phenomenon ... The sharp discrepancy between idea and reality, intellectual radicalism and political backwardness in Germany during the nineteenth and twentieth centuries came to a head in Hitler's double revolution, the regime's absolute triumph in 1933 and total defeat in 1945. The nineteenth-century "German problem" was the breeding-ground of Hitler's ideas; despite their worldwide effects, Hitler was above all a German – and Austrian – phenomenon.' Then, approaching the problem on a wider basis, Bracher continues: 'This is an experiment and a warning for all nations and politicians ... The lesson must not be forgotten, misunderstood or misused: extreme political conceptions, held up as "final solutions" for all possible problems, can never serve human aims, but degrade mankind and its values into mere instruments of a power-crazy, destructive and barbaric regime. Today, in the face of old and new extremisms, Hitler's defeat and ruin must give us ground for hope that such extreme conceptions are doomed to failure whencesoever they come' (Bracher, 1976b, pp. 99–100).

Chronology

1933

30 Jan.	Hitler appointed Reich Chancellor.
27 Feb.	Reichstag fire.
28 Feb.	Presidential decree 'for the protection of the nation and state'.
5 Mar.	Reichstag election. Main results: NSDAP (Nazis) 43·9 per cent, DNVP (Nationalists) 8 per cent, Catholic Centre 11·2 per cent, SPD (Social Democrats) 18·3 per cent, KPD (Communists) 12·3 per cent.
13 Mar.	Goebbels appointed Reich Minister for Popular Enlightenment and Propaganda.
21 Mar.	Potsdam ceremony: 'Day of National Rising'.
23 Mar.	Law for Removing the Distress of People and Reich (Enabling Act).
31 Mar.	First law for *Gleichschaltung* of the *Länder* (constituent states).
1 Apr.	Organised boycott of Jewish shops.
7 Apr.	Second law for *Gleichschaltung* of the *Länder*: appointment of governors (*Reichsstatthalter*). Law for the Restoration of the Professional Civil Service.
2 May	Dissolution of trade unions.
10 May	Public burning of 'un-German writings' by Nazi student leaders (in Goebbels's presence) on the Opernplatz in Berlin.
June–July	(Self-)dissolution of all parties except the NSDAP.
14 July	Law forbidding the revival of parties.
20 July	Concordat between the Reich and the Vatican.
22 Sept.	Creation of the Reich Chamber of Culture.
29 Sept.	Law on Hereditary Farms.
4 Oct.	Press law (*Schriftleitergesetz*).
14 Oct.	Germany withdraws from the Disarmament Conference and from the League of Nations.
12 Nov.	Reichstag 'election' and plebiscite.

1934

20 Jan.	Law for the Organisation of National Labour.
26 Jan.	Non-aggression pact with Poland.
30 Jan.	Law for the Reconstitution of the Reich.
20 Apr.	Himmler appointed head of the Prussian Gestapo.
24 Apr.	Creation of the People's Court.
14–15 June	First meeting between Hitler and Mussolini at Venice.
17 June	Von Papen's speech at Marburg.
30 June	The 'Röhm revolt'.
25 July	Nazi coup in Austria; Chancellor Dollfuss murdered.
2 Aug.	Death of von Hindenburg. Hitler, as Führer, assumes the combined offices of President and Reich Chancellor. On the same day, the *Wehrmacht* swears a personal oath to him as its supreme commander.
19 Aug.	Plebiscite approving the law of 2 Aug.

1935

13 Jan.	Plebiscite in the Saar area: 91 per cent vote for return to the Reich.
16 Mar.	Reintroduction of conscription; Hitler denounces the military provisions of the treaty of Versailles.
11–14 Apr.	Stresa conference; resolution to oppose 'any unilateral denunciation of treaties'.
21 May	Hitler's Reichstag speech: 13-point 'peace programme'.
18 June	Anglo-German naval agreement.
26 June	Introduction of compulsory labour service.
15 Sept.	German Jews deprived of rights and subjected to discrimination by the Nuremberg Laws on Reich citizenship and 'for the protection of German blood and honour'.

1936

7 Mar.	In violation of the Locarno treaty, German troops occupy the Rhineland area demilitarised by the treaty of Versailles.
29 Mar.	Reichstag 'election': Hitler's policy approved by 99 per cent of voters.
11 July	German-Austrian agreement.
25–26 July	Hitler decides to intervene in the Spanish Civil War which broke out on the 17th.
1 Aug.	Opening of Olympic Games in Berlin.
24 Aug.	Introduction of two years' compulsory military service.
9 Sept.	Inauguration of Four-Year Plan announced at the Nuremberg party rally (8–14 Sept.).
25 Oct.	German-Italian treaty ('Berlin–Rome Axis').
25 Nov.	Anti-Comintern Pact between Germany and Japan.
1 Dec.	Membership of Hitler Youth made compulsory (*Staatsjugend*).

1937

30 Jan.	The Enabling Law extended for four years.
14 Mar.	Pope Pius XI's encyclical *Mit brennender Sorge* ('With deep anxiety').
25–28 Sept.	Mussolini visits Germany.
5 Nov.	Hitler addresses the three service chiefs and the Foreign Minister on his foreign-political aims (the 'Hossbach memorandum').
6 Nov.	Italy accedes to the Anti-Comintern Pact.
19 Nov.	Lord Halifax visits Hitler on the Obersalzberg.
26 Nov.	Schacht replaced as Reich Economic Minister by Walther Funk.

1938

4 Feb.	Dismissal of the War Minister, von Blomberg, and the army commander-in-chief, von Fritsch. Hitler becomes supreme commander of the *Wehrmacht* (defence forces). The *Oberkommando* (high command) of the *Wehrmacht* set up under Gen. Keitel. Von Neurath replaced as Foreign Minister by von Ribbentrop.
12 Feb.	The Austrian Chancellor von Schuschnigg visits Hitler on the Obersalzberg.
12 Mar.	German troops enter Austria.
13 Mar.	Law 'reuniting Austria with the Reich' (the *Anschluss*).
10 Apr.	Plebiscite confirming the *Anschluss*.

24 Apr.	The Sudeten German Party under Konrad Henlein demands autonomy for the Sudeten area of Czechoslovakia.
20 May	Czechoslovak mobilisation (the 'weekend crisis').
30 May	Hitler's directive to the *Wehrmacht* for the destruction of Czechoslovakia.
18 Aug.	Resignation of Gen. Beck, chief of the general staff.
15 Sept.	Prime Minister Neville Chamberlain flies to Berchtesgaden to confer with Hitler on the Sudeten crisis.
22–24 Sept.	Chamberlain–Hitler conference at Bad Godesberg on the Sudeten crisis.
26 Sept.	Hitler, speaking at the Sportpalast in Berlin, gives an assurance that the Sudetenland is his last territorial demand in Europe.
Sept.	Members of the conservative opposition, especially army chiefs, plan an anti-Hitler coup, which, however, comes to nothing.
29 Sept.	Munich conference: Hitler, Mussolini, Chamberlain and Daladier agree as to the cession of the Sudetenland to Germany.
30 Sept.	Hitler–Chamberlain declaration: 'peace in our time'.
1 Oct.	German troops begin to occupy the Sudeten area.
21 Oct.	Hitler's first directive on 'settling what is left of Czechoslovakia'.
7 Nov.	Herschel Grynszpan, a Jewish refugee, shoots Ernst vom Rath, a junior diplomat in the German embassy in Paris. Vom Rath dies two days later.
9 Nov.	'Night of broken glass': organised excesses against Jews throughout Germany.
12 Nov.– 3 Dec.	Collective punishment and special measures against German Jews.
6 Dec.	Franco-German declaration of non-aggression signed in Paris.

1939

20 Jan.	Schacht dismissed from presidency of the Reichsbank.
30 Jan.	Hitler 'prophesies' to the Greater Germanic Reichstag that the Jewish race in Europe will be destroyed in the event of a world war.
15 Mar.	German troops invade Czechoslovakia.
16 Mar.	Creation of the Reich Protectorate of Bohemia and Moravia.
21 Mar.	Hitler's demands to Poland: the return of Danzig and an ex territorial autobahn and railway across the Corridor. He offers a long-term guarantee of the German-Polish frontier.
23 Mar.	Slovakia places itself under the 'protection' of the Reich.
27 Mar.	Spain accedes to the Anti-Comintern pact.
31 Mar.	British and French guarantee of Polish independence.
22 May	German-Italian military alliance ('Pact of Steel').
23 Aug.	German-Soviet non-aggression pact, with secret protocol (the 'Hitler-Stalin' pact).
25 Aug.	Hitler's 'generous offer' to Britain for co-operation after settlement of the dispute with Poland.
27 Aug.	Food rationing in Germany.
1 Sept.	German invasion of Poland.
3 Sept.	Britain and France declare war on Germany.
27 Sept.	Surrender of Warsaw. Reich Central Security Office (RHSA) set up.
6 Oct.	Hitler's 'peace appeal' to the Western powers.

7 Oct.	Himmler appointed 'Reich Commissar for the Consolidation of German Nationhood'.
9 Oct.	Hitler's first directive for the Western campaign.
12 Oct.	Hans Frank appointed governor-general of rump Poland (the *Generalgouvernement*).
Oct.	Führer decree on the euthanasia programme, backdated to 1 Sept.
8 Nov.	Georg Elser's attempt on Hitler's life in the Bürgerbräu cellar at Munich.

1940

11 Feb.	German–Soviet economic agreement.
1 Mar.	Hitler's first directive for the occupation of Denmark and Norway (operation 'Weser exercise').
18 Mar.	Hitler and Mussolini meet at the Brenner Pass.
9 Apr.	Occupation of Denmark. Norway invaded.
10 May	Invasion of Belgium, The Netherlands, Luxemburg and France.
15 May	Surrender of Dutch forces.
28 May	Surrender of Belgium.
10 June	Italy enters the war. Surrender of Norwegian forces.
18 June	Hitler and Mussolini meet in Munich.
22 June	Franco-German armistice signed at Compiègne.
16 July	Hitler orders preparations for the invasion of Britain (operation Sea-Lion).
19 July	Hitler's Reichstag speech: final 'peace appeal' to Britain.
31 July	Hitler's conference at the Berghof with von Brauchitsch, Halder, Keitel, Jodl and others. His intention to attack the Soviet Union begins to take shape.
13 Aug.	Battle of Britain begins.
27 Sept.	Tripartite Pact signed by Germany, Italy and Japan.
4 Oct.	Hitler and Mussolini meet at the Brenner.
12 Oct.	Preparations for 'Sea-Lion' suspended.
23 Oct.	Hitler meets Franco at Hendaye.
24 Oct.	Hitler meets Pétain and Laval at Montoire.
28 Oct.	Italy invades Greece. Hitler and Mussolini meet at Florence.
12–13 Nov.	Molotov in Berlin.
18 Dec.	Hitler signs directive No. 21 for operation Barbarossa (invasion of the Soviet Union): preparations to be completed by 15 May 1941.

1941

19–20 Jan.	Hitler and Mussolini meet at the Berghof.
2 Mar.	German troops enter Bulgaria.
30 Mar.	Hitler, addressing over 200 senior officers, announces the principles of the 'Commissar order' (6 June 1941) as part of the planned 'war of annihilation' against the Soviet Union.
31 Mar.	Rommel's 'Africa Corps' in action in Cyrenaica.
6 Apr.	German invasion of Yugoslavia and Greece.
17 Apr.	Yugoslavia surrenders.
23 Apr.	Greece surrenders.
10 May	Hitler's deputy Rudolf Hess flies to Scotland.
12 May	Martin Bormann succeeds Hess as head of the party chancellery.
13 May	Hitler's decree, in anticipation of 'Barbarossa', sanctioning crimes by the military against the Soviet civil population.

2 June	Hitler and Mussolini meet at the Brenner.
6 June	The 'Commissar order' lays down directives for the treatment of political commissars of the Red Army.
11 June	Draft of 'Führer directive No. 32' by the *Wehrmacht* planning staff, on strategy to be followed after the completion of 'Barbarossa'. Not signed by Hitler.
22 June	Invasion of the Soviet Union. 'Task forces' (*Einsatzgruppen*) of the SD (security service) and Sipo (security police) begin the systematic extermination of Jews in the conquered Eastern territories.
June	Himmler, invoking Hitler's authority, orders Hoess, commandant of the camp at Auschwitz (Oświęcim), to prepare gas chambers.
8 July	Hitler's decision to 'raze Leningrad and Moscow to the ground'.
14 July	Confident of victory over the Soviet Union, Hitler orders the emphasis in arms production to be shifted from army needs to those of the navy and air force, in preparation for the next phase of the war against Britain and America. To the Japanese ambassador Oshima he proposes a general offensive alliance for the destruction of the Soviet Union and the USA.
15 July	In accordance with an order from Himmler dated 24 June, Meyer-Hetlich, chief planning officer of the Reich Commissariat for the Consolidation of German Nationhood, submits the draft of a 'General Plan for the Eastern Territories' (cf. 12 June 1942).
16 July	In the presence of Rosenberg, Göring, Keitel, Lammers and Bormann, Hitler proclaims his political objectives in the East, including the parcelling of the Soviet Union into four Reich commissariats.
17 July	New Ministry for the Occupied Eastern Territories set up under Rosenberg; Himmler made responsible for the 'political security' of the area.
21 July	Hitler informs Kvaternik, the Croatian Defence Minister, of his intention to eliminate Jews from Europe.
31 July	Heydrich instructed to make plans for a 'general settlement of the Jewish question in Europe'.
Aug.	The 'euthanasia programme' is suspended and reduced in scope.
19 Sept.	Jews in Germany obliged to wear the Star of David.
19 Nov.	As the advance in the East comes to a standstill, Hitler concedes that 'the two groups of adversaries cannot destroy each other'.
1 Dec.	General Field Marshal von Bock, commander-in-chief of Central Army Group in Russia, reports that 'the troops' energy will soon be completely exhausted'. German advance halted before Moscow.
Dec.	Gassing of Jews begins in the camp at Chelmno.
7 Dec.	Hitler's 'Night and Fog' decree.
11 Dec.	Germany and Italy declare war on the USA. Attacked by the Japanese at Pearl Harbor on 7 Dec., the USA had declared war on Japan on the 8th.
19 Dec.	Hitler takes over personal command of the army.
1942	
6 Jan.	President Roosevelt declares that it is America's war aim to destroy German militarism.

14 Jan.	End of the 'Arcadia' conference at Washington between Churchill and Roosevelt: the Allied war effort to be concentrated on defeating Germany in Europe.
18 Jan.	Military agreement between Germany, Italy and Japan: the respective spheres of operations to be divided at longitude 70° East.
20 Jan.	At the Wannsee conference, attended by senior officials of the principal ministries, Heydrich, head of the RSHA, announces the 'final solution of the Jewish question' in Europe by 'evacuation' eastward and 'other measures'.
8 Feb.	Fritz Todt, Minister for Arms and Munitions since 17 Mar. 1940, is killed in an accident and succeeded by Albert Speer.
23 Feb.	Stalin's Order of the Day No. 55 declares that 'Hitlers come and go, but the German people and the German state remain'.
21 Mar.	Gauleiter Sauckel appointed commissioner-general for labour allocation.
26 Apr.	The Reichstag acknowledges Hitler as 'supreme judicial authority'.
29–30 Apr.	Hitler and Mussolini meet at the Berghof.
7 May	Hitler's decree for the unified direction of arms production.
26 May	Heydrich (now deputy Reich Protector of Bohemia and Moravia) attacked by Czech resisters in Prague. He dies of his wounds on 4 June.
30–31 May	Major British air raid on Cologne (first thousand-bomber attack on a German city).
10 June	Czech village of Lidice destroyed in retaliation for Heydrich's death.
12 June	Himmler approves the 'General Plan for the Eastern Territories' (deportation of Poles, Czechs, Ukrainians and Byelorussians to Siberia).
3 July	The German-Italian advance in North Africa comes to a stop at El Alamein, 65 miles west of Alexandria.
21–22 July	Beginning of the systematic deportation of Jews from the Warsaw ghetto (who number some 350,000 in all) to the extermination camp at Treblinka.
20 Aug.	Roland Freisler appointed president of the People's Court. His predecessor, Otto Thierack, becomes Minister of Justice in place of Franz Gürtner, who died on 29 Jan. 1941.
25 Aug.	Hitler gives orders for the construction of the Atlantic Line.
3 Nov.	The Africa Corps begins to retreat following the British victory at El Alamein.
11 Nov.	German troops enter the hitherto unoccupied zone of France as a counter-move to the Allied landing in North Africa on 7–8 Nov. (Operation Torch).
19 Nov.	Soviet counter-offensive at Stalingrad.
23 Nov.	Stalingrad encircled by the Red Army.

1943

13 Jan.	Hitler's decree on the liability of men and women for defence duties.
14–25 Jan.	Casablanca conference: Roosevelt and Churchill demand 'unconditional surrender'.
27 Jan.	Sauckel, commissioner-general for labour, issues order for 'total war'.
31 Jan.–2 Feb.	Surrender of the Sixth Army at Stalingrad.

11 Feb.	School pupils aged 15 and over are called up for auxiliary service with the air force.
18 Feb.	Goebbels announces 'total war' in a speech at the Sportpalast in Berlin. Arrest of Hans and Sophie Scholl, leaders of the 'White Rose' resistance group of Munich students.
27 Feb.	Jews working on arms production in Berlin are deported to Auschwitz.
13 Mar.	Unsuccessful attempt on Hitler's life by the military resistance movement.
21 Mar.	A second unsuccessful attempt on Hitler's life in Berlin.
8–9 Apr.	Hitler and Mussolini meet at Klessheim.
13 Apr.	The mass graves of over 4,100 Polish officers, murdered by the Soviet NKVD in the spring of 1940, are discovered by the Germans at Katyń near Smolensk.
19 Apr.	Uprising in the Warsaw ghetto, savagely suppressed; resistance ceases on 16 May.
19 May	Berlin declared 'cleared of Jews' (*judenrein*).
24 May	Turning-point in the U-boat war: cessation of attacks on Atlantic convoys.
10 June	Beginning of the combined Anglo-American bombing offensive against Germany, decided on at Casablanca (14–25 Jan.).
5 July	Beginning of operation 'Citadel' (German attack on the Soviet salient at Kursk).
10 July	Allied landing in Sicily.
12 July	Red Army opens its summer offensive (against Orel).
12–13 July	'National Committee for a Free Germany' set up at Krasnogorsk near Moscow.
13 July	Failure of operation 'Citadel'.
19 July	Hitler and Mussolini meet at Feltre.
24 July– 3 Aug.	Large areas of Hamburg destroyed by bombing.
25 July	Fall of Mussolini and collapse of the Italian fascist regime.
6 Aug.	Goebbels announces partial evacuation of the population of Berlin.
14–24 Aug.	Allied summit conference at Quebec; plans for the invasion of France.
24 Aug.	Himmler becomes Reich Minister of the Interior.
2 Sept.	Hitler's decree for the concentration of war production; Ministry for Arms and Munitions transformed into Reich Ministry for Armaments and War Production.
8 Sept.	Publication of the armistice (concluded secretly on 3 Sept.) between the Allies and the new Italian regime. German troops begin to occupy northern and central Italy.
19–30 Oct.	Moscow conference of foreign ministers (Molotov, Eden, Hull) on postwar planning.
28 Nov.– 1 Dec.	Tehran conference (Roosevelt, Churchill, Stalin). War aims and planning for the future of Germany. Stalin informed of the date set for the invasion of France (1 May 1944).
22 Dec.	Introduction of National Socialist Leadership Officers (*Führungsoffiziere*).

1944

19 Mar.	German troops occupy Hungary.
6 June	Allied landing in northern France.
10 June	The French village of Oradour-sur-Glane destroyed and its inhabitants murdered as a reprisal for atrocities by French partisans.
22 June	Opening of Soviet summer campaign against Central Army Group.
3 July	Collapse of Central Army Group.
20 July	Von Stauffenberg's attempt on Hitler's life. Abortive coups in Berlin and Paris.
23 July	The 'Hitler salute' made compulsory in the army.
28 July	Speer's second memorandum (the first was dated 30 June) informing Hitler of the desperate state of synthetic fuel production due to Allied bombing of hydrogenation plants since 12 Apr. 1944.
1 Aug.	Hitler's decree on the arrest of offenders' kinsfolk (*Sippenhaft*). Uprising of the Polish Home Army in Warsaw.
23 Aug.	Change of regime in Romania, which surrenders to the Red Army.
8 Sept.	Bulgaria declares war on Germany.
11 Sept.	American troops reach the German frontier.
11–16 Sept.	Second allied summit conference at Quebec. Signature of first protocol delimiting zones in Germany.
25 Sept.	Hitler's decree (promulgated on 18 Oct.) calling up all able-bodied men between 16 and 60 for the militia (*Volkssturm*).
2 Oct.	Surrender of the Home Army in Warsaw.
end Oct.	End of gassing operations at Auschwitz.
26 Nov.	Himmler's order for destruction of the Auschwitz crematoria.
16–24 Dec.	Hitler's Ardennes offensive.

1945

3 Jan.	Allied counter-offensive in the Ardennes.
12 Jan.	Red Army crosses the Vistula.
14 Jan.	Soviet advance into East Prussia.
23 Jan.	Soviet troops reach the Oder in Silesia.
4–11 Feb.	Yalta conference, including decisions on Germany's future.
12 Feb.	Women conscripted as auxiliaries to the militia.
13–14 Feb.	Allied bombing of Dresden.
7 Mar.	US troops cross the Rhine at Remagen.
19 Mar.	Hitler's scorched-earth ('Nero') order; nullified in practice by orders of the Wehrmacht high command dated 30 Mar. and 4 Apr.
2 Apr.	Appeal to form 'Werewolf' units.
12 Apr.	Roosevelt dies suddenly and is succeeded by Harry S. Truman.
25 Apr.	American and Soviet troops meet at Torgau on the Elbe.
30 Apr.	Hitler commits suicide.
2 May	Dönitz succeeds Hitler as 'Reich President', with headquarters at Flensburg.
5 May	'Provisional government' formed under Count Schwerin von Krosigk.
7–8/9 May	German surrender signed at Reims and Berlin-Karlshorst. Cessation of hostilities in Europe.
23 May	All members of the Dönitz government and the *Wehrmacht* high command arrested and imprisoned at Flensburg-Mürwik.

List of Principal Works Cited

In cases where English translations of German works exist, these have been cited in the present edition in preference to the originals. For abbreviations see p. xii.

Abendroth, W. (ed.) (1968), *Faschismus und Kapitalismus. Theorien über die sozialen Ursprünge und die Funktion des Faschismus*, 3rd edn, Frankfurt am Main.

Adam, U. D. (1972), *Judenpolitik im Dritten Reich*, Düsseldorf.

Aigner, D. (1978), 'Hitler und die Weltherrschaft', in W. Michalka (ed.), *Nationalsozialistische Aussenpolitik*, Darmstadt, pp. 49–69.

Arendt, H. (1958), *The Origins of Totalitarianism*, New York and London.

Bettelheim, C. (1946), *L'Économie allemande sous le Nazisme*, Paris.

Binion, R. (1976), *Hitler among the Germans*, New York.

Birkenfeld, W. (1964), *Der synthetische Treibstoff 1933–1945. Ein Beitrag zur nationalsozialistischen Wirtschafts- und Rüstungspolitik*, Göttingen.

Bollmus, R. (1970), *Das Amt Rosenberg und seine Gegner. Studien zum Machtkampf im nationalsozialistischen Herrschaftssystem*, Stuttgart.

Bracher, K. D., with W. Sauer and G. Schulz (1962), *Die nationalsozialistische Machtergreifung. Studien zur Errichtung des totalitären Herrschaftssystems in Deutschland 1933/34*, 2nd edn, Cologne.

Bracher, K. D. (1970), *The German Dictatorship. The Origins, Structure and Effects of National Socialism*, New York.

Bracher, K. D. (1971), *Die Auflösung der Weimarer Republik. Eine Studie zum Problem des Machtverfalls in der Demokratie*, 5th edn, Villingen.

Bracher, K. D. (1973), *Der Faschismus. Sonderbeitrag aus Meyers Enzyklopädischem Lexikon*, Mannheim, pp. 547–51.

Bracher, K. D. (1976a), *Die Krise Europas 1917–1975*. Propyläen-Geschichte Europas, Vol. 6, Berlin.

Bracher, K. D. (1976b), *Zeitgeschichtliche Kontroversen – Um Faschismus, Totalitarismus, Demokratie*, Munich.

Bracher, K. D. (1977), 'Zeitgeschichte im Wandel der Interpretationen. Zur Neuausgabe von K. D. Erdmann, Die Zeit der Weltkriege', *HZ*, vol. 225, pp. 635–55.

Broszat, M. (1970), 'Soziale Motivation und Führer-Bindung des Nationalsozialismus', *VfZg*, vol. 18, pp. 392–409.

Broszat, M. (1977), 'Hitler und die Genesis der "Endlösung". Aus Anlass der Thesen von David Irving', *VfZg*, vol. 25, pp. 739–75.

Broszat, M. (1981), *The Hitler State. The Foundation and Development of the Internal Structure of the Third Reich*, London.

Bullock, A. (1962), *Hitler: A Study in Tyranny*, London; 1st edn 1952.

Czichon, E. (1968), 'Das Primat der Industrie im Kartell der nationalsozialistischen Macht', *Das Argument*, Berlin, vol. 10, pp. 168–92.

Dahrendorf, R. (1961), 'Demokratie und Sozialstruktur in Deutschland', in his *Gesellschaft und Freiheit. Zur soziologischen Analyse der Gegenwart*, Munich, pp. 260–99.

Dawidowicz, L. (1975), *The War against the Jews 1933–1945*, New York.

Dehio, L. (1948), *Gleichgewicht oder Hegemonie. Betrachtungen über ein Grundproblem der europäischen Staatengeschichte*, Krefeld, n.d.

Dehio, L. (1961), 'Der Zusammenhang der preussischdeutschen Geschichte 1640–1945', in Clément, A., *et al.*, *Gibt es ein deutsches Geschichtsbild?*, Würzburg, pp. 65–91.

Deuerlein, E. (1969), *Hitler. Eine politische Biographie*, Munich.

Dülffer, J. (1967), 'Bonapartism, fascism and National Socialism', *JCH*, vol. 11, pp. 109–28.

Ehlers, D. (1964), *Technik und Moral einer Verschwörung*, Frankfurt am Main.

Eichholtz, D. (1969), *Geschichte der deutschen Kriegswirtschaft 1939–45*, Vol. 1, 1939–41, Berlin (East).

Eichholtz, D., and Gossweiler, K. (1968), 'Noch einmal: Politik und Wirtschaft 1933–1945', *Das Argument*, Berlin, vol. 10, pp. 168–92.

Erbe, R. (1958), *Die nationalsozialistische Wirtschaftspolitik 1933–1939 im Lichte der modernen Theorie*, Zurich.

Erdmann, K. D. (1976a), 'Deutschland unter der Herrschaft des Nationalsozialismus und der Zweite Weltkrieg', in his *Die Zeit der Weltkriege*, Stuttgart.

Erdmann, K. D. (1976b), 'Nationalsozialismus-Faschismus-Totalitarismus', *GiWuU*, vol. 27, pp. 457–69.

Farquharson, J. E. (1976), *The Plough and the Swastika. The NSDAP and Agriculture in Germany 1928–1945*, London and Beverly Hills, Calif.

de Felice, R. (1975), *Il Fascismo* (interview with M. A. Leeden); German trans., Stuttgart, 1977.

Fest, J. C. (1974a), *Hitler*, New York and London.

Fest, J. C. (1974b), introduction to Smith, B. F., and Peterson, A. F. (eds), *H. Himmler, Geheimreden, 1933 bis 1945*, Berlin and Frankfurt am Main.

Fischer, W. (1968), *Deutsche Wirtschaftspolitik 1918–1945*, Opladen.

Forstmeier, F., and Volkmann, H.-E. (eds) (1975), *Wirtschaft und Rüstung am Vorabend des Zweiten Weltkrieges*, Düsseldorf.

Fraenkel, E. (1941), *The Dual State*, New York.

Friedrich, C. J., and Brzezinski, Z. K. (1956), *Totalitarian Dictatorship and Autocracy*, Cambridge, Mass.; rev. edn 1965.

Georg, E. (1963), *Die wirtschaftlichen Unternehmungen der SS*, Stuttgart.

Haffner, S. (1979), *The Meaning of Hitler*, London.

Hassell, U. von (1947), *The von Hassell Diaries, 1938–1944*, New York and London.

Hauner, M. (1978), 'Did Hitler Want a World Dominion?', *JCH*, vol. 13, pp. 15–32.

Heiden, K. (1936–7), *Adolf Hitler. Das Zeitalter der Verantwortungslosigkeit*, 2 vols, Zurich; first vol. translated as *Hitler: A Biography*, London, 1936.

Hennig, E. (1973), *Thesen zur deutschen Sozial- und Wirtschaftsgeschichte 1933 bis 1938*, Frankfurt am Main.

Heuss, Th. (1932), *Hitlers Weg*, repr. with introduction by Jäckel, E., Stuttgart, 1968.

Hildebrand, K. (1969), *Vom Reich zum Weltreich. Hitler, NSDAP und koloniale Frage 1919–1945*, Munich.

Hildebrand, K. (1973), 'Hitlers Ort in der Geschichte des preussisch-deutschen Nationalstaates', *HZ*, vol. 217, pp. 584–632.

Hildebrand, K. (1974), 'Innenpolitische Antriebskräfte der nationalsozialistischen Aussenpolitik', repr. in Michalka, W. (ed.), *Nationalsozialistische Aussenpolitik*, Darmstadt, 1978, pp. 175–97.

Hildebrand, K. (1976), 'Hitler. Rassen- contra Weltpolitik. Ergebnisse und Desiderate der Forschung', *MGM*, vol. 19, pp. 207–24.

Hildebrand, K. (1978), 'Die ostpolitischen Vorstellungen im deutschen Widerstand', *GiWuU*, vol. 29, pp. 213–41.

Hill, L. E. (ed.) (1974), *Die Weizsäcker-Papiere 1933–1950*, Berlin.

Hillgruber, A. (1965a), *Hitlers Strategie. Politik und Kriegführung 1940–1941*, Frankfurt am Main.

Hillgruber, A. (1965b), 'Der Faktor Amerika in Hitlers Strategie 1938–1941', repr. in his *Deutsche Grossmacht- und Weltpolitik im 19. und 20. Jahrhundert*, Düsseldorf, 1977, pp. 197–222.

Hillgruber, A. (1967), *Deutschlands Rolle in der Vorgeschichte der beiden Weltkriege*, Göttingen.

Hillgruber, A. (1972), 'Die "Endlösung" und das deutsche Ostimperium als Kernstück des rassenideologischen Programms des Nationalsozialismus', repr. in his *Deutsche Grossmacht- und Weltpolitik im 19. und 20. Jahrhundert*, Düsseldorf, 1977, pp. 252–75.

Hillgruber, A. (1973a), 'Zum Forschungsstand über die Geschichte des National-sozialismus', in *Auswärtiges Amt – Informationsdienst für die Auslandsvertretungen –* 240–312.73.

Hillgruber, A. (1973b), 'Grundzüge der nationalsozialistischen Aussenpolitik 1933–1945', *Saec.*, vol. XXIV, pp. 328–45.

Hillgruber, A. (1974), 'Kontinuität und Diskontinuität in der deutschen Aussenpolitik von Bismarck bis Hitler', in his *Grossmachtpolitik und Militarismus im 20. Jahrhundert. 3 Beiträge zum Kontinuitätsproblem*, Düsseldorf, pp. 11–36.

Hillgruber, A. (1977), *Gutachten zur nationalsozialistischen Judenverfolgung auf dem Territorium der Sowjetunion (betr. Strafverfahren gegen Manfred R. K. Roeder)* (legal opinion, ref. Js 175/77 (KLs)).

Hillgruber, A. (1978), 'Tendenzen, Ergebnisse und Perspektiven der gegenwärtigen Hitler-Forschung', *HZ*, vol. 226, pp. 600–21.

Hofer, W. (1955), *War Premeditated 1939*, London; rev. German edn 1964, Frankfurt am Main.

Hofer, W., Calic, E., Stephan, K., and Zipfel, F. (eds) (1972), *Der Reichstagsbrand*, Berlin.

Hofer, W., and Graf, Chr. (1976), 'Neue Quellen zum Reichstagsbrand', *GWuU*, vol. 27, pp. 65–88.

Hofer, W., and Michaelis, H. (1965), *Deutsche Geschichte der neuesten Zeit von Bismarcks Entlassung bis zur Gegenwart, Part II: Von 1933–1945*, Frankfurt am Main.

Hüttenberger, P. (1977), 'Vorüberlegungen zum "Widerstandsbegriff" ', in Kocka, J. (ed.), *Theorien in der Praxis des Historikers*, Göttingen, pp. 117–34 (discussion, pp. 134–9).

Irving, D. (1977), *Hitler's War*, New York; previously published (1975) as *Hitler und seine Feldherren*, Frankfurt am Main.

Jäckel, E. (1969), *Hitlers Weltanschauung. Entwurf einer Herrschaft*, Tübingen.

Jäckel, E. (1977), 'Rückblick auf die sogenannte Hitler-Welle', *GWuU*, vol. 28, pp. 695–710.

Jacobsen, H.-A. (1968), *Nationalsozialistische Aussenpolitik 1933–1938*, Frankfurt am Main.

Jasper, G. (1962), 'Über die Ursachen des zweiten Weltkrieges: Zu den Büchern von A. J. P. Taylor und David L. Hoggan', *VfZg*, vol. 10, pp. 311–40.

Kele, M. H. (1972), *Nazis and Workers. National Socialist Appeals to German Labor 1919–1939*, Chapel Hill, NC.

Kessel, E. (1961), 'Adolf Hitler und der Verrat am Preussentum', in *Aus Politik und Zeitgeschichte*, supplement to the weekly *Das Parlament*, 15 Nov. 1961, pp. 649–61.

Kuhn, A. (1973), *Das faschistische Herrschaftssystem und die moderne Gesellschaft*, Hamburg.

Loock, H.-D. (1970), *Quisling, Rosenberg und Terboven. Zur Vorgeschichte und Geschichte der nationalsozialistischen Revolution in Norwegen*, Stuttgart.

Mann, G. (1961), *Deutsche Geschichte 1919–1945*, Frankfurt am Main.

Martin, B. (1976), *Friedensinitiativen und Machtpolitik im Zweiten Weltkrieg 1939–1942*, 2nd edn, Düsseldorf.

Maser, W. (1973), *Hitler: Legend, Myth and Reality*, New York.

Mason, T. W. (1966), 'Der Primat der Politik – Politik und Wirtschaft im Nationalsozialismus', *Das Argument*, vol. 8, pp. 473–94.

Mason, T. W. (1968), 'Primat der Industrie? – Eine Erwiderung', *Das Argument*, vol. 10, pp. 193–209.

Mason, T. W. (1975), *Arbeiterklasse und Volksgemeinschaft. Dokumente und Materialien zur deutschen Arbeiterpolitik 1936–1939*, Düsseldorf.

Mason, T. W. (1977), *Sozialpolitik im Dritten Reich. Arbeiterklasse und Volksgemeinschaft*, Opladen (revised version of the introduction to preceding item).

Meinecke, F. (1950), *The German Catastrophe: Reflections and Recollections*, Cambridge, Mass., and London.

Messerschmidt, M. (1969), *Die Wehrmacht im NS-Staat. Zeit der Indoktrination*, Hamburg.

Michalka, W. (1976a), 'Die nationalsozialistische Aussenpolitik im Zeichen eines "Konzeptionen-Pluralismus". Fragestellungen und Forschungsaufgaben', in Funke, M. (ed.), *Hitler, Deutschland und die Mächte. Materialien zur Aussenpolitik des Dritten Reiches*, Düsseldorf, pp. 46–62.

Michalka, W. (1976b), *Joachim von Ribbentrop und die deutsche Englandpolitik 1933–1940. Studien zur aussenpolitischen Konzeptionendiskussion im Dritten Reich* (thesis), Mannheim.

Michalka, W. (1978), 'Wege der Hitler-Forschung: Problemkreise, Methoden und Ergebnisse. Eine Zwischenbilanz', *Quaderni di storia* (Bari), vol. 8, pp. 157–90, and vol. 9 (1979).

Moltmann, G. (1961), 'Weltherrschaftsideen Hitlers', in *Europa und Übersee. Festschrift für E. Zechlin*, Hamburg, pp. 197–240.

Mommsen, H. (1971), 'Nationalsozialismus', in *Sowjetsystem und demokratische Gesellschaft. Eine vergleichende Enzyklopädie*, Freiburg, vol. 4, cols 695–713.

Mommsen, H. (1972a), 'The Reichstag fire and its political consequences', in Holborn, H. (ed.), *Republic to Reich: The Making of the Nazi Revolution*, New York.

Mommsen, H. (1972b), 'Die Auflösung der Weimarer Republik und die nationalsozialistische Machteroberung', in 'Faschistische Diktatur in Deutschland. Historische Grundlagen – gesellschaftliche Voraussetzungen – politische Struktur', in *Politische Bildung* (Munich), vol. 5, pp. 37–52.

Mommsen, H. (1976), 'Ausnahmezustand als Herrschaftstechnik des NS-Regimes', in Funke, M. (ed.), *Hitler, Deutschland und die Mächte. Materialien zur Aussenpolitik des Dritten Reiches*, Düsseldorf, pp. 30–45.

Mommsen, W. J. (1970/1), 'Das nationalsozialistische Herrschaftssystem', *Jahrbuch der Universität Düsseldorf*, pp. 417–30.

Müller, Chr. (1970), *Oberst i. G. Stauffenberg*, 2nd edn, Düsseldorf.

Müller, K.-J. (1969), *Das Heer und Hitler. Armee und nationalsozialistisches Regime 1933–1940*, Stuttgart.

Neumann, F. (1944), *Behemoth: The Structure and Practice of National Socialism*, New York; 1st edn, 1942.

Nolte, E. (1965), *The Three Faces of Fascism: Action Française, Italian Fascism, National Socialism*, London.

Nolte, E. (1968), *Die Krise des liberalen Systems und die faschistischen Bewegungen*, Munich.

Petzina, D. (1968), *Autarkiepolitik im Dritten Reich. Der nationalsozialistische Vierjahresplan*, Stuttgart.

Petzina, D. (1977), *Die deutsche Wirtschaft in der Zwischenkriegszeit*, Wiesbaden.

Plum, G. (1972), 'Widerstandsbewegungen', in *Sowjetsystem und demokratische Gesellschaft. Eine vergleichende Enzyklopädie*, Freiburg im Breisgau, vol. 6, cols 961–83.

Rauschning, H. (1939a), *Germany's Revolution of Destruction*, London.

Rauschning, H. (1939b), *Hitler Speaks*, London

Reinhardt, K. (1972), *Die Wende vor Moskau. Das Scheitern der Strategie Hitlers im Winter 1941/42*, Stuttgart.

Rich, N. (1973–4), *Hitler's War Aims*, New York (2 vols).

Ritter, G. (1948), *Europa und die deutsche Frage. Betrachtungen über die geschichtliche Eigenart des deutschen Staatsdenkens*, Munich.

Ritter, G. (1958), *The German Resistance. Carl Goerdeler's Struggle against Tyranny*, London.

Röhl, J. C. G. (ed.) (1970), *From Bismarck to Hitler. The Problem of Continuity in German History*, London.

Roon, G. van (1971), *German Resistance to Hitler: Count von Moltke and the Kreisau Circle*, London.

Rothfels, H. (1962), *The German Opposition to Hitler. An Appraisal*, Chicago.

Schärer, M. R. (1975), *Deutsche Annexionspolitik im Westen. Die Wiedereingliederung Eupen-Malmedys im Zweiten Weltkrieg*, Frankfurt am Main.

Schieder, Th. (1970), 'Das Deutsche Reich in seinen nationalen und universalen Beziehungen 1871 bis 1945' in Schieder, Th., and Deuerlein, E. (eds), *Reichsgründung 1870/71. Tatsachen, Kontroversen, Interpretationen*, Stuttgart, pp. 422–54.

Schieder, Th. (1972), *Hermann Rauschnings 'Gespräche mit Hitler' als Geschichtsquelle*, Opladen.

Schieder, W. (1968), 'Faschismus', in *Sowjetsystem und demokratische Gesellschaft. Eine vergleichende Enzyklopädie*, Freiburg im Breisgau, vol. 2, cols 438–77.

Schieder, W. (1976), 'Spanischer Bürgerkrieg und Vierjahresplan. Zur Struktur nationalsozialistischer Aussenpolitik', in Schieder, W., and Dipper, Chr. (eds), *Der Spanische Bürgerkrieg in der internationalen Politik (1936–1939)*, Munich, pp. 162–90.

Schleunes, K. A. (1970), *The Twisted Road to Auschwitz. Nazi Policy towards German Jews, 1933–1939*, Urbana, Ill.

Schmitthenner, W., and Buchheim, H. (eds) (1970), *The German Resistance to Hitler*, London.

Schoenbaum, D. (1966), *Hitler's Social Revolution: Class and Status in Nazi Germany 1933–1939*, New York.

Scholder, K. (1977), *Die Kirchen und das Dritte Reich*, Vol. 1: *Vorgeschichte und Zeit der Illusionen 1918–1934*, Frankfurt am Main.

Schulz, G. (1974), *Faschismus-Nationalsozialismus. Versionen und theoretische Kontroversen 1922–1972*, Frankfurt am Main.

Schulz, G. (1975), *Aufstieg des Nationalsozialismus. Krise und Revolution in Deutschland*, Berlin and Frankfurt am Main.

Schulz, G. (1976), *Deutschland seit dem Ersten Weltkrieg 1918–1945*, Göttingen.

Schumann, W., and Nestler, L. (eds) (1975), *Weltherrschaft im Visier. Dokumente zu den Europa- und Weltherrschaftsplänen des deutschen Imperialismus von der Jahrhundertwende bis Mai 1945*, Berlin (East).

Schweitzer, A. (1965), *Big Business in the Third Reich*, 2nd edn, Bloomington, Ind.

Smith, B. F., and Peterson, A. F. (eds) (1974), *Himmlers Geheimreden 1933 bis 1945 und andere Ansprachen*, Berlin and Frankfurt am Main.

Stachura, P. D. (ed.) (1978), *The Shaping of the Nazi State*, London.

Stegmann, D. (1973), 'Zum Verhältnis von Grossindustrie und Nationalsozialismus 1930–1933', *Arch. f. SozG*, vol. 13, pp. 399–582.

Stephenson, J. (1975), *Women in Nazi Society*, London.

Thamer, H.-U. (1977), 'Ansichten des Faschismus', *NPL*, vol. 22, pp. 19–35.

Thamer, H.-U., and Wippermann, W. (1977), *Faschistische und neofaschistische Bewegungen. Probleme empirischer Faschismusforschung*, Darmstadt.

Thies, J. (1976), *Architekt der Weltherrschaft. Die 'Endziele' Hitlers*, 2nd edn, Düsseldorf.

Tobias, F. (1964), *The Reichstag Fire Trial*, New York.

Treue, W. (1966), 'Die Einstellung einiger deutscher Grossindustrieller zu Hitlers Aussenpolitik', *GiWuU*, vol. 17, pp. 491–507.

Trevor-Roper, H. R. (1960), 'Hitlers Kriegsziele', *VfZg*, vol. 8, pp. 121–33; part trans. in Röhl (ed.) (1970), pp. 172–5.

Trevor-Roper, H. R. (1971), *The Last Days of Hitler*, 4th edn, London; 1st edn 1947.

Turner, H. A., Jr (1972), *Faschismus und Kapitalismus in Deutschland. Studien zum Verhältnis zwischen Nationalsozialismus und Wirtschaft*, Göttingen.

Turner, H. A., Jr (1975), 'Grossunternehmertum und Nationalsozialismus 1930–1933. Kritisches und Ergänzendes zu zwei neuen Forschungsbeiträgen', *HZ*, vol. 221, pp. 18–68.

Weisenborn, G. (ed.) (1974), *Der lautlose Aufstand. Bericht über die Widerstands-bewegung des deutschen Volkes 1933–1945*, 4th edn, Frankfurt am Main.

Winkler, H. A. (1972), *Mittelstand, Demokratie und Nationalsozialismus. Die politische Entwicklung von Handwerk und Kleinhandel in der Weimarer Republik*, Cologne.

Winkler, H. A. (1976), 'Mittelstandsbewegung oder Volkspartei? Zur sozialen Basis der NSDAP', in Schieder, W. (ed.), *Faschismus als soziale Bewegung*, Hamburg, pp. 97–118.

Winkler, H. A. (1977), 'Der entbehrliche Stand. Zur Mittelstandspolitik im "Dritten Reich" ', *Arch. f. SozG*, vol. XVII, pp. 1–40.

Winkler, H. A. (1978), 'Die "neue Linke" und der Faschismus: Zur Kritik neomarxistischer Theorien über den Nationalsozialismus', in his *Revolution, Staat, Faschismus*, Göttingen, pp. 65–117 and 137–59.

Wippermann, W. (1976), ' "Deutsche Katastrophe" oder "Diktatur des Finanz-kapitals"? Zur Interpretationsgeschichte des Dritten Reiches im Nachkriegs-deutschland', in Denkler, H., and Prümm, K. (eds), *Die deutsche Literatur im Dritten Reich. Themen, Traditionen, Wirkungen*, Stuttgart, pp. 9–43.

Index

Printed in Great Britain
by Amazon.co.uk, Ltd.,
Marston Gate.